HOW TO CARVE WILDFOWL
Book 2

HOW TO CARVE WILDFOWL
Book 2

Best-in-Show Techniques of 8 Master Bird Carvers

Roger Schroeder

STACKPOLE BOOKS

Copyright © 1986 by Stackpole Books

Published by
STACKPOLE BOOKS
5067 Ritter Road
Mechanicsburg, PA 17055

First paperback printing August 1997

Printed in the U.S.A.

Library of Congress Cataloging-in-Publication Data
(Revised for book 2)

Schroeder, Roger, 1945-
     How to carve wildfowl.

     Book 2 lacks subtitle.
     Includes bibliographies.
     1. Wood-carving – United States. 2. Waterfowl in art.
3. Decoys (Hunting) – United States. 4. Wood-carving –
Technique. I. Arnold, Eldridge. II. Title.
NK9712.S3   1984   731.4'62   84-2598
ISBN 0-8117-2802-1

to Bill, Bob, Jett, Habbart,
John, Marc, Louis, and Manfred.

Contents

Introduction

In 1923 there occurred a novel exhibit of waterfowl in a small town on the south shore of New York's Long Island. The *Patchogue Advance* wrote about it in the August 30 edition of that year. In part it read:

> Long Beach and Atlantic City may have their beauty shows in which the fair young chickens smirk before the camera and outdare each other in abbreviation of costume, but Bellport has a beauty show in which nary a chicken appears, but only wild ducks and geese – wooden ones at that – making up an exhibit which is believed to be the first of its kind in history and which will no doubt bring the fame of Bellport before the whole sporting world. . . .

> Some months ago some of the leading sportsmen of Bellport got to discussing the fine points of decoy making and management, and there came into being an idea that as men brag some about the superiority of their dummy ducks it would be well to have a competition and award prizes to those whose entries were adjudged by competent authority the best. . . .

> Some of the decoys have been finished off in marvelous detail and the grace of their shapes and poise would do credit to a classic style sculptor, while others are rather impressionistic in finish though depicting well the general natural outlines and coloring. . . .

It was a historic and changing time for decoy makers. Only five years earlier, a United States Congressional act made into law the Migratory Bird Treaty Act, which severely limited the hunting of wildfowl. Decoys were already falling into disuse from the Maine Coast to the Chesapeake, westward to the Great Lakes, the Illinois and Mississippi Rivers, and beyond. It was a law to save waterfowl and birds of all kinds, though at the same time it encouraged the outlaw gunner and later the decoy collector.

Many other events have occurred between that first show and the competitions held today that include no less than a World Championship. In the interim, great decoy makers like Elmer Crowell, Joe Lincoln, the Ward brothers and Ira Hudson have passed on, leaving a legacy of folk art perhaps unrivaled in this country.

Decoy competition was to remain a curiosity until the 1960s when real interest arose in having carved birds, primarily duck decoys, "adjudged by competent authority."

During that same decade, however, decoy makers once again got together to test the superiority of their carvings. From that interest came a World Championship Wildfowl Carving Competition, and the Ward

Foundation, which promotes the making of wildfowl and preserves the heritage of birdcarving. Today, the World Championship is the most prestigious of the nearly 100 shows and competitions held around the country, and it attracts some 2,500 entries and an estimated 10,000 visitors. No fewer than 800 carvers enter this show, three of whom can gain the award Best in World for their work. That awesome title is applied to the best decorative life-sized bird, the best waterfowl pairs, and the best miniature bird. These are coveted awards, not to mention remunerative ones, with the decorative life-size winner alone being awarded $20,000.

The art displayed at the World Championship today is a legacy of those early decoys. Even in the early 1970s, birds were relatively smooth-bodied with details done stiffly, still imitating the serviceable decoy. But a few carvers dared to bring to the shows birds that not only were off their flat bottoms, but were in the air – suspended not like mobiles, but carefully engineered to be held by cleverly designed bits of habitat such as reeds, branches, even cornstalks.

Two of these men were Grainger McKoy and his friend and mentor, Gilbert Maggione, both of South Carolina. But they were more than engineers. They were artists who depicted birds such as hawks and pheasants in natural conflict as prey and predator, frozen in a drama that would rarely if ever be seen by a human being.

I met Grainger McKoy in 1980 when I was a freelance writer in the woodworking field, putting together an article for *Fine Woodworking* magazine. At the time, he was working on a covey of 13 quail breaking into flight. No carver or artist up to that time, nor since, has put so many birds into a sculpture or for that matter into the air.

I was impressed with this man who talked about carving as an art form. He was not looking to duplicate a bird exactly. He called that "taxidermy art." Instead, he was looking to achieve an artistic expression. More of his pieces, he said, would lack details and even paint, with some emerging partially carved from blocks of wood.

I realized that people like McKoy were not only artists, but also philosophers. They had attitudes about the materials they worked with and their subject matter. They were looking at birds as they may never have been looked at before, and they looked to transcend the medium they worked in.

But my thoughts about the field did not fully take shape until I was asked to interview nine of the top bird carvers in North America, photograph their techniques and work in progress, and put the results into a book. The book was *How to Carve Wildfowl*, published in 1983, exactly 60 years after the first decoy competition.

I found nine men I thought had made significant contributions to the field of bird carving. My choices were based on works I had seen and, in particular, how they had done in competition at the World Championship Wildfowl Carving Competition. They had done remarkably well, I discovered, with one of them winner of seven Best-In-World awards during the first 15 years of the show's existence, not to mention some 700 blue ribbons.

Still, there was more to be learned than blue-ribbon techniques. I was to discover artistic statements and views ranging from realism to expressionism over and over again. So what I had learned from McKoy was not unique to him. There were philosophies that these men connected to their carved birds.

The eight men I interviewed during the summer of 1985 for this book are an impressive group. They have easily won not just blue ribbons but also Best in Shows. It is this award that is an achievement far more significant than a blue ribbon for it is the most coveted award a carver can take home from a competition. These eight have won more than 100 Best-in-Show awards.

They are well versed in their art form and are decidedly opinionated about how birds should be carved and painted. But interestingly, their techniques for achieving remarkable results are quite different. So diverse are those techniques that the tools, the paints, and even the very wood they choose are decidedly different from one to the other.

Some of these men use motor-powered grinding tools that come from jewelers and dental technicians. The names used throughout the chapters are the Foredom Tool and the Dremel Moto-Tool. Yet, others disdain the grinders and use only knives, chisels, and gouges. And while one carver opts for acrylic paints, another will use nothing but oil-based paint. Even electric burning tools, used to define feather quills and barb lines with heat-controlling boxes and pen-like handles, the descendents of the woodburners many of us used as children, are not unilaterally used.

As you follow my chapters, you will begin with William Koelpin of Hartland, Wisconsin. He talks about design and an abstract approach to sculpting birds while he works within the bounds of his medium, which is wood. He also contributes a concise history

For removing large amounts of wood from a cutout, and even putting in refined details, many carvers use The Foredom Tool. Note the removable handpiece, the flexible shaft, and the cannistered motor. Most suppliers of carving accessories carry it. See the appendix for a list of them.

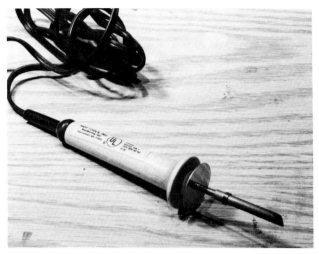

The Hot Tool is another burning instrument used by many bird carvers. Many dealers of bird carving tools carry it.

A hand-held grinding tool with a high rpm motor can remove small amounts of wood. This is the Dremel Moto-Tool. Most suppliers of woodworking and carving tools carry it.

Carvers will use heavy abrasive burrs or cutters impregnated with carbide grit as well as fluted cutters, rotary rasps, and sanding rolls to remove wood.

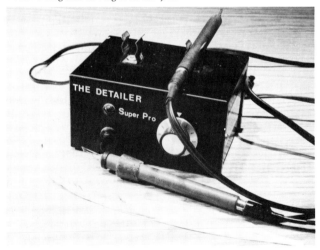

Generically called a burning tool, burner, and burning pen, this is The Detailer, manufactured by Colwood Electronics. The metal box houses a rheostat which varies the heat carried to the handle. The tip, which is interchangeable with other shapes, puts in feather details.

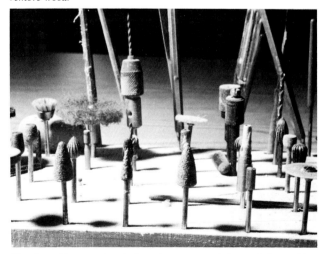

Here is another assortment of wood removers and shapers to be used in a Foredom or Dremel. Finer burrs or cutters will have ruby and even diamond grit on their surfaces.

These bits are called ruby carvers, used for fine detailing. (See appendix for supplier.)

Many carvers paint their birds with acrylic paints. These are water based and fast drying. They are available from any artist supply store and most bird carving catalogs.

A holdover from the tradition of making working decoys, glass eyes are still used today by carvers. A large assortment of sizes and colors is available, and many suppliers of carving accessories sell them.

Bird carver, painter, and sculptor, William Koelpin was a pioneer in bringing realism into wildfowl and later turning wildfowl sculpture into an art form.

Koelpin has much to say about designing a composition. These willow ptarmigans are among birds he has done.

of decoy making and why carvers turned from water-fowl to other wildfowl – with his help.

You move on in the following chapter to Robert Guge, of Carpentersville, Illinois. From a partially formed indigo bunting to a completed carving with textured body, metal feet, aqua and blue-violet colors, a branch to stand on, and a turned base, you will follow him step by step with text and photos.

Next, it is south to Galliano, Louisana, the Cajun home of Jett Brunet. Work is in progress on a mallard and canvasback drake. He talks about "bumping" or defining feathers, shows you how he burns in feather patterns, and makes a sizable bird from a single piece of wood without inserts.

Then head east for a visit with Habbart Dean of Bishopville, Maryland. He is working on a least tern and a hooded merganser hen. He shares with you his thoughts on capturing the expressions of wildfowl through their heads and wings, and he shows you how to make feather inserts, while teaching you how to use a variety of tools. In addition, he discusses the meaning of winning a Best in Show, comparing it to earning a degree from a university.

A bird featured in Guge's chapter is this indigo bunting. Its detailing is achieved with a variety of grinding, sanding, and burning tools. Making legs and feet is well explained in that same chapter.

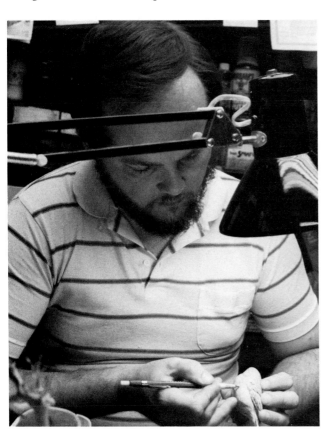

Robert Guge is a leader in achieving personality in his birds.

The indigo bunting has been put on a piece of discarded bonsai bush.

Here is the finished indigo bunting. Guge will describe in detail how to paint this song bird.

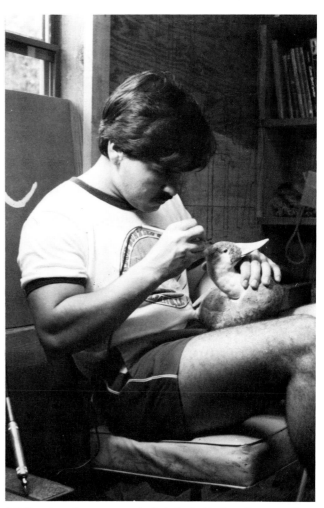

Jett Brunet works on a canvasback drake in his shop. Brunet, a Cajun carver of Louisiana, won Best in World at the 1985 World Championship Wildfowl Carving Competition with a pair of floating ruddy ducks. This is the most prestigious prize a carver can win. Along with it goes a $10,000 purchase prize.

Another of Guge's birds is this bluebird, perched on a piece of barbed wire he made from a common household item.

Some of the finest waterfowl ever carved were made at this table in the shop of Jett Brunet and his father Tan.

This cinnamon teal drake was carved by Brunet. You will see this and other ducks in various stages of completion in his chapter.

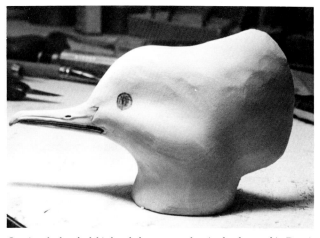

Carving the head of this hooded merganser hen is also featured in Dean's chapter.

Habbart Dean, a carver of waterfowl and shore birds, is shown here working on a hovering least tern, a project he discusses at length.

A hooded merganser hen made by Dean.

Back to Illinois, John Gewerth of Alsip talks more about texturing and shaping the body of a mallard, pointing out how to organize feather groups and how to paint them with acrylics. He also discusses how he animates birds like ruddy ducks and widgeons.

It is also back to Wisconsin to learn from Marc Schultz of the town of Denmark. He discusses how he combines feather burning with oil paints to produce depth and a softness of color while he works on a black-bellied plover. He also shares a wealth of insights on how to capture the personality of birds as he has with wood ducks, widgeons, and canvasbacks.

In Richmond, Virginia, lives Louis Kean, Jr. From him you will discover how to make habitat such as leaves, cattails, and grass, and how to make birds like pintails and blackbirds part of that environment.

The last stop is with Manfred Scheel of Quakertown, Pennsylvania. Scheel talks about how to make

Here Dean has made separate wings and feathers for the tern. He will explain how to make them and how they convey or express an aspect of a bird's personality.

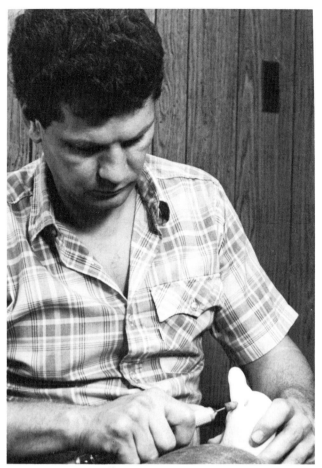

Marc Schultz, a carver who well understands avian personality, is as at home out of doors as he is in his shop.

John Gewerth, a highly regarded waterfowl carver, is shown here working on a mallard drake's head. His chapter features how to make feather patterns and animate birds.

Typical of Schultz's work is this wood duck hen. This quiet pose is a favorite of his.

Gewerth carved this mallard hen. How to paint a bird like this is also featured in his chapter.

Also carved by Schultz is this canvasback drake.

Louis Kean, Jr., a skilled carver who has mastered making habitat as well as birds, is seen here working on a pintail drake. The duck is featured in his chapter in various stages. Photo by Edward M. Burrell.

Kean also creates songbird compositions. These are redwing blackbirds and cattails, the latter fashioned from strips of wood. How to make the cattails and the birds is discussed by Kean.

A widgeon hen carved by Kean.

The drake of the widgeon pair. Though Kean once carved working decoys for hunting trips, he now carves finely rendered birds like these.

Here is the female redwing blackbird of the composition.

Manfred Scheel has several enclosures, called aviaries, for birds that he studies firsthand. Here he is holding a duck from one of them.

Another miniature of Scheel's is this kestrel or sparrow hawk.

A miniature wood duck he carved.

birds smaller than life-size, make habitat displays of stones and plants for them, and even create for them eyes and feet from glues and lead, respectively.

Reading these chapters, you will discover a part of history being made as a new art form takes hold in this country. Where it goes from here is difficult to

say, but some of these men make predictions. Read about them and how they are turning wood into wildfowl.

The journey is not quite over for me. I still remember watching chickadees feed outside Robert Guge's window while we ate breakfast. Nor will I forget harvesting tupelo gum in an alligator-infested swamp, or walking the shores of Lake Michigan under low-weeping willows and stiff cottonwoods, or looking up at the Milky Way on Marc Schultz's farm.

As in *How to Carve Wildfowl*, there are over 800 black-and-white and color photos, nearly all of which I took. They are close-ups of men sculpting masterpieces in basements, laundry rooms, dens, and garages. You will view tools at work and paints applied. You will see metals and paper transformed into unique shapes, and you will also be able to study finished carvings.

I would also like to bring you up to date on the previous nine wildfowl artists I interviewed. Larry

After the publication of How to Carve Wildfowl, *one of the featured carvers, Ernest Muehlmatt, won the coveted Best in World prize with this composition of quail he titled "Needles, Feathers, & Bone." In the collection of the North American Wildlife Art Museum, the Ward Foundation, Salisbury, MD.*

Barth went on to win the 1985 Best-in-World award for a decorative life-size composition he titled "Winter Lakeshore – Snowy Owl and Bonaparte's Gull." That same year Gary Yoder won Best in World with his miniature cooper's hawk and flicker.

Runners up to Barth were Anthony Rudisill and Ernest Muehlmatt. But in 1984, Muehlmatt won Best in World with five life-size bobwhite quail in a desert setting. He titled the piece "Needles, Feathers, & Bone."

And the others? John Scheeler, Lynn Forehand, and Eldridge Arnold continue to compete, taking ribbons with their fine variety of shorebirds, gamebirds, and birds of prey.

James Sprankle, with whom I coauthored *Waterfowl Carving with J.D. Sprankle,* carves his Best-in-Show ducks at his new home on Kent Island, Maryland.

And Larry Hayden still elicits the best from his carv-

Another carver featured in How to Carve Wildfowl *is John Scheeler. An inspiring pioneer in wildfowl carving, Scheeler won Best in World in the 1981 World Championship Wildfowl Carving Competition with this goshawk and crow. In the collection of the North American Wildlife Art Museum, the Ward Foundation, Salisbury, MD.*

ing students as he himself continues to paint waterfowl on canvas.

My thanks to these men who set the standards for *How to Carve Wildfowl, Book 2.*

Finally, I would like to make some acknowledgments and at the same time apologize that this portion of a book too often reads like an office building directory. But they are a way of expressing appreciation for those who help in such an undertaking. In fact, I compare doing a book like this and its predecessors to carving a piece for the World Championship Wildfowl Carving Competition.

First, my appreciation goes to Judith Schnell, my editor at Stackpole Books, who, with an almost maternal interest, insists on the best throughout the production of one of my projects. She has been a great asset.

Second, my thanks go to Richard Meek and Paul Olivelli, whose advice has helped make possible the fine photographs in this book. I do not have to be convinced that good pictures are more than worth their space in words.

Third, I wish to thank Denny Rogers, graphic designer and illustrator, for the fine drawings in the front of the book. I have yet to find anyone else who so thoroughly presents a bird on paper.

And last I would like to thank the members of the Long Island Wildfowl Carvers and the Long Island Woodcarvers Association. The enthusiasm and encouragement of their members make the long hours spent at a typewriter or word processor truly worth it.

You are now ready to follow my birdcarving odyssey, stopping off to sit down at the elbows of this country's master bird carvers.

1

William Koelpin
Within the Bounds of the Medium

William Koelpin, a pioneer in the field of decorative bird carving, is also a painter and historian of wildfowl hunting in this country.

An Artist of Many Mediums

Not satisfied with working only in wood, William Koelpin is a wildlife artist who has also mastered canvas and bronze. He is an ardent sportsman who has brought into his art forms the traditions and history of wildfowl hunting. Among the major exhibitions that have included his work are the Leigh Yawkey Woodson "Birds in Art" Exhibit, those put on by the National Geographic Society, the National Collection of Fine Arts in Washington, D.C., the Carnegie Museum of Natural History in Pittsburgh, Pennsylvania, the Royal Scottish Academy of Edinburgh, Scotland, and the British Museum of Natural History of London, England. He has been called one of America's premier artists by the Leigh Yawkey Woodson Museum, and his awards include Best in World from the 1974 World Championship Wildfowl Carving Competition.

Koelpin is a native of Wisconsin, a state where dairyland merges into wooded terrain and lake country, an ideal environment for his subject matter. Yet he will travel to the Western states to study such species as magpies and roadrunners, birds that will later become carvings, paintings, or even bronzes. Of these three mediums, he says, "Paintings and carvings are subject to deterioration. But a bronze sculpture can

This painting of a pintail pair became a Wisconsin duck stamp in 1982.

This greated horned owl and prey is a pencil sketch by Koelpin.

last a thousand years. It seems to me to be an important way to preserve our wildlife heritage for future generations."

History of a Unique Art Form

Koelpin is well acquainted with the history of the decoy in North America. He believes that only three true art forms evolved in this country. One would be the art of scrimshaw, or the inscribing of scenes and figures on whalebone. Another is jazz music. And the third, not coincidentally, is the art of decoy carving.

"Decoys," he says, "were done as utilitarian objects that later evolved into floating and flying sculpture." He explains that there is sufficient evidence that early American colonists learned decoy-making from the Indians. "When the settlers came to these shores, their firearms were ineffective on birds since you have to get the birds in close, even though there were probably billions of wildfowl on the East Coast alone. But the Indians decoyed birds with nothing more than clumps of mud and stuffed bird skins mounted on blocks of wood that could be floated out into the water. Then, with just ladles or throwing sticks, they could kill wildfowl."

Koelpin continues that even as far west as Nevada, Indians were using reed decoys thousands of years ago. Of the canvasback duck decoys found there in a cave in 1923, he says, "I have never seen a better representation of that species, though I've seen technically perfect models with individual feathers." He adds, "In fact, many of those contemporary carvings left me flat because there was no life imparted to them."

This is what decoys made by American Indians looked like two thousand years ago. This painting, by Larry Hayden, became a Nevada duck stamp in 1979. Hayden titled it "Tule Canvasback Decoy."

He notes that decoy collectors and historians have searched other cultures and countries for decoys but have found nothing predating our own Colonial period. He points out, though, that carved birds have existed from Paleolithic times for decorative and religious purposes.

Reflecting on the transition from the decoy as utilitarian object to art object, Koelpin says, "I'd like to think that some early colonist made his decoy a little better than the next fellow's and didn't want to put it out into the water. But nothing has survived from that time. We have furniture dating back to the Plymouth Colony, but no carved birds."

More years were to pass before decoys would be displayed as decorative pieces. Koelpin says that in the sixteen and seventeen hundreds, hunting wildfowl was done for survival because birds were an important source of food before farms were established. But it was the nineteenth century that saw this kind of hunting become a business. "It was once said that any restaurant worth its salt would have wildfowl on its menu, from ducks to shore birds."

The man who was to become known as a market hunter of that era turned to carving his own decoys, with as many as 500 in what was termed a rig, or stool.

Hull Designs and Regional Differences

Decoys are interesting because of their regional differences, Koelpin notes. Areas where carving decoys was prolific, such as the Illinois River or Barnegat Bay (New Jersey) or Lake Erie or the Chesapeake Bay, had uniquely designed birds. "Hull design is a term I use to describe how decoys were made for fast water, slow water, shallow or deep water, even icing conditions. The Barnegat Bay decoys had higher breasts on them because they had to break ice when they rode on winter water. Illinois River decoys, for example, were designed to ride in fast water, so their bodies were designed almost like sailboats."

Deadly Miniatures?

Oversized decoys have been turned up by collectors. Were these regional? Koelpin answers that they were designed in different parts of the country for visual effect. And what of miniature decoys? He relates a story he heard from friends, though he will not guarantee how much truth there is to it.

"Somewhere on a lake hunters utilized miniature decoys. They were easy to carry. You could bring along hundreds, and they were so effective that hunters didn't even need to use guns. The ducks would simply fly over, see the miniatures, misgauge the altitude, and die when they crashed into the water."

The Decorative Decoy and the Competitions

When market hunting was banned in 1918, and wildfowl hunting of all kinds was severely limited, Koelpin believes that decoy making had no other outlet except into an art form. But there was still another historic period for the decoy, one which as of today has no end in sight – and that is the competition.

"Back in the 1920s, carvers got together to see who could design the best decoy. That's when the carving shows started. But even when I started in the late sixties, it was by and large still a decoy competition. Decorating the bird to make it more than a good gunning decoy was still unheard of, though fellows like the Ward brothers were getting away from the stiff poses you associate with the floating decoy."

But Koelpin admits that there were categories at the competitions for birds that were not decoys. These were often carvings crudely or poorly done, he says. "I looked at this area as one I could get my teeth into. It interested me. But when I started, there were only a few of us doing decorative birds that didn't float."

Was this, then, the beginning of bird carving as an art form? Koelpin believes it was, saying, "People started to compose a piece. This is the essence of sculpture." But perhaps more significantly, "The shows picked this up because it was popular with the public. They were fascinated with those decorative pieces." But there were problems, he admits. "There were just too many different kinds of birds on the same table. So the competitions, which were still governing what carvers were doing, started coming up with rules so that you didn't have birds of prey and songbirds in the same competitive category. Apples and oranges just don't compare."

Dividing birds into species and categories helped as did the competitions themselves in making bird carving an art form. Yet Koelpin wonders, "Have the shows stymied creativity? Do carvers today carve for individual shows or even for judges?"

He points out that yet another forum for bird carving has been the exhibition or museum show, the Leigh Yawkey Woodson Exhibition being one of them. Many of these he has contributed to. "Here birds can be displayed for the enjoyment of the public. And perhaps these shows help bring what we do into the realm of fine art."

But Koelpin admits, "No one really knows whether this is fine art. We won't know that for another fifty or a hundred years how some of our carvings will be taken. Will they be seen as quaint knickknacks of the period, as folk art, an art form of some kind, or fine art? For that matter, just what are we creating? Will these be remembered just as models for museum or natural history exhibits to show what birds look like in their ecology, or are we creating a unique art form to be respected for generations?"

A Blue-Ribbon Artist?

"I'm not damning the shows," Koelpin explains further. "For a young carver the competitions are still a good forum for his work. And the public does relate to ribbons or awards. But a carver has to decide whether he wants to be a competitive type who goes for ribbons or whether he wants, at least in his own mind, to create something he believes to be artistic. I think it has to do with creativity. There are those who will diminish their creativeness because they want to be show artists. And I'm saying that you can go off and do great work without competing." He refers to South Carolina artist Grainger McKoy as one who does not go to competitions yet is known as a leading carver of wildfowl.

Douglas Miller, An Early Patron

Koelpin credits Douglas Miller, art collector and founder of Wildlife World Art Museum in Monument, Colorado, as being a significant influence on decorative bird carving. When Koelpin first met Miller, it was a time, he recalls, "when I was carving species like prairie chickens that no one ever thought of doing. Well, I sat down with Miller and told him that what I and others were doing was an American phenomenon with some pretty long historical roots; and that it could become a leading American art form; and someone like him could get in on the ground floor as a collector. He seemed receptive and later asked me if I wanted to work for him full time." Soon Miller was a patron for other carvers who wanted to make a living carving wildfowl, one of them being William Schultz, whose son is featured in chapter 6.

"Now there are other patrons," Koelpin says. "But we still owe a great deal of gratitude to that early patron who was receptive to carvers doing birds that were neither waterfowl nor even of this country. He was what a good patron should be. He didn't dictate what

the artist does, so his was a time when the creative powers came forward."

A Painter of History

In addition to his own impact on the history of North American bird carving, Koelpin may well have a lasting influence on wildlife painting. He says, "Being a hunter, I've come to realize there's a great hunting history in this country which really has not been documented historically." He refers again to the American Indian when explaining that history, which has been the subject matter of his paintings. "The reed and mud decoy wasn't the only means of fooling waterfowl. The North American Indian, in the fall, would float pumpkins out into a pond. When the ducks became accustomed to them, he would put a hollowed-out pumpkin over his head and swim out into the water. When an unsuspecting duck would come by, the Indian would grab it by the legs and drown it. This was a fascinating means of hunting ducks that has not been put on canvas."

Koelpin painted a long-recognized decoy carver named Joe Wooster.

This painting, titled "Coffee Break," depicts the frustration sometimes experienced by wildfowl hunters. Koelpin did this work in 1982.

Titled "Slim Pickens," this painting by Koelpin depicts the plight of the buffalo and these prairie birds called magpies.

Koelpin has also succeeded as a bronze sculptor. This composition he titled "Damn the Wind!" The sculpture suggests an impending storm.

He has done paintings of contemporary duck hunting, some even comical. In one, entitled "Fowl Tip," a Labrador upsets a boat while retrieving a duck. In another, "Coffee Break," a hunter pours coffee on his dog's head while ducks fly off behind him. In another, more serious scenario that was put on canvas and also sculpted in bronze, there is a hunter and his dog facing the possibility of being swamped in a small skiff. It is entitled "Damn the Wind!" Koelpin explains, "Per-

haps it reflects the Wisconsin disaster of 1940. It was a warm day that brought hunters out in shirt-sleeves. When there was a freakish change in weather with freezing temperatures and strong winds, many on the water could not escape and perished."

Koelpin believes we are nearing the end of our hunting history, making it all the more important to record these experiences on canvas or even in bronze. "Ducks can't take the pressure of hunting, breeding grounds are drying up, and we're losing the wetlands in this country. So there's no place for ducks to go. I feel sad over this," he laments, "because I love hunting."

Perhaps even more symbolic of Koelpin's despondency over changes in our wildlife is a painting he did that depicts neither hunter nor duck. Titled "Slim Pickens," a pair of scavenger birds called magpies rest on top of a buffalo skull. The birds' stark black color is in even starker contrast to the gray of the bone. With the background painted to give the impression of prairie fading into nothingness, Koelpin describes his work as "a mystic piece symbolizing the passing of the buffalo. Yet, the painting shows as well the tragedy

A pencil sketch of one of the magpies.

Koelpin will use traditional tools like these for carving wildfowl.

and hardship to the birds, no longer able to feed off an occasional carcass."

An American Culture

Few Americans hunt, so why, then, the growing interest in wildfowl and wildlife art? Koelpin answers, "I base a lot of that on our country growing up. For the first two hundred years, the prime forces behind people were surviving and making a living. Now leisure time is a reality. So what do Americans become interested in during their spare time? Well, twenty years ago you couldn't give wildlife art away. And what there was of it went into magazines like *Field & Stream*. But all of a sudden it broke loose. There was a market created for it by print and publishing houses. But at the same time, we were becoming interested in our own culture, which meant looking not to Europe for our art forms but instead to what Americans were doing." And, coincidentally, he adds, we were also becoming concerned with the ecology movement and bird carving.

"Americans are finding that there is more than one way to enjoy wildlife. They can take a walk in the woods and observe it, they can paint it, they can carve it, or view what others have painted and carved. And when collecting bird carvings or prints of paintings," Koelpin adds, "people want to find out more about the field. So that's where books come in, including this one."

Traditional Tools and Learning the Process

"People ask me how to start carving. I advise getting a knife and a piece of wood. Then get a set of tradi-

He will also use a Foredom Tool and grinding bits to shape a somewhat massive piece of habitat, such as this trillium.

tional gouges and chisels. Learn the process," Koelpin says.

He is critical, then, of carvers who start with grinding tools such as the Foredom. "I've seen people who never carved before in their lives run out and get some power equipment. I believe the big enjoyment in carving should be the process of removing wood, and if you can do that with handtools, so much the better. Aesthetically, it isn't pleasing using a big grinder that tears wood away. In fact, it can be disastrous to the surface of the wood." Still, he admits, it does the job faster, and he does rely on the Foredom Tool for much of his carving these days. How then does he resolve this apparent contradiction?

Koelpin uses power tools and their bits not to replace but to simulate traditional carving effects. With

A typically abstract base made by Koelpin has a trillium as part of its flora.

Koelpin carved the wood in this composition abstractly.

Note that the flower is somewhat massive. Koelpin is not concerned with a very realistic and delicate-looking trillium but with one that suggests a flower.

the concave cuts he can achieve with power bits, he has learned to fake the marks of traditional carving tools while achieving speed. Still, he confides, "A good sharp gouge gives the most beautiful cut in the world. It's finished; it's polished."

Mixed Media and Ersatz Materials

Koelpin points out that the trend in carving today has been to use a variety of materials for the habitat on a base and even for the bird itself. (For more on ersatz materials, see chapter 2 with Robert Guge, chapter 7 with Louis Kean, and chapter 8 with Manfred Scheel).

"Take a large standing bird and you'll discover it's pretty hard to carve out of wood a set of legs to hold it up," he says. "So now we accept metal or soldered legs in this field. Then carvers got to putting an environment on a base because it was no longer satisfactory to stick a bird on a piece of driftwood. So we started experimenting with different materials for bases such as gravel and sand. It was part of the evolution. Then ersatz materials were found even for the sand and gravel.

"So today you have paper, or brass, or plaster to make an environmental display of flowers or leaves, and putties and epoxies to make rocks. Granted, you may say that the end justifies the means, that if it's something of beauty, what difference does it make what it's made out of? But I ask, are we still woodcarvers? To me, this mixed media approach has created a problem in defining what we are and what we're doing."

German Woodcarving and the Bounds of the Medium

"I admire the German tradition of woodcarving, their stylized representations of objects." And what is that interpretation? Koelpin says, borrowing from this tradition, that for him to make something like grass he would not use pieces of ersatz materials or bits of wood glued to a base. Instead, he would carve it from a solid block of wood. He says, "I prefer, then, to interpret or stylize grass, make it abstract. The next step would be deciding what the wood is capable of doing and what the tools can do to achieve the effect I want. You can only get wood so fine before it breaks. So you have to keep its tensile strength. I believe, then, that

Another view shows a trillium leaf.

Abstract sketches of a trillium become more refined.

woodcarving, in the German tradition, tends to be a little massive in its proportions." On the other hand, "Some carvers get a little flimsy with the material. That I call overstepping the bounds of the medium."

Abstract Art

Koelpin believes that to create in wood what other carvers use ersatz materials for, and still stay within the bounds of what the wood can withstand before losing its strength, he must carve abstractly. This applies particularly to his bases, which have featured a variety of environmental studies from a nest to rocks, to flowers, all done in wood.

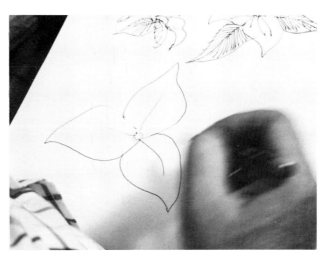

A basic top profile is decided upon.

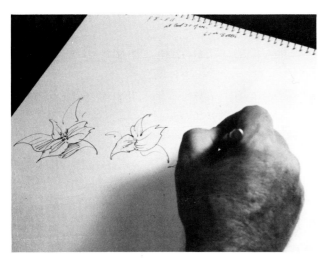

Koelpin starts with sketches of a flower he wants to carve.

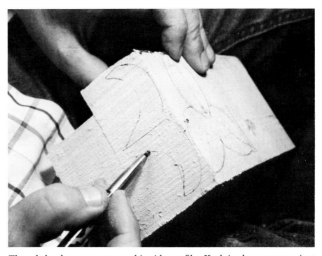

Though he does not cut out this side profile, Koelpin demonstrates just how massive a block is needed for him to make a flower as traditional carvers have made them for centuries.

Here Koelpin works at a band saw, a tool used by all the carvers featured in this book.

To demonstrate, he sketches out on a thick piece of jelutong the shape of a trillium flower. Removing waste wood on a band saw, he uses his Foredom Tool and a variety of grinding bits to shape the petals. With ball-shaped, conical, and other bits, the flower took on its distinctive shape.

"Understanding the construction of the flower is more important than taking wood off," explains Koelpin. "I want the petals to undulate and have ripples. This is the way a trillium is. Knowing that, I start with bigger bits for rough work and smaller ones for the finer work."

Koelpin will not cut out a side profile, saying, "The more massive the wood remains, the more details I can work in without pieces breaking off."

The rest of his shaping is what he calls "modeling." He says, "I'm modeling the surface to give it light and dark shadows. At the same time I can change the design and effects without being committed to the pattern. This is modeling, controlling the effects without letting the pattern dictate to me. Carving, then, can be a loose process of creation." Koelpin adds that he will do no texturing on the surfaces of the flower. "I can get my effects by modeling alone, with the light and dark textures ultimately producing soft and hard effects. European woodcarvers effectively achieve hard and soft effects with an effective use of folds and no paint. I appreciate this, because if the medium isn't obvious, what's the sense of using it?"

There is a massiveness to the petals to allow them a floppy shape while avoiding fragility. He finds precedent for this not only in German carving but also in

The profile of the flower is cut to shape.

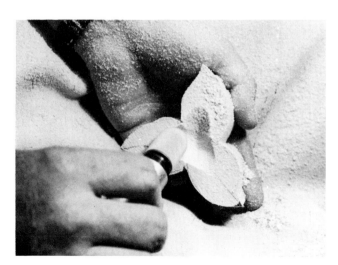

Koelpin demonstrates that grinding bits can simulate the cuts made by traditional carving tools like this gouge.

He works toward the points of the flower petals.

More refining is done with the previous bit.

Here he makes ripples in the surface of the petals.

Koelpin begins with a sizable grinding stone, one seven-eighths inches in diameter, at the center of the cutout.

A large conical stone can also make ripples.

A fluted cutter reduces this area to show that the petals will overlap.

Koelpin removes wood in the center to give more dimension to the flower.

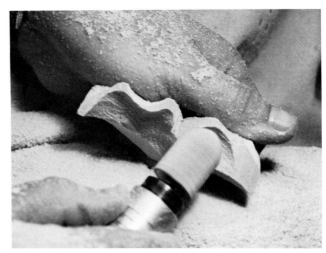

Note that he keeps the petal edges fairly thick.

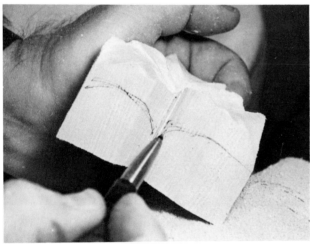

Here he decides how thick the trillium will be.

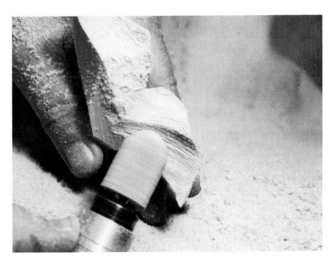

Koelpin gives the underside of the petals a V shape.

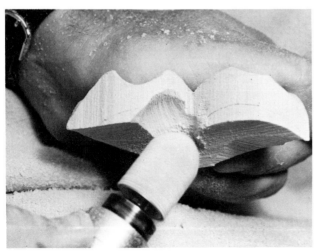

Koelpin begins to remove wood from underneath the petals.

Lines are drawn to indicate where the petals overlap.

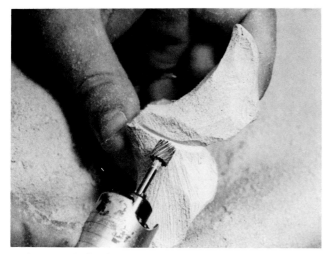

Koelpin uses the fluted cutter to remove wood where the petals overlap on the underside.

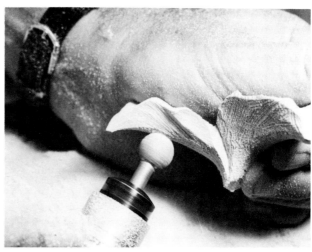

Here he demonstrates how the round stone can reduce the thickness of the petals.

The fluted cutter continues on the faces of the petals.

He gives a concave shape to the underside of the petals.

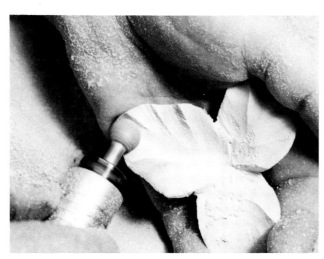

Koelpin gives some roundness to the ripples.

The thickness is reduced from the top.

Note that there is still a certain massiveness to the flower. Koelpin says this is within the bounds of the medium, wood, which cannot be shaped too thinly and still retain its strength.

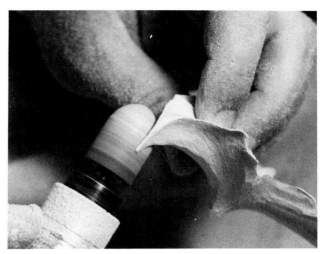

The points of the petals can be "sharpened."

With the large, cone-shaped stone, he can give the petal more of a drooping appearance.

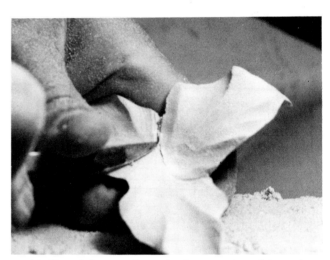

A knife can help create the overlapping appearance of the petals.

Variations can be made in the outlines of a petal..

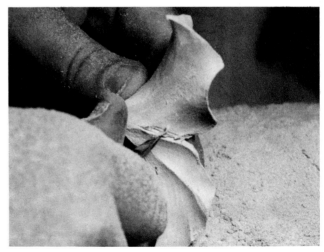

The overlapping or underlapping is also refined on the underside.

Koelpin draws in the veins on the petals.

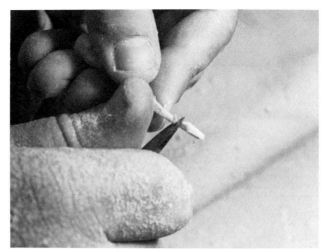

Here Koelpin carves one of the flower's stamens.

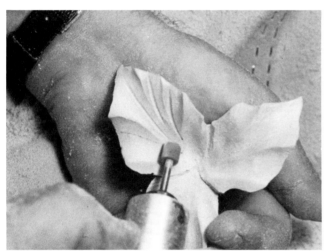

The fluted cutter defines the vein lines.

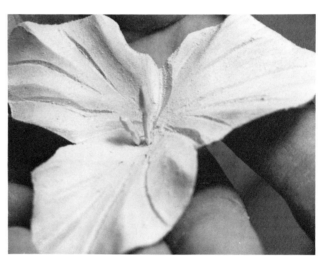

He then inserts the stamens into the center of the flower.

A V-parting tool can also be used to make veins.

Here is the finished trillium.

stone sculpture. "Look at a stone figure with its arm outstretched. You'll find some kind of drapery or clothing acting as a truss between part of the arm and the body. That's the only way to give that arm strength against its own weight." Of his trillium, he says, "It is impressionistic and representational because I have not made it out of paper or metal foils."

But the abstractness Koelpin employs is not limited to his bases. He will create a bird that has little feather texturing and no insertion of separate pieces of wood for feathers. (Compare Jett Brunet's techniques in chapter 3.) Koelpin says, "Today I enjoy taking a block of wood and carving an entire wing rather than inserting feathers. Perhaps I regressed after having been through all the stages of carving. In fact, I may have been one of the innovators of feather inserts, but I enjoy the abstract qualities of the traditional approach." He has also gotten away from burning and texturing much of the wood's surface on a bird, claiming, "I don't want to disguise the wood, which is my medium."

Wood Staining, Oil Paints, and a Wax Medium

Koelpin is not the only carver to use oil paints. (For more on them, see chapter 6 with Marc Schultz.) But he is the only one using a staining technique and a wax medium. The coloration of the bases, in particular, is done by staining them. "This goes back to traditional wood carving that employed oil paints thinned down with turpentine. I wash them on certain areas, then wipe the stain so that the wood still shows through." He calls this "working on a colored background," pointing out that many carvers work on a stark white background produced by gesso, a primer for paint.

He adds that he may be unique in that he uses a wax in his oil paints. "Dorland's Wax Medium is a pure, white fossil wax, soft and malleable. I'll mix it with a little turpentine and mix that with my oil paints." Adding that it is an ancient medium, he says, "In the past, an oil painting would be put into an oven and its colors would fuse together with the help of this wax. This is called encaustic painting." He says that it is a highly protective medium, and many paintings have been coated with it.

Koelpin believes, however, that many people are trying their hands at bird carving because oil paints have been replaced by acrylics. He calls these paints "a great innovation. Many people got sick from using oil paints and turpentine. With acrylics, they dry right away, there's no smell, little mess, and you can paint over them almost immediately."

Yet he himself disclaims the use of acrylic paint. "Maybe I'm a sentimentalist, but I don't like acrylics because they're plastic. I like wood and oil, the latter which will change, discolor, and even crack. It's like a 500-year-old painting that has those cracks in it. That's the patina of age."

Painting for a Visual Effect

"I can paint a feather a whole lot better than I can carve one," says Koelpin. "So a lot of texturing ruins the surface for the effect I want, though I've burned in feathers in the past and I appreciate good burning." Even simulating feather groups with grinders as most other carvers do may be detrimental to the effects he wants. What he calls his own style of working on a surface is "loose." He explains, "I like the carving to project a bit, meaning it doesn't have to be a perfect representation of the bird. So when I paint, I'm after a visual effect. I stylize, then, some areas, subdue others, even exaggerate in places."

But whatever the painting technique, Koelpin warns against doing too much with the bird or its setting. He explains, "Most great pieces are very simple. You don't need the whole woods or shore in the piece." (Compare Marc Schultz's remarks in chapter 6.) He adds, "Don't be theatrical. That's the mark of an amateur, being complicated to prove you can do something."

He refers to his friend John Scheeler (featured in *How to Carve Wildfowl*) as a master of achieving simplicity with a bird carving yet being able to project the feeling that there is more to the piece than the senses are willing to admit. He refers to a pair of Louisiana herons Scheeler carved. The base is part of a log and material shaped and painted to simulate mud. Yet, Koelpin says, "With that piece, you might think an entire swamp is present. You want to woo people's emotions, and that's what Scheeler does." Koelpin asks of all art, "Can an onlooker soar with the work? Can the art move something inside him?"

Koelpin praises Scheeler as "an abstract painter who can pull off more with one brush stroke than the average person can with fifty."

Believing that great carving should, like great painting, need no signature to be recognizable, Koelpin laments that many carvings done today are not distinguishable from one another. "You must go beyond techniques which are very mechanical. That's why neophytes ask me where to buy a Foredom before they've learned the basics, or they want to know how to burn in feathers before they even learn how to carve." Another solution to the dilemma of sameness is obviously the painting. This, he says, is more of a personal technique. "You take fifty good painters in our field and they'll all paint a feather differently. Take fifty carvers who haven't applied the paint yet, and you'll find many more similarities. That's the great fascination with what we're doing. It's a combination of two art forms, painting and sculpture."

It should not be surprising that Koelpin supports those who do not paint their carvings. He says, "I know great carvers who complain that they cannot paint. Yet, does a great carving need paint? Is it possible that we have ruined good woodcarving? Is it in fact possible to get away with bad woodcarving because of a good paint job?"

Sculpting with a Chainsaw

Koelpin claims that when he begins carving, he is not especially analytical. Roughing is done with an axe, an adze, or even a chainsaw. These, he says, keep him from a highly finished look prematurely. He muses, "I wonder if the more mature an artist becomes, the looser he becomes, the more abstract?

"I see beginning art students being very methodical and tightly rendering their work. Later, though, one brush stroke may become a tree. Things become more suggestive. This is probably why, every time I start a carving, I'll use different tools. That's part of my looseness and why I enjoy the effects of different tools."

Sketching in the Field

Koelpin, in spite of his loose approach in carving, is not casual in his research of birds. For both his prairie chickens sculpture and painting, he in fact sat in a blind watching these birds engage in a kind of dance. He describes it as "a primeval ceremony, going on for eons of time." Males perform the dance on what are called "booming grounds," called that because of the sound they make. This is done for the benefit of the hens. "I can picture the American Indian watching these birds," he says, "and imitating them in their dances."

He may watch a bird such as this through binocu-

Koelpin did field sketches of these prairie chickens and later applied watercolors for reference.

This is a watercolor field study of a pied-billed grebe.

Koelpin did these sketches of a live barn swallow and a road kill.

lars, quickly making what he describes as "attitude sketches." He can literally turn the bird around, capturing different poses. Later he may even go over them with watercolor washes. "It's amazing the retention you'll have watching birds. I advocate drawing what you see no matter how crude the sketches turn

This is a field study sketch that Koelpin converted into a pattern.

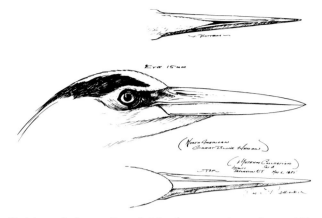

Koelpin made these pattern sketches from a specimen of a great blue heron head in a museum collection.

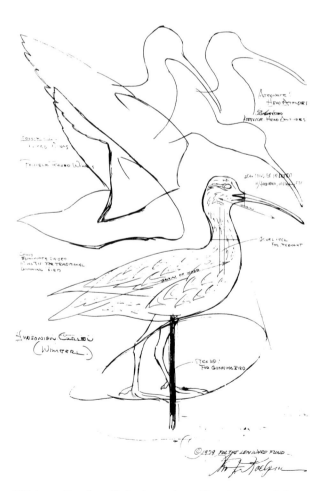

This is a pattern for a Hudsonian curlew with various presentations.

out. Even photographs cannot replace what you can get being there watching that bird. I want to know how a bird runs, walks, flaps its wings."

From there, he will do studies of real or dead birds for feather sizes and anatomy. He says, in fact, that he would not carve without the study skin of a bird in front of him.

But he warns against using illegal birds. Many specimens, he says, can be obtained from museum collections, and he points out the remarkable array of rare and exotic birds done by William Schultz, who worked for the Milwaukee Public Museum.

Solving Problems in Three Dimensions

Despite the fact that Koelpin works from field sketches and study skins, he will resort to yet another aid. "Sketches won't solve your three-dimensional problems. But in a medium like clay, you can work out a form very quickly and achieve a strategy when changing from two dimensions." Sometimes he will even use wax, which has a tensile strength greater than clay, but is more difficult to sculpt.

Contending with Grain

"A lot of times I'll draw a pattern and it will look great, but then I'll go to a medium like clay or wax to see if it works." Still, the pattern will have yet another function besides giving a shape. Grain problems have to be dealt with, and patterns can help solve them. Grain patterns were critical with his spruce grouse

Koelpin says that modeling clay is an excellent tool for solving problems in three dimensions. This is the clay model of a pintail.

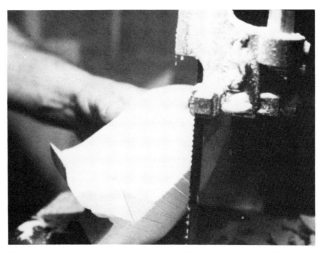

Koelpin can do some shaping of a large bird on a band saw. Photo by William Koelpin.

Here is a suggestion of wooded habitat made in clay.

Compare how much shaping was done with a couple of passes through the band saw blade. Photo by William Koelpin.

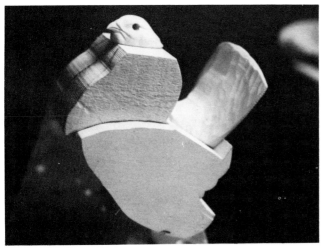

To contend with grain changes, Koelpin used separate pieces of wood for this spruce grouse. Photo by William Koelpin.

More shaping with the band saw is shown here. Photo by William Koelpin.

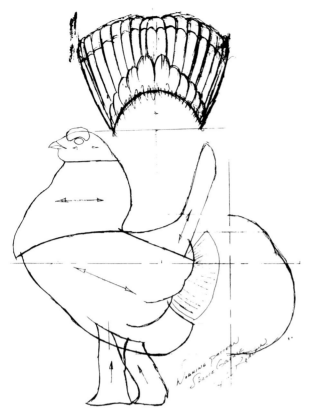

This is Koelpin's pattern for his spruce grouse. The arrows indicate grain direction of the individual pieces.

Koelpin decided to laminate two pieces of wood together to accommodate this green-winged teal sketch and pattern.

carving on which the head jutted straight out, the wings were extended, and the tail was up. But once he decided how the grains of the different parts of the anatomy would run in the carving, he cut out separate pieces. Each was shaped separately, using his band saw as a shaping tool, a carpenter's chisel, and fishtail gouge. Finally, they were glued together.

The Prevailing Woods for Carvers

There are really only three woods used by bird carvers today, all of which will be discussed at length in succeeding chapters. They are basswood, jelutong, and tupelo gum. The first is a carryover from our European heritage where, under the aliases of linden and limewood, it has been worked for centuries by such masters as Grinling Gibbons of England. Jelutong is a wood from Malaya, but imported to this country in great quantities for use by pattern makers. The wood has remarkable stability and can be carved into anything from steel struts to ships' propellers, from which castings can be made. And tupelo gum is a wood native to the South, probably first employed for bird carving by the Cajuns of southern Louisiana.

Though Koelpin has tried basswood, he has recently been working with jelutong. He enjoys the way it takes shape with grinding tools, but admits that it has limitations. He says that it is not very strong and he cannot achieve delicate features with it. He says he has never tried tupelo. "Perhaps I don't want to discover I really like it only to find I can't have a ready source for it. But I hear it works great with power or hand tools."

A Regal Spruce Grouse

"In terms of design," says Koelpin, "I think my spruce grouse is one of my most successful carvings. It has a regal look, it's in a strutting posture, and the plumage is in a display position." And though the base is abstractly carved, it does capture the flora and fauna of the spruce grouse's environment. Koelpin admits, however, that he did not have a specimen of the bird until after this carving was completed. "But if a fellow wanted to carve such a bird, and didn't have a skin, he could learn a lot from a chicken. It has the same construction, the same anatomy, and both are galinaceous birds."

A Quiet Long-eared Owl

Koelpin notes that an owl is a successful hunter and predator because of the soft feathering that allows it to fly with very little sound. "Most birds make quite a bit of noise when flying. But the owl can sneak up on its prey because of the soft edges of its feathers."

He points out that a problem with carving a species like this one is giving it a soft appearance. "One successful aspect of this piece is the contrast between the owl and the roughly carved base, which accentuates the softness of the bird." He adds that he did a minimum of texturing to maximize that soft look.

Had something inspired him to do this particular bird? Koelpin answers, "It's one I actually saw sitting on a post one day. The post was higher than the one I carved, but I took artistic license, as people say, and made a short, stumpy post. I used an actual piece of barbed wire I found on the original post. It adds interest and compositionally it pulls the piece together." (Compare a similar piece done by Robert Guge in chapter 2.) How is that achieved? "Whereas there is a strong line that runs through the post and the owl, the piece of barbed wire breaks that up yet ties the components together."

Koelpin comments on the feather in the owl's talon. "Perhaps it's a gimmick, though it's not as gimmicky as, say, drops of water on a duck's bill; and I don't advocate gimmicks particularly if the carving is done well. Perhaps it would better be described as a trick. I observed that the owl had a kill at the foot of the post. There were feathers present. Well, the public accepted it. But one problem wildlife artists have is showing a dead bird. So when people asked me at shows about the prey, I'd respond that the owl missed the bird and it got away."

A Secretive Saw-whet Owl

Koelpin describes this owl as secretive and not readily seen. Yet, he says, it is quite common, and anyone walking through a wooded area has probably heard one. "You hear a little buzzing sound," he says, "and that's the owl. Hence, its name."

Koelpin feels this is also a successful piece because of its simplicity. "There's no gimmickry whatsoever," he says. "It's simply a bird standing on a very abstract base carved to give the impression of woodland country. There's a little stone and roots and trumpeter flowers to add color to what would otherwise be a drab scene." The owl, Koelpin says, is not very colorful

Koelpin sees this carved spruce grouse as a regal bird in a strutting position.

The saw-whet owl Koelpin carved in 1985.

The owl is an unseen occupant of the woods.

Part of the owl's base comprises carved trumpeter flowers.

Koelpin prefers the look of heavy feathers done without burning.

The base suggests a woodland country of roots, rocks, and flowers.

The feathers for the primaries, secondaries, and the tail are all inserted.

nor is the woodland floor of its habitat. "But that flower enlivens the piece, yet keeps it simple without attracting much attention." He adds, "It's also very balanced, which has a lot to do with composition."

Audubon's Mourning Doves

"I would, in all honesty, have to call these Audubon's doves because the composition is literally taken from one of his paintings. Though I wouldn't say this is plagiarism, I tried to interpret a painting as a carving," adding that there were other birds and foliage in the Audubon picture.

Though the base is a lathe-turned piece of walnut, Koelpin tried to give the impression of the birds being high up in a dogwood tree in bloom. "Realistically,

This is the pattern for Koelpin's saw-whet owl.

These mourning doves were inspired by a John Audubon painting. The flowers are those of a dogwood tree.

these birds don't nest on the ground. So the base hopefully gives the transition from the ground to the top of the tree."

As for the nest, Koelpin carved it abstractly. He explains, "Rather than take individual sticks and try to reconstruct a nest, I carved it as a whole. I believe it was successful."

A Believable Roadrunner

Koelpin enjoys this piece because it comes from the desert country he feels at home in and where the roadrunner is well known. But a problem arises, Koelpin says, when trying to make the bird believable. "It's hard to pull off something that may look artificial in real life because it's such a funny-looking creature." Yet, he has observed these birds running alongside vehicles or appearing along a foot trail.

"I tried to give the piece a feeling of a desert setting. The earthy tones I used help; also the prickly pear cactus, which holds the composition together."

A roadrunner is a difficult bird to do, says Koelpin, because in real life it still appears a caricature of itself. The scene, typical of a desert, includes a cactus and even a lizard.

Koelpin explains that the tail of the roadrunner acts like a pointer, leading the viewer's eye away from the piece. In the lower left-hand corner is a small lizard. "This is not a gimmick because it's a natural prey for the bird. But the roadrunner doesn't know that the lizard is there. People at shows liked that because the underdog got away. Also, it's natural history with a little story."

Koelpin carved these willow ptarmigans in 1984.

Mottled Willow Ptarmigans

Koelpin describes the base for his willow ptarmigans as showing an "advanced style of undercarving and depth. It's obviously abstract, but it gives the impression of high country and glacial rocks and lilies that make up the habitat of these birds."

He notes, "Birds of this type are difficult to pull off. What I mean by that is, these ptarmigans are in their spring plumage, giving them a mottled appearance, whereas in the winter they are pure white. So they look unfinished. People will ask, then, 'When are you going to finish the piece?' Perhaps a piece like this would appeal only to those very knowledgeable about birds."

The pair comprises a male and female. Koelpin says he was taking artistic license here. "I'm not sure these particular birds would be associated with each other at this time of year." But he feels that too many wildlife

Koelpin says he can do more with paint than he can with texturing a surface, as he did on this lower ptarmigan.

These ptarmigans are birds found in northern latitudes, though their habitat will have vegetation and even flowers.

Koelpin suggests feathers on the flank of this ptarmigan with paint and gouge marks.

By the ptarmigan's foot is a glacial lily.

A ptarmigan has a mottled look in the spring, but is all white in the winter.

This is a full-size pattern for one of Koelpin's willow ptarmigans.

Koelpin carved the birds' habitat to give the impression of high country, with rocks and northern flowers.

This is a pattern sketch for the upper ptarmigan.

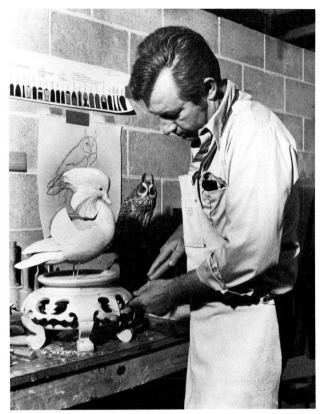

Here Koelpin is working on a mandarin duck on an Oriental-style base, carved in basswood but finally painted to look like rosewood.

These are prairie chickens Koelpin studied in central Wisconsin.

artists are concerned with being ornithologically correct in their compositions. "Bird design," he says, "should be done for visual effect. I wanted to show a male and a female bird, and they make a good design."

A Mandarin Drake

Describing this as an Oriental bird, Koelpin says it is only natural to have the duck on an oriental-type base, with its design coming from a teacup holder.

Achieving the shape of the base from turning a piece of basswood on a lathe, Koelpin then did incise work on it. "Orientals tend to use a lot of rosewood, so I stained the basswood with ochres and reds, then blacks." He adds, "I believe that the realism of the bird is accentuated by the oriental feeling of the base."

On the bird itself, primary and scapular feathers were inserted while the feet were carved out of wood. A piece of steel supports the one leg the bird is standing on.

Prairie Chickens

This carving was done in conjunction with a painting. Koelpin had observed these birds on a marsh in upper Wisconsin performing what he describes as a ritual mating dance. He says that these birds inflate orange air sacs on the sides of their necks to produce a booming sound. With the base, he simulated prairie land and grass with some pasque flowers to add an accent of color.

The prairie chickens also made for a carved composition, with a very abstract base. These birds have sacs on their necks which, when inflated, emit a booming sound.

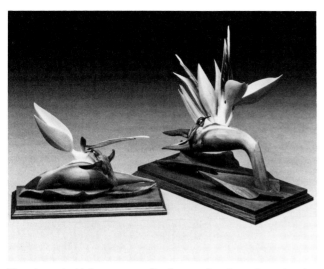

These hummingbirds are on paradise flowers, though one flower is only a bud. The bird on the left is a rufous, the one on the right a ruby-throated hummingbird.

Hummingbirds

The bird of paradise flower would seem to be as much a part of the piece as the hummingbirds, one of which is the ruby-throated, the other a rufous. The inspiration to use the flower came from a trip to lower California where it can be found growing. Also, Koelpin points out, hummingbirds are attracted to these flowers.

Bobwhite Quail in Flight

"Flight is a violent, fast reaction in most cases, so you don't even see the action of wings; they're a blur," Koelpin explains. "This is more easily depicted in a painting. So I feel it goes against the rules of good sculpture to show violent action that is suddenly stopped. You get the uneasy feeling of what's going to happen next." For that matter, he questions the ability of any sculptor to successfully show flight.

Yet, Koelpin attempted to portray his bobwhite quail exploding from a woodland setting, using the elongation of the composition to help depict movement. And the setting? Koelpin carved mushrooms and fungus, both of which add some extra color to the base.

Ungainly Kingfishers

Koelpin describes this as an older piece, saying that it was typical at the time to put a bird on an object

Koelpin has two bobwhite quail in flight, though he says flying birds are difficult to make look realistic.

An early piece, this composition has two kingfishers. Koelpin says he enjoyed the challenge of carving the minnow in the upper bird's mouth as much as he did the birds themselves.

These California quail were inspired by a hunting trip to the Baha Peninsula. The flowers are those of the prickly pear cactus.

such as a piece of driftwood. The bird itself, he says, is ungainly with a large head and small feet. Interestingly, he feels that the minnow in the one bird's mouth may be the most interesting part of the piece.

"I don't think this holds up too well in terms of composition. It would have been more successful with only one bird. In fact, I took artistic license because two of these birds wouldn't be together to begin with."

Calling it one of his original decorative carvings, Koelpin says he enjoyed dealing with the problems of the crests, trying to make them loose, as if caught by the wind.

California Quail

This piece was inspired by a hunting trip to Baha, California. "I tried to indicate some of the flora of the Baha Peninsula with chip carving on the base. The brush and sandstone are abstractly carved to simulate desert." But the upturned arms of the prickly pear cactus, explains Koelpin, "give the feeling of a continuous circle that holds the composition together because the birds are directional."

This woodcock has a great deal of insertion work and burning done. Note the more realistic habitat of Koelpin's earlier work.

One of the smallest ducks, this hen ruddy duck lays eggs that seem out of proportion to its body.

Hen Ruddy Duck

Koelpin says this piece is a favorite of many people. It is one of our smallest ducks, he explains, yet it lays an exceptionally large egg for its size. "I feel the importance of the piece comes with the tiny hen ruddy laying those tremendous eggs."

He adds that these ducks make floating nests of cattails and reeds. Koelpin's carved nest "is an abstract indication of tangled weed matter that does not distract from the bird and its eggs."

A Woodcock in Flight

This composition was a transitional one for Koelpin. It was done at a time when he did extensive burning and insertions; yet, he was attempting to get away from a realistic rendering of flora, retaining many of the original gouge marks with little sanding.

"It's a realistic rendering of the bird, but like the bobwhite quail, achieving flight in a sculpture isn't always successful, though a carver like John Scheeler seems to capture flight well." Aside from the issue of stopping flight, Koelpin says, "You have to hold the bird up somehow, attached to a branch or whatever, and I feel that's artificial. Only blurring the wings without attachment can truly simulate flight, and that's impossible. My theory is, you show the very beginning of takeoff, or the end, but not the action of flight itself. And that holds true for other wildlife art. I've seen painters make deer suspended over a log. This is ludicrous. A good artist shows the deer still on the ground before the jump or returning to the ground."

Still, how did Koelpin suspend the woodcock? The bird was attached to the main trunk on the base with a steel pin.

Pied-billed Grebes

Koelpin describes this as a triangular composition. (For more on this, see chapter 8 with Manfred Scheel.) "It's a good construction that holds everything together. The eye just can't wander off the piece."

He describes the base as secondary, not even wanting people to notice it. His reasoning is rooted in the coloring of the birds. "The young of these birds are quite colorful. There are strong reds and ochre colors. And they're cute birds that have been called helldivers because of the speed in which they dive."

This pied-billed grebe and chick form a triangular composition. Note the very abstract base.

These mourning doves are in a typical pose, says Koelpin. The butterfly gives color to an otherwise drab base, he adds.

Koelpin sketched a design for a pair of shorebirds called greater yellow-legs on a very abstract base.

More Mourning Doves

"I wanted these birds to have a compatible relationship, looking at each other," Koelpin says. "People should relate to them as loving, homey birds. I used a few carved rocks and a stump in the base and carved grass to contrast with the color of the birds. I've even added little spots of color by putting in a butterfly. It gives life and color to an otherwise drab scene."

This, like the pied-billed grebe sculpture, Koelpin describes as a triangular composition. "It would be vertical except that the butterfly brings the eye around. It becomes, then, a solid shape."

Koelpin points out that the directional features generated by anatomy is a problem with many bird carvings. "Many of our birds are very directional. The bill and tail themselves are directional. So you need other elements to hold the piece together."

More on Abstract Art

Questioning the realism of today's bird sculptures, many of which may include finely rendered and exacting habitat, from water to rocks to grass, Koelpin says, "A human being, when looking at a lawn, doesn't see every blade of grass. Instead of seeing fine details, he sees the overall, which is really a blurred abstraction. It's the same with decorative bird carving, and that's why I question an overabundance of detail. I keep things suggestive, while staying within the bounds of my medium."

2

Robert Guge
Landscaping and Painting Wildfowl

Growing Up in the Fox River Valley

In 1984, Robert Guge won Best in World with a pair of miniature mourning doves. The coveted prize came after some 60 blue ribbons and 20 Best in Shows for a variety of wildfowl.

He relates a story, perhaps half seriously, that seven years ago an important catalyst to helping him make his decision to carve full time was seeing a well-known carver, feet propped up on his desk, casually working on a decoy. Yet, Guge is not opposed to putting in 14 hours a day on a piece, nor spending 60 hours on a carving to be contributed, without compensation, to an auction raising money to save wetlands.

Interestingly, with the exception of his father having carved decoys, and a brief association with a legendary carver of the Illinois River School, Harold Haertel, little in Guge's background would indicate that he would ultimately carve wildfowl that is among the most sought after by collectors. At one time, he was a drummer in a band, and he was an industrial painter. But he has been a highly astute observer of birds, able to capture in his carvings an essence that goes beyond the techniques of wood sculpting and painting.

What has undoubtedly helped to shape his under-

Though Robert Guge is a top carver of finely rendered wildfowl, he will occasionally do a primitive like this loon, imparting to the wood the patina of age. Photo by Kurt Butcher.

Guge enjoys doing what he calls "fat little birds." This miniature male cardinal is one example.

standing of wildfowl has been the area he grew up in. Called the Fox River Valley of Illinois, it is a territory rich with birds, especially waterfowl and songbirds. Guge has seen nearly every species of inland North American waterfowl, even coastal scooters. In his own backyard, which is close to the Fox River, he has found wood ducks and mallards. There are nearly sixty species of songbirds in the area. Birds of prey such as great horned, screech and long-eared owls frequent the valley, not to mention a year-round migration of geese. Even a nature center, one place where he does some of his bird-watching, is only twenty minutes away.

Knowing the Bird Personally

Revealingly, Guge describes a tree sparrow he had observed for weeks outside his kitchen window, where feeders attract two dozen species or more of songbirds. "I'll get to know a bird personally before I carve one. And I did with this tree sparrow that was feeding on my deck. In fact, we had four of them that one winter. I really enjoyed seeing them all puffed up.

But when I found that particular one dead one morning, I felt like my best friend had died, I knew that bird so well. But that's what made the final carving so good. And it came quickly because it all came so naturally."

Fat Little birds

"I love fat little birds," says Guge, "especially the puffiness that comes with winter. So if I see that, then that's the way I'll portray the bird."

That is not the only criterion Guge uses when creating a bird in wood. He points out that accuracy is a main criterion for birds in competition. Yet, he admits to breaking tradition, saying, "I have become looser with my carvings, even to the point of changing colors in places. Getting away from total accuracy was a turning point in my career. I realized I was doing the bird for me, not for someone else such as a judge. I now make a bird reflect what I want to show, so if something is not totally accurate but looks good, I'm satisfied."

He refers to the face. "I try for more expression in the face than a real bird has. I'll put in cheek lines or a raised area I call a 'mustache.' It's an exaggeration. Now sometimes these things show, and sometimes they don't. But if this is going to be an art form, we have to express the bird the way we see it and feel it."

He goes on to say that he strives for life in the face. "The most important thing on a carving is the face. If you can capture a look there, you've succeeded with the carving." What kinds of looks does he try to cap-

The female miniature cardinal shows the puffiness that comes with a winter day.

Guge says the most important part of a carving is the face. Imparting personality is important, he says. This is the head of a miniature goshawk.

ture? "You may want a startled look, even a sad or depressed look. A hawk or an owl may have a mean face, and you have to capture that. Each bird, in fact, can have its own particular face."

Unique Individualism

But even after Guge has created the look he wants in a bird's face, he is not content to leave the body with a stiff or uninteresting pose. "If you want the bird to look alive, you don't want a lot of straight angles and lines. In fact, a bird doesn't sit around with both wings straight down its back, the tail perfectly straight, and everything lined up." He adds, "I'm trying to show a uniquely individual bird without having to carve it in conflict with prey or predator, or even one in flight."

The Restraints of Composition

Guge is aware of many of the rules of composition used by artists, ones that speak of the eye following

geometric patterns or being brought to a focal point. But, he says, "I don't want to have to read a book of rules to compose. I can take a branch and put my bird on it, and if it looks good, then I'm content." What is important, he says, "is that my feelings about a bird, especially one I've built up a relationship with, come across."

Perhaps in defiance of traditional rules of composition, Guge says that a composition may even come from a piece of wood. A rotted-out knot and surrounding wood from a willow tree will someday generate an owl and nest composition.

High Up on a Wire

A member of the finch family, an indigo bunting is the only small North American finch to appear blue

Guge is aware of compositional design elements such as S curves. This white-breasted nuthatch is actually part of an S curve that forms at the tail and ends at the base of the wood.

Guge says that not everything lines up perfectly in nature. Hence, he likes to give his carvings individuality. To help achieve this, he avoids symmetry where he can. He'll also turn a head or have tail feathers out of line. Shown here is an unfinished indigo bunting.

Featured in this chapter is an indigo bunting, a bird Guge sees as territorial and prone to perching high up. He also sees it as a stocky bird.

A composition may be prompted by a piece of habitat such as this willow knot. Guge says one day it will be the base for an owl.

on nearly all its body. Though it nests in bushes and thickets, and does much of its feeding on the ground, during the nesting season it is often seen on utility wires and other high perches. Guge describes the bird as very territorial. He says, "When I see an indigo bunting sitting on a wire, I see this little stocky bird watching over its area. So I want my indigo bunting to have a waiting kind of look, watching over his own piece of space."

The branch, then, for the indigo bunting composition, was nothing more than a piece of a discarded bonsai bush found in a trash can. Guge chose it not so much for its curving shape, but because it simply gave the bird height.

Sketching on a Board

Much like William Koelpin (chapter 1) and Jett Brunet (chapter 3), Guge makes use of study skins and other references, but he does not want to be too constrained by patterns. He goes so far as to say, "The day I decided not to use patterns was one of the best days of my career. I felt too regimented. If I didn't follow the pattern, I was going to ruin the bird." But, he admits, "You must go to the band saw with something."

Instead of drawing detailed preliminary patterns, or sketches as Koelpin does, he will go right to the wood and draw the outline of the bird. "They're just a few lines," he says, "to get a design." Still, after sawing, he will take more accurate measurements from a specimen.

Turning a Head

One way to achieve what Guge calls unique individualism is to have the head of a bird turned to one side or the other. "I'll make gouge marks with a Foredom and a small carbide bit to show where a turned head will be." (Compare Jett Brunet's techniques for working from a solid block of wood in chapter 3.)

Many carvers, including those featured in this book, will shape the head and body of a bird from a single piece, then sever the head, turn it, and glue it in place. (Compare Louis Kean's and Manfred Scheel's techniques in chapters 7 and 8 respectively.) This is done not only because it is easier first to carve a head symmetrically aligned with the body, but also a separate head can compensate for changes in grain that occur from upright body to tilted head. A bill or beak oriented with the grain of a separate head will have some inherent strength. But if carved from the original block at a severe angle to the body, that strength will be lost.

Guge points out, however, that wood, by the nature of its pores, expands and contracts with changes of humidity. Simply put, it moves. "So you put two pieces of wood together, and there's definitely going to be movement." But more importantly, he says, "I still would rather deal with a potential grain problem than have a seam come back and haunt me later on." He adds, "I feel very strongly about making pieces of art to last."

Feather Insertions and the Loss of Continuity

"I don't like inserting feathers any more than I like turning a head and having a seam as a result. I think you lose the feel of the bird; I guess the continuity is lost somehow. And when people say they insert feathers because it's stronger that way than it is trying to undercut them or carve them from the body block, well, I disagree. I undercut and cross my primaries

Guge will not carve a bird, sever its head, then turn and glue it. Rather, he carves the bird with its head turned from the solid block of wood. This is the beginning of a redpoll.

Note that the primaries are also carved from the original block of the wood he prefers—jelutong.

This bluebird carved by Guge shows a well-turned head.

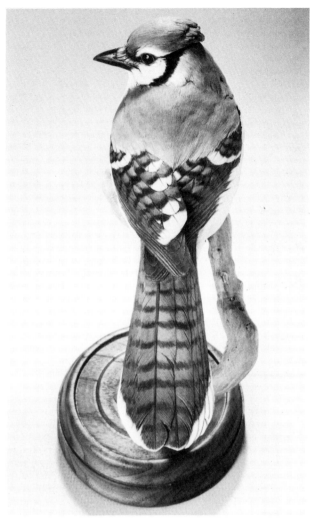

Here is a bluejay done by Guge. He says that adding separate feathers breaks up the continuity of a composition. There are no inserts on this bird. Also note that the tail feathers do not line up perfectly and note how the head is turned.

Guge begins on the indigo bunting a process he calls "landscaping." This first entails penciling in feather groups.

without problems. Now I'll admit that the wood is fragile in that area, but then that's part of the art form. A carved bird is not meant to be played with."

Molding Jelutong Like Clay

Guge uses jelutong almost exclusively. He says, "I haven't found a wood that does a better job. I've tried tupelo, but I didn't have a whole lot of success with it. There's only a small portion of the tree that's good, especially the heartwood (the inner core cells which, being dead, give strength to a tree), and I don't think I've had good wood.

"People claim that pores are a problem with jelutong. But they don't show up on my work. In fact, I don't try to hide the pores. They go away by themselves with the style I use." (See "Filled Pores" below.)

He continues, "Jelutong is brittle, and that's the worst part about it, but I grind almost exclusively, except for some scalpel work." But that is where an advantage comes in, he maintains. "This wood will grind without fuzzing up, and that's a problem I find with a wood like basswood. Also, it's very stable, especially when bone dry. I find you can almost mold it like clay."

Landscaping

Once Guge has shaped his bird in jelutong, head turned if necessary, more design must be put into it. A carbide bit will give shape to the wings, while main feather groups such as primaries, secondaries, and scapulars are defined with a small ruby carver, one of a series of grinding stones literally impregnated with ruby grit. "I'll landscape the rest of the body with muscles and bumps. Landscaping is a term I borrowed from Larry Barth (featured in *How to Carve Wildfowl*)." These too can be made with a ruby carver. (See appendix for supplier).

"You want everything to flow from the head back," Guge says. "But what I draw on the bird is my own design, be it muscles and bumps or feather flow. On the back of the indigo bunting, I start with some rows of feathers. Even though it's a solidly colored bird, you can still see individual feathers on a specimen. So some I'll carve, others will be burned into place, some just painted. But let me point out that the lines I draw are only a rough draft to follow. They do not fix me to a certain landscape. I may change them or see something differently as I'm working."

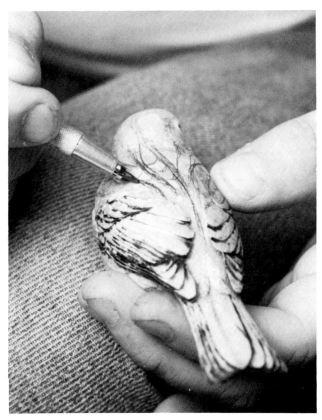

Landscaping also means making what he calls muscles and bumps. Here he roughly outlines them, and he may make many changes along the way.

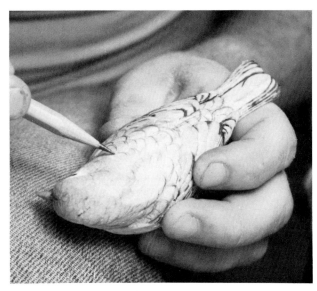

Guge says that muscles and bumps must flow from the head back.

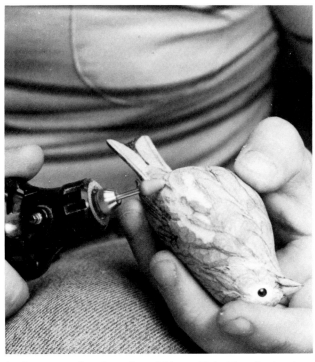

A ruby carver sculpts the surface of this songbird without leaving sharp divisions or ridges. (See appendix for supplier.)

Here is the landscaping on the underside of the indigo bunting.

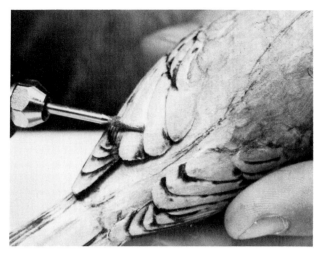

Guge demonstrates how a grinding stone with carbide grit can layer feathers. Guge prefers this to using a knife.

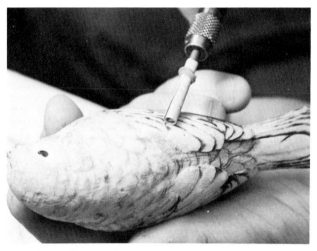

What Guge calls a "sanding stick" is used for defining feathers. It is a strip of sandpaper wrapped around a mandrel and held with a rubber band.

Here the sanding stick is used on the indigo bunting's primaries.

A Bent Grinding Stone

Guge is quick to point out that a bird's soft, fluffy feathers do not have sharp edges. So a small stone with a rounded edge will give them definition. But with feathers that have a definite edge, such as on a wing, he will still avoid sharp divisions.

Many carvers will make stop cuts, which are straight-in cuts made with a sharp tool to define an area that will be carved higher or lower than an adjacent one. Guge will avoid them. "I don't like to make stop cuts because once you've made them, there's no changing your design. And if you should try, there's a small line in the wood to contend with." What Guge uses is a small, thin stone, but with a difference: He has bent it slightly, "just enough so that one side is hitting the wood with each revolution. Believe it or not, it gives me more control and cuts faster." Without the stop cuts, then, he is "shaping feathers with one motion, eliminating the extra step of the stop cut."

A Sanding Stick

Also useful for defining individual feathers, especially their edges, is what Guge calls a sanding stick. Its core is a one-eighth-inch-diameter steel rod, the top portion of which has been cut down its middle. A strip of sandpaper is then inserted into the slot, wrapped around the shaft, and held with a rubber band.

Grinding vs. Burning

Guge says he would do all his surface texturing with grinding tools and bits if he could, but he admits that some feathers, such as flight and tail feathers, have definite, sharp edges. These, he says, cannot be achieved with a stone. "You can't get tight enough into corners with a stone."

He does look, though, for small stones and bits, finding many in dental supply catalogs, which, he says, are full of neat tools." (See appendix for suppliers.) He continues that he enjoys grinding or stoning in texture more than burning. "The stone lines hold the paint better, and you're not searing the wood, which makes too flat a surface. With stoning, you're rippling the surface, which is a nicer one to hold paint. Also, with burning, you end up with sharp lines that you can't change. But a blunter stone line can be altered.

A conical grinding stone is used to make texturing lines.

Here a burning-pen tip gives sharp definition to primary feathers.

Guge would prefer not to do any burning, but in an area such as this sharply defined tail feather he must.

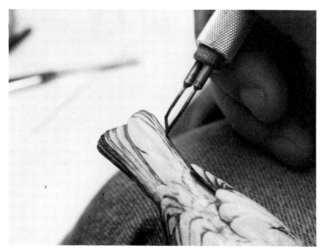

Another burning tip can be used to define tail feather separations.

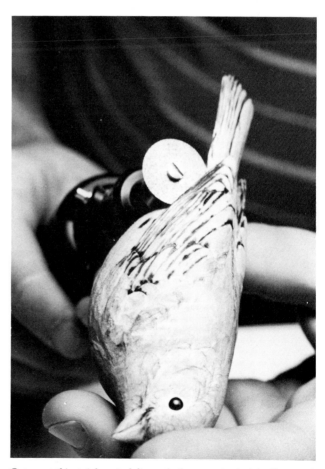

Guge says this stainless steel disc, only three-quarter inch in diameter, is excellent for separating the primaries from the body. Fine diamond grit is bonded to the metal.

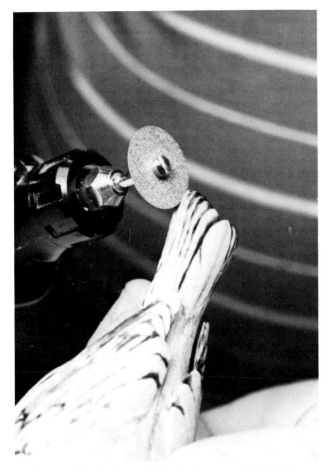

The same disc in a Dremel Moto-Tool can separate tail feathers.

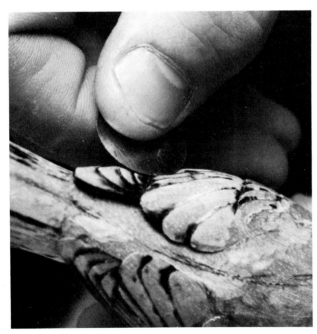

This small diamond disc can even be hand-held to separate feathers.

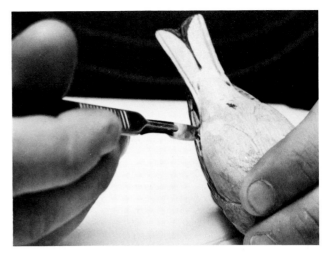

Guge demonstrates that a scalpel can reach far in to separate the primaries from the body.

"I think a lot of people overdo texturing. Over the last couple of years, I've gone from fine, tightly burned detail to a smoother, looser surface. This gives me more freedom in painting and a softer, more realistic surface." He adds, "If every feather is burned perfectly, you can't change anything."

Filled Pores

Guge had stated that the pores inherent in jelutong, and a disadvantage to many carvers, do not reveal themselves with his techniques. He explains that those very pores, which can show through even heavy painting, become filled. "Through the sanding and grinding I do, those pores end up being filled with sawdust. And I want to leave that where it is. I will use a rotary bristle brush to remove some of the roughness left by the texturing process, but not enough to lift the dust from the pores."

Sanding devices include not only the sanding stick and bristle brush, but also de-fuzzing or sanding pads (available from Craft Cove), which he uses after the initial shaping. (Address in appendix.)

Dremel Moto-Tool Preferred

Though Guge will use the Foredom Tool for achieving the bird's basic shape, he prefers the Dremel, especially for landscaping and texturing. "With the Dremel, I like its balance and the lack of back pressure from the flexible shaft that the Foredom has."

He also appreciates the faster speed of the Dremel

Guge says dental catalogs are filled with useful tools he can use for shaping a bird.

This wood de-fuzzer, available from Craft Cove, removes any edges left by the ruby carver used in a previous step. (See appendix for address.)

over the Foredom, 30,000 rpm for the Dremel as opposed to 14,000 for the Foredom. He finds that with the higher speed, he has more control over his texturing, while making cleaner cuts.

The Hot Tool

Guge uses The Hot Tool to edge his feathers after they have been cut with a stone. (See appendix for manufacturer.) He will, however, use other burning pens for different effects. One puts in the fine feather lines around the beak. Another accentuates a break between feathers on an area like the tail. But he is critical of some burning tools that allow too much heat into the pen handles.

Hairy Beginnings

Guge points out, when burning in detail, that feather separations are barely visible at the base of the tail and at the base of the secondary feathers. "You can't differentiate one feather from another in these areas," he says, describing them as having hairy beginnings. "They blend into each other and then spread out into individual feathers. So it's important to capture such subtleties in your carving."

The Foot Bone Connected to the Leg Bone?

"You don't realize how similar the foot anatomy of a bird is to a human's leg," Guge says, though he points

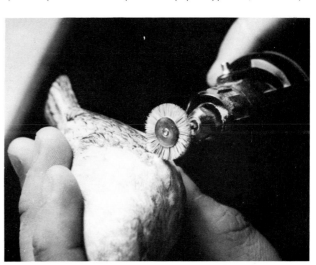

Surface dust is removed with this rotary bristle brush, but not the dust that fills the pores of the jelutong. That dust will help seal the wood.

One of the burning tools Guge prefers to use is the Hot Tool. Here he defines and smooths the edges of the flight feathers. (See appendix for manufacturer.)

Shown here is the finished texturing and burning on the indigo bunting.

Guge points out on a specimen the hairy beginnings at the base of the secondary feathers. These make the separations barely visible. This is something carvers must be conscious of when making a bird, he says.

Note the stoning done on the breast area.

This view of the partially finished bird shows how sharply the tail feathers were defined with the burning tool.

Guge studies the foot of an indigo bunting specimen. He says that the entire structure up to the first joint is the foot. The rest is the leg.

out that what seems to be the leg is still part of the foot up to the first joint. And making feet is an aspect of bird carving Guge particularly enjoys.

"Stand in front of a mirror," he suggests, "and lift up one leg. Watch what happens to your body, to the angle of the leg. It's going to be the same with the bird. The body will shift its weight over that one supporting leg. And this leads to a problem I see with birds at competitions. Carvers will have a bird standing on one leg without any compensation for the mass above. So you end up ruining the look of a bird that is not balanced properly."

Guge advises taking time to study foot and leg anatomy and even handling easily obtainable birds such as chickens.

He demonstrates how most of the leg can disappear into the belly feathers. This is a consideration when making legs and feet, he notes.

Wire Feet

To make the feet, Guge chooses wire, the gauge of which will be equal to the diameter of the foot bones. Since there are tendons in the rear of the feet, he also selects wire with a smaller diameter for those, which will later be soldered to the backs of the feet.

"Depending on how the bird is standing," he says, "you will see a lot of leg bone, or very little. Also, that will depend on whether the bird is standing on an inclining or declining branch. What happens is that some of one leg or both get concealed in the belly feathers." But, he cautions, the foot wires, no matter how they are bent or shaped, have to be the same length.

Still another problem is where the feet wires come out of the bird's belly, because of partial concealment that may occur. In addition, a bird may be tipped slightly forward or backward. Guge's indigo bunting is slightly forward, suggesting it is ready to take off.

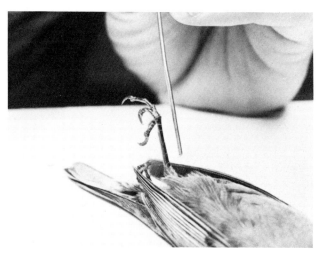

Guge chooses a piece of copper wire, the gauge of which equals the thickness of the foot bone.

Removing the Bird from Its Feet

Guge says that some carvers will make the feet after the bird has been painted, but he prefers to handle the bird as little as possible after that final preparation. What he must do, then, is position the feet on the branch as he makes them, making sure he can remove the bird easily once the feet are positioned. He says, "I drill both holes into the underside at the same angle – up and sideways. That way I can slip the bird off to paint it."

To straighten a bent piece of wire, Guge rolls it on a milled surface under a block of wood.

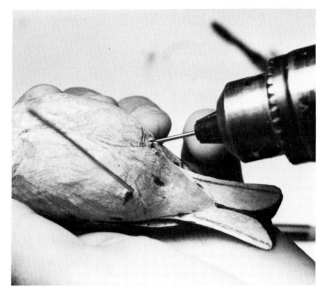

Drilling the holes to accept the foot and leg wire is crucial and should be done at the same angle if the bird is to be removed from feet made stationary on a base or branch.

A measurement of the foot bone is taken and transferred to the copper wire.

Guge has bent the wire to shape, now comparing it to the shape of the foot and leg bones.

Guge decides how the indigo bunting will perch on its branch.

Making Toes

Two methods have traditionally been used to make toes, both involving individual pieces of wire. One has been to epoxy them to the foot, the other to solder them. Guge says of the latter, "When you do that and try to bend them to fit the shape of the branch, you'll end up breaking all the solder joints. What I do is make the four toes for each foot out of two pieces of copper wire, bending them and soldering them around the foot armature. This way, you're bending against copper rather than a solder joint."

Working on a block of wood he calls a soldering block, Guge builds the toe structure, following two steps before joining the toes. One is that he makes a slight hollow in each foot to accept the separately bent toe wires. "It's really a notch," he says, "to make a better solder joint." The other step is stapling the toes to the soldering block. This will prevent their moving when being soldered to the feet.

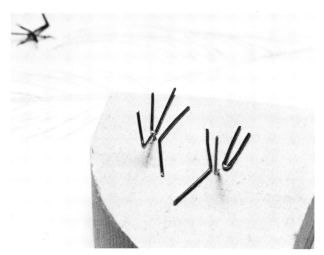

Guge lays the feet and toes on what he calls a soldering block, where he will join them. Note that two bent wires comprise four toes.

The wires have been cut to length. The vertical ends will be inserted into the branch and will hold the feet in place.

A slight notch is cut in the toe wires so that they will better join the foot wires.

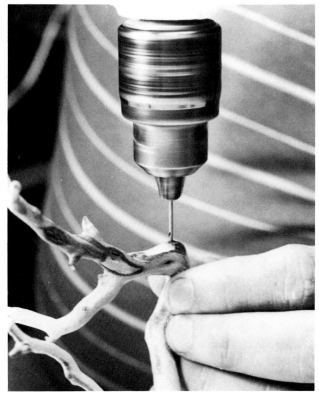

A small drill bit makes the holes in the branch to accept the ends of the feet.

Before soldering, Guge staples the toe wires in place. This prevents movement.

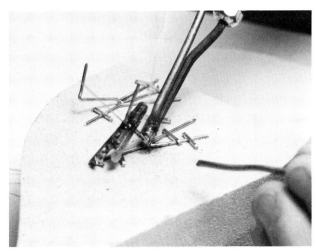

Soldering provides a stronger bond than epoxy putty, which many other carvers will use to attach toes to feet.

Here we see the result of the soldering.

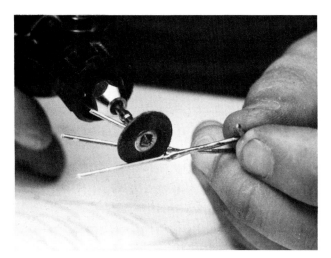

Excess solder is ground off with a sanding disc. He says a small cutter can also be used.

The solder joint is cleaned up with a de-fuzzer in a Dremel. Cleaning is important because Guge will seal the metal with lacquer. Metal oxidizes and will otherwise bleed through the paint, he says.

Guge is seen here working in his shop on the toes for the indigo bunting. The books above his head are for reference.

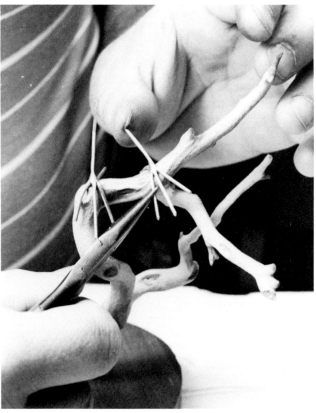

He bends the toe wires around the perch. He says that if he had used a single piece of wire for the toes, they would have broken off with this procedure.

The indigo bunting is joined to the leg and toe wires, but it can be removed easily and put back into place. This allows Guge to paint it off its perch. And if he attached the legs after painting, he would run the risk of rubbing paint off the bird.

The bent toes of the indigo bunting.

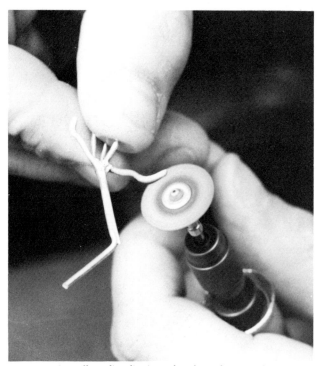

A small sanding disc is used to shape the toe nails.

A de-fuzzer removes small filings around the toes.

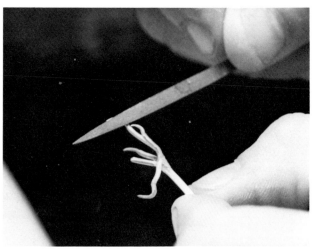

A needle file puts in the toe joints.

Detailing with Epoxy Putty

While detailing of the toes can be accomplished with small bits and a rotary sanding disc, forming of the surface of the feet can be achieved with epoxy putty. In two parts, the putty, a Duro product, can be worked and shaped with any number of instruments before it hardens. With it, Guge can affect scales on the feet and the pads on the bottom of the toes, which help the bird grasp something. Guge does advise, though, to use a fresh mix as much as possible, none older than fifteen minutes. He also says that the epoxy will adhere to the copper feet and toes better if the metal parts are warmed, suggesting that a light bulb will do the job. After the putty does harden, which can take up to 12 hours, he seals it with a lacquer to harden it even more.

Spackled Eyes

For setting in the glass eyes of his birds, Guge has a unique technique. When he cuts in the eye holes, he makes a continuous channel instead of shallow depressions. He then fills this through-cavity with spackle. When the eyes are set into either side of the head, he can get them perfectly balanced, for "pushing one in will squeeze out the other." But he cautions that this is a small bird technique. "I wouldn't want to fill a large head with this water-based material," he says, citing the possibility of the material chipping or cracking. He adds that he will also use the spackle for making eyelids.

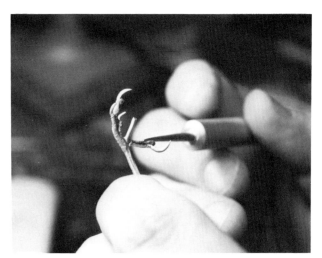

The bottom of birds' toes have pads which help the bird grip its perch. To simulate these, Guge uses epoxy putty and shapes it with a dental probe.

Pads applied, the toes show the results of filing their joints.

Guge seals the wire with a mix of 70 percent lacquer and 30 percent lacquer thinner.

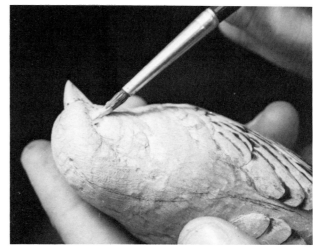

Guge fills the eye cavity with spackle before inserting the glass eyes. The cavity actually goes through the head.

Here is the finished foot for a chickadee.

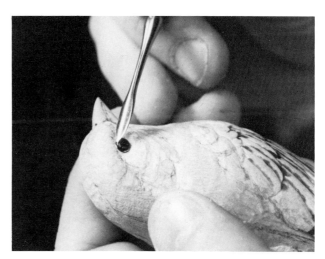

Here he shapes the eyelids with a dental tool.

This epoxy-covered foot was made for a burrowing owl, one of a composition of three birds Guge made the 1985 World Championship Wildfowl Carving Competition.

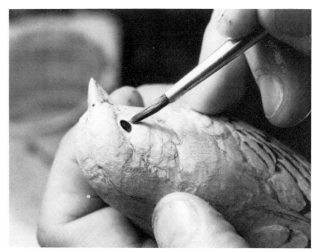

A brush and water smooth out the spackle paste around the eye sockets.

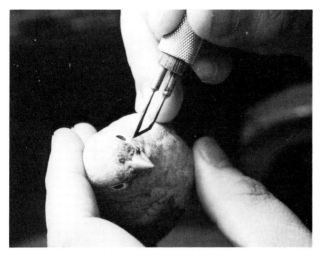

Burning around the eyes is done with a skew-tipped burner.

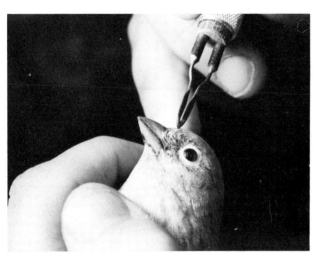

A sharp tip makes deep lines on the forehead.

Guge mixes his paints on glass, with white paper underneath. The glass cleans easily and the paper simulates white gesso.

A Wet Palette

At one time, Guge mixed his colors only on glass with white paper underneath – the glass being a smooth and easily cleaned surface, the white imitating the color of the paint primer. Now Guge uses both that method and a wet palette. "It has a special paper that you put on foam pad. You soak the foam and the paper wicks up the water." Its biggest advantage, he says, is that it keeps paint mixes up to five days without drying out, a long time considering that the acrylics he uses dry in less than an hour in most cases.

A Sanding Sealer and Gesso

Before Guge starts to paint, he first seals the wood of the bird with his own sanding sealer mix, one that

Guge also uses a wet palette. A special paper on water-soaked foam rubber wicks up the water and keeps the acrylics he uses from drying out.

Guge has laid out blobs of acrylic colors on the wet palette.

will allow the primer to flow on more smoothly. Two parts satin lacquer and one part paint thinner, it is fast drying, leaves no brush marks, and soaks evenly into the wood.

The next step is to apply gesso, a clay-based primer that can be used before acrylics or even oil paints. Guge says he primes the entire bird with a number of thin coats of four parts water to one part gesso. He uses a fairly stiff brush, he says, and even dry-brushes the primer onto the wood. He explains that he does not want the pigment in the gesso to clog up too much of the lower parts of the textured surface. But he admits that this pigment may well explain why the pores of the jelutong don't show on his carvings.

A Holding Tool

Decoy carvers often employ a keel or scrap of wood temporarily glued to the bottom of the duck, allowing the wood scrap and not the bird to be held. Guge has devised his own holding device. It is nothing more than a dowel with a screw epoxied into one end. The threaded part can then be inserted into the bottom of the bird. And what of the hole made by the screw? Spackle again comes into use.

Painting in One Sitting

While several of the carvers featured in this book use oil paints, Guge prefers acrylics, paints that are water soluble. He admits that oils can be blended exceptionally well, but the drying time is considerable.

Guge uses a stiff brush to apply the gesso primer. He is careful to spread the gesso pigment evenly, getting into all the crevices and texturing lines.

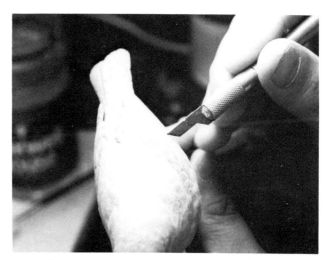

During the priming, he may scrape away some imperfections with an X-acto knife.

Guge prepares to paint the indigo bunting and even the branch, which came from a bonsai bush. In the jar is the lacquer and paint thinner he uses to seal the bird.

The indigo bunting has been completely covered with gesso.

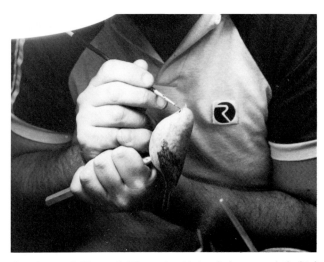

Guge has made his own holding tool so his hands do not touch the bird. It is nothing more than a dowel with a screw epoxied into one end.

(Compare Marc Schultz's application of oils in chapter 6.) With acrylics there is not a lot of time to blend because of their fast drying properties. Yet, with oils, "You have to plan out what you're doing because you can't paint over what you've just done. And if an oil doesn't cover well, you still have a long wait. I went from acrylics to oil because I didn't know how to use acrylics. But when I mastered the blending methods with washes of color (or colors mixed with water), I went back to them. Now I can paint a bird in one sitting."

Basic Colors for an Indigo Bunting

Guge uses a few basic acrylic colors for the indigo bunting, with water as a medium for each. Then each of those colors is divided up, using other colors, to produce different values or intensities of the original color. He starts with the darker indigo color, which is a mix of thalo blue and alizarin crimson. He creates a lighter blue by mixing thalo blue, cobalt blue, and cadmium crimson. Into those mixes he adds different amounts of white and burnt umbers to change the degree of color. For the black areas on the bird, he will use a mix of ultramarine blue and burnt umber.

"You may want to take the same liberties in painting the bird that you took in forming it," Guge says. He points out, "Everyone sees colors differently, so paint what you feel."

Even different lighting affects the visible colors. "Take a study skin and put it under incandescent light, which is your household bulb, and then under fluorescent. The differences are remarkable. The incandescent light will project a yellow tone, while a fluorescent bulb will project a blue or cooler color. This certainly creates problems in deciphering colors."

Another problem is the nature of the bird itself. He says, "I can't find two birds of the same species colored exactly alike, but there do seem to be some basic averages of color. So I strive for an average feather color to give the general idea of an indigo bunting."

Wet on Wet

Guge says the transition from one color to another is important. "I use a wet-on-wet method so that one color blends right into the next. Many people will paint one color of acrylics, wait until it dries, then go back with another color and paint next to it. For me, I blend my colors while the entire bird is wet, adding color here and there. You get a good transition this way."

He continues, "There's no special skill using this method. I study my bird ahead of time to know where I'm going, and I have all my colors mixed ahead of time."

Painting Notes

"I start with a burnt umber and ultramarine blue. From there, I add a little more burnt umber and white to come up with a warmer black. Still more white and burnt umber achieve a browner color for the primaries.

Guge compares his first wash of an indigo blue to his specimen.

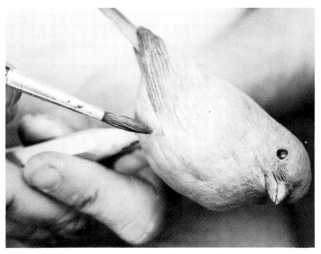

Here he applies a mix of thalo blue and alizarin crimson.

Guge checks the tail feather colors.

Guge checks his progress with his specimen.

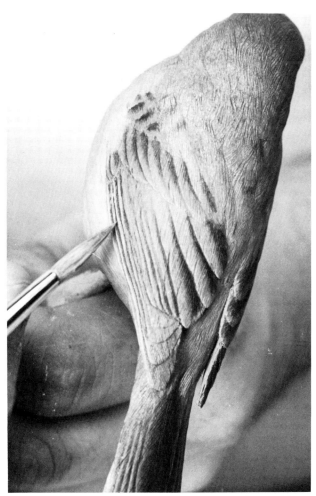

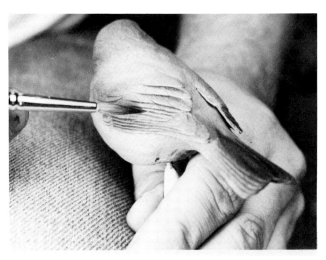

On the primaries he applies a medium blue color.

The dark bars he is painting are a mix of ultramarine blue and burnt umber.

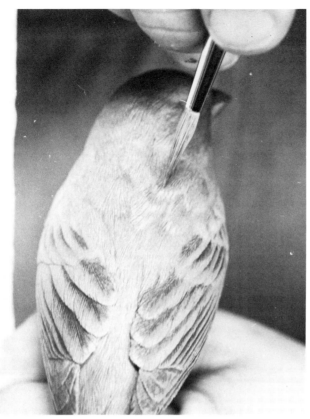

On the back, he applies a mix of the indigo color he used on the rest of the body and thalo green with white.

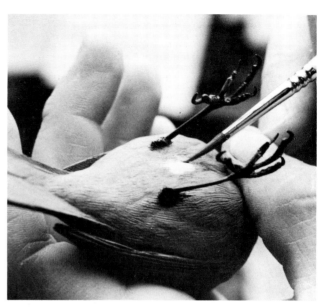

The hole made by the holding tool's screw is spackled over and painted.

These dark patches are made from a mix of ultramarine blue and burnt umber.

The indigo bunting is finished.

Note the splits on the primary feathers. Some are scalpel cuts, while others Guge made with a burning tool.

Another view of the finished bird shows muscles, bumps, and undercut primaries. The feet were painted black with a white and burnt umber glaze.

Note the lack of symmetry in the tail feathers and how other feathers are neither equal in size nor are they positioned the same way on either side of the back.

Guge may paint a stickup profile like this one as a guide or study aid.

The stickup is made from one-half-inch jelutong.

Using a Brush

Guge, who uses Grumbacher and Langnickel brushes, says that paint lodged in the heel or base of the bristles and allowed to dry will ruin a good brush. He advises that a simple way to keep paint out of the heel is to saturate the brush with the medium before painting, water being the case for acrylics. It will keep the stronger mix of paint from getting into that area.

Peterson's Field Guide

Guge uses dead specimens of birds loaned to him by a nearby nature center. He will also use a combination of photos and even Peterson's Field Guide. "It can be helpful because Peterson's already worked out the bird and deciphered the colors for you." He adds that even black and white photos are helpful for seeing what he calls "color boundaries." As for seeing an indigo bunting outdoors, he says, "If he's sitting up on a wire facing you, all you're going to see is a dark blue color."

Unnatural Wood

Interestingly, Guge did not leave the branch on which the indigo bunting perches in its natural state. He explains, "Any time you take a natural thing and put an unnatural thing with it, the unnatural component looks more unnatural. But putting a carved bird

Guge will reshape branches used as perches and even paint them. He says that a natural object does not complement an unnatural one—that is, a carved and painted bird. Here he is using a Karbide Kutzall abrasive burr. Available from P.C. English Enterprises, Inc.

"There is an aqua color, formed from the blue and green mix, that I use to create airy feathers, ones that suggest light passing through them. These I'll highlight with a blue-green mix that has more of the white I've used in all the mixes added to it.

"I work for a medium tone of blue on the wings, then come back with the darker tones, then highlight the edges with lighter tones where I want the feathers to be airy-looking.

"Basically, then, I start with my medium tones of color, then develop out from that, with both light and dark tones of color. This method gives more roundness to areas. (Compare John Gewerth's techniques in chapter 5.)

"I make my birds to look good under artificial light, basically incandescent. That's the way most art is displayed, particularly from a single light source.

"I paint transparently. That means I keep my colors thin, allowing the gesso to show through and help create the colors. That's one of the reasons I don't like my pieces shown in daylight. Too much of the white would show through. I could paint over and over until I got a nice solid color over the gesso. But I would also get a solid sheen that's too shiny."

on something that has also been carved and textured and painted brings the two things together."

Guge often reshapes his own wood branches by removing pieces or joining smaller branches to larger ones. For the indigo bunting branch, he shaped and textured a piece of wood, which previously had been sandblasted, with a wire brush in a Foredom to duplicate the texture of real wood. Next, he covered the wood with gesso. Finally, to achieve what he describes as "the nice gray patina typical of bleached-out wood," he used a combination of burnt umber, ultramarine blue, white, and a small amount of yellow. "By painting it, I can get just the tone I want, perhaps even a color to complement the bird," he says.

Turning a Base

Though lathe-turned bases are readily available to carvers, with many different shapes and profiles, Guge prefers to turn his own. Using walnut, he made the base for the indigo bunting with a variety of traditional tools including a gouge, a skew chisel, and even an old file he ground to shape. "I'll make my base as close to the size of the carving and branch as I can," he says, adding that by making his own, he can achieve the profile he wants. "Also, I'll have something that fits the carving just right." Yet he has become dissatisfied with the turned bases so frequently used by himself and other bird carvers today. A future project he is planning will have two juncos on a bittersweet branch with no base at all.

Guge first paints the branch with gesso. After that he will apply thin coats of grays and browns.

A wide gouge begins to shape a walnut base for the indigo bunting on a wood lathe.

A wire bristle brush in a Dremel creates a textured surface on the branch.

A parting tool begins to put definition into the profile. Guge makes his own bases so that they are the exact shape and size he desires.

A reshaped rattail file is used to put an ogee curve into the edge of the base. This homemade tool acts like a gouge.

A parting tool puts a flat profile at the top of the base.

A skew chisel finishes the edge profile.

A de-fuzzing pad smooths the edge of the base.

Guge drills a hole through the base so that a wood screw secures the branch.

Guge uses a scrap piece for a temporary base. Note the wood screw that holds the branch in place.

The branch is located on the walnut base.

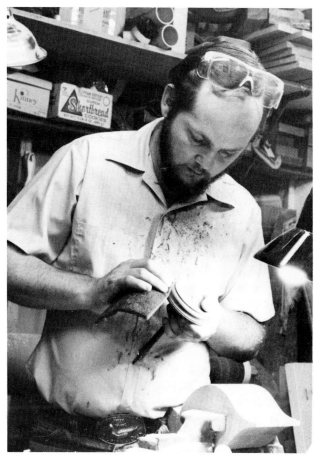

Between coats, Guge polishes the finish with a de-fuzzing pad. He says this gives the finish a hand-rubbed look.

The base is sprayed with Tester's Dull Cote, a flat varnish.

Posting a Bird

Guge points out that there have been notable and damaging accidents when carvings have been shipped through the U.S. mail service or even with private carriers. He believes that while no packing system is foolproof, he has designed a package that will considerably reduce damage.

Using Styrofoam pellets as the basic packing material, Guge first puts his composition into a plastic bag to prevent the pellets from rubbing against the carving. He warns, though, against packing the pellets too tightly. "I first put pellets into the bottom of the box, then lay the bird in the box and pour more pellets over it." But the packing does not stop there. He then puts that box within a larger box with a layer of pellets between. Guge says this prevents a "whiplash" effect. "I pack it this way so that if the box stops abruptly, the bird doesn't."

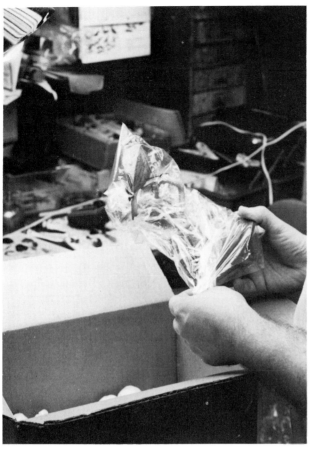

Posting a bird to prevent damage takes some care. Guge first puts his indigo bunting and base in a plastic bag.

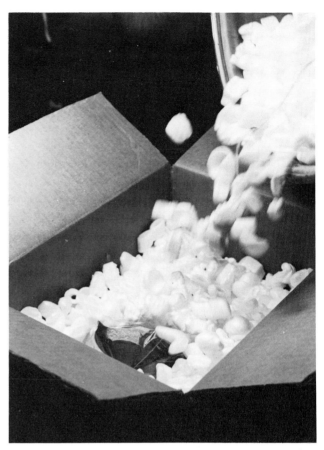

Next, he fills the box to its top with pellets.

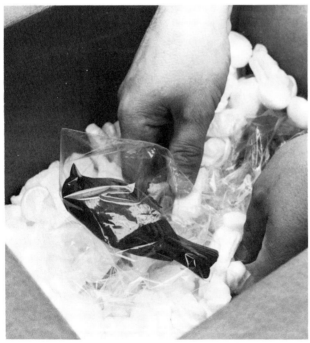

He next places the carving in a box half filled with Styrofoam pellets.

The box is sealed with packing tape.

The last step is to place the sealed box into a larger box with a layer of Styrofoam pellets on all sides. This prevents a whiplash effect, Guge says.

Hazards of the Art Form

Guge wonders just how conscious carvers are of the hazards of the tools, chemicals, and even the woods they use. He points out the fine dust produced by grinding, and asks whether it is a latent carcinogen, appearing as a cancer a decade or two later. And he reminds carvers of the health risks involved with using cyanoacrylate glues, epoxies, paints, lacquers, and other chemicals. He says even the grinding tools, though not especially dangerous, can cause tendonitis from their vibrations.

Another Medium?

"Will wood survive as a medium for this art form?" Guge asks. He believes it is possible that artists might well go to some other medium that will take a better texture, be more stable, "maybe something that can be fused together when making separate parts, or big enough and strong enough that you can carve from a single piece."

He refers to a product called Super Sculpey, a clay-like material Guge has used when making reference models of birds to be carved, and available from Craft Cove. See appendix for address. He says it can be molded easily, dries rock hard, and can be painted only hours later. He adds that some carvers have been incorporating Super Sculpey into their work, though birds' feet, cast in pewter, have been sold for some time to carvers wanting to avoid making their own.

Another reason he questions the future of wood as a medium is the way it is treated. "You've put pieces of

Guge may make a model before carving. This one, for an indigo bunting, is made from a ceramic-like sculpturing compound called Super Sculpey. Available from Craft Cove, Inc. (See appendix for address.)

When Super Sculpey is heated at 300 degrees for thirty minutes, it dries ceramic hard and becomes chip-proof and shatter-proof.

wood together with glue, you've burned it, then you've put a clay primer [gesso] over it. On top of that, you put plastic [acrylics], and we don't even know the life-time of that material. Can we expect all of these things to hold up equally well or for that matter hold up together?"

Two for Approval

A composition Guge made for the World Championship Life-size Decorative Division is made of three burrowing owls. Only nine to eleven inches long, these owls can be found in the American West and even in Florida, usually residing on prairies and feeding on insects and small mammals.

Guge says he was always fascinated with these diminutive owls. "I wanted all the eyes of the birds to meet at a central point, though that's not something you can see."

The design of Two for Approval has one bird, the

Also made from Super Sculpey are these diminutive models for a burrowing owl composition.

adult female, higher up than the two juveniles. "The two young birds are bringing home one of their first catches, a grasshopper, for the mother's approval. The piece makes more sense when you know the title."

But there is little on the base except material simulating earth. "I wanted to show the barrenness of their lifestyle, a prairie perhaps. So I didn't want bushes or grass or shrubs. I wanted a plain setting." To get the effects of packed earth, Guge used Durham's Rock Hard Water Putty, while he made the rocks out of wood and covered them with a mix of gesso and the Durham putty. (Compare Manfred Scheel's use of the product in chapter 8.)

The base was turned from a large piece of two-inch-thick walnut, with a slight recess made in the top. But the Durham putty did not go directly into that recess. As Guge points out, "Whenever you're working with this putty or a plaster material, you face the problem of warpage from water escaping from the mix into the wood. Ultimately, warped wood will crack the putty or plaster." Guge's solution? "By putting the putty mix on Styrofoam, the water stays in the putty." An added advantage of the Styrofoam is that less putty has to be used, thus reducing the weight of the composition.

Of the Durham Rock Hard Water Putty, he says it will take paint almost like a stain, though he can add colors to the mix itself.

The entire composition was put on a turntable, making the piece "art in the round," Guge says. "It's now a total sculpture." It was also something he used while composing the piece, and he will probably use the turntable with more carvings.

The finished sculpture Guge calls "Two for Approval." It portrays two immature owls returning to the mother with a grasshopper. All eyes of the birds meet at a central point.

Guge made life-size models of the owls, as shown here.

This is one of the immature burrowing owls, made from Super Sculpey.

Mirroring Your Work

Another aid to the sculpturing of Two for Approval was a mirror. Set up behind the work in progress, Guge was able to see the front and back of the composition at the same time. Guge says that it eliminated a lopsided effect because he could see how the backs of the birds related to their fronts. (Jett Brunet also uses this technique in chapter 3.)

Best-in-World Mourning Doves

As mentioned previously, Guge won Best in World in 1984 for his mourning dove composition. Guge describes the birds, male and female, as being at a mountain runoff stream, each looking at the other. The water is a plastic casting resin in a walnut base, and the stones are jelutong. (Compare Louis Kean's use of this resin in chapter 7.) Did Guge have anything particular in mind when he planned out the piece? He answers, "There was no deep thought involved. It just looked good on paper during some sketching."

Winter Cardinals

Guge has these birds in what he describes as a simple winter setting. "This is typical of the way you see them," he says. "I also used the snow to show the cold and help reflect the puffiness of the birds, to give more reason for it. I see cold in the piece," he adds.

The snow is a mixture of plaster and gesso with some iridescent white acrylic and a gloss medium added. For the wood the birds are perched on, he used

Winner of Best in World for the 1984 Decorative Miniature Wildfowl Carving category, this mourning dove composition is in the collection of the North American Wildfowl Art Museum, The Ward Foundation, Salisbury, Maryland.

This female dove might possibly be getting ready to take a drink, says Guge.

The male of the pair, only five inches long, is looking at the female. Note the stoned texture.

Here is a view of the back of the male dove. The branch was handmade, says Guge, and painted with gray acrylics.

One pouring of plastic casting resin filled the base to represent a mountain runoff, where birds come to drink.

The rocks and stones are made from jelutong. Some of the texture was carved in, some pounded in.

Done in 1983, these cardinals are depicted in a winter setting. The snow is a mix of plastic, gesso, and a gloss medium. They are from the collection of Dr. and Mrs. Stan Matusik, Dundee, Illinois.

Guge preferred stoning to burning on the body of this male cardinal.

Guge gave the bird what he describes as a calm and rested look.

Shown here is the primary feather layout for the male cardinal.

Note the puffiness of the male.

Here is the back of the male. For the basic red color, Guge mixed cadmium red, burnt umber, and white.

This shows the layout of the back of the female. Note the turn of the head and the non-symmetrical tail feathers.

Here are the primaries for the female.

different pieces joined together, saying, "This way, I ended up with just the shape I wanted."

As for the miniature birds themselves, male and female, Guge consciously kept the texturing to a minimum, aiming for a smoother shape.

A Friendly Bluejay

"Disliking the normally mean, aggressive nature of the bluejay, I wanted to carve the bird to be softer, cuter, more friendly perhaps. I also took some liberties with color to achieve this," Guge explains. "Rather than making the back such a dark purple color, I put more blue into it to blend better with the rest of the bird."

The flight and tail feathers of the bird he burned, but he stoned the rest.

This bluejay was carved in 1983. It was picked for the national tour of the Leigh Yawkey Woodson Art Museum.

Carved in 1983, this piece was chosen by the Leigh Yawkey Woodson Museum to travel on a year-long national tour of bird art.

A Spiraling Composition

"This is a spiral composition which supports the bird. The shape is pleasing because it points your eye right up to the bird," says Guge.

Rather than employ a real strand of barbed wire in the composition, Guge made his own. Using wire from a coat hanger, he first glued sawdust to it and painted it to look like rust, using burnt sienna and washes of raw umber.

"I wanted the old wood and the barbed wire. It's typical of the habitat of a bluebird."

Here can be studied the head and face of the bird. He separated the crest feathers using a burning tool and a diamond disc.

Note the muscles and bumps on the back of the bird.

Guge gave his bluejay a friendlier look than a real bird actually has.

This shows the layout of the tail feathers. Note the use of splits.

This bluebird is on a strand of barbed wire Guge made from a coat hanger. It's from the collection of Mr. and Mrs. Stephen Keibler, Dundee, Illinois.

Here can be studied the layout of the back. Note that no inserts were used.

Guge describes this as a spiraling composition.

Guge used sawdust, burnt sienna, and a wash of raw umber to create the look of rusted wire.

A White-breasted Nuthatch

"The design for this piece came from the wood, though at one time it was a bigger piece. In the twist of the wood, I envisioned a nuthatch walking down it," Guge explains. "So I designed the bird to 'repeat' the shape of the wood, an S shape. It starts with the tail and ends with the head."

A Petite Upland Sandpiper

"This is an elegant bird that doesn't need a lot of anything else with it. It looks good by itself. So when I did it, I had no thought of composition. It's nice and petite and is a well-scaled miniature." No doubt the judges agreed, for it won Best in Show at the International Decoy Contest.

Guge gave this bird an inquisitive look.

The design for this white-breasted nuthatch came from the shape of the wood. It is in the collection of Mr. and Mrs. Stephen Keibler, Dundee, Illinois.

The shape of the nuthatch's body reflects the S curve of the wood.

Here can be studied the underside of the bird.

Guge used basswood for this bird with copper feet and legs.

This simple upland sandpiper, a miniature carved in 1982, won Best in Show at the International Decoy show held in Davenport, Iowa. This bird is in the collection of Dr. and Mrs. Stan Matusik, Dundee, Illinois.

Here one can study the side.

Note how the bird balances itself.

This shows the feather patterns for the back.

Guge carved this miniature goshawk in 1985. It is in the collection of Mr. and Mrs. Tom Rossetter, St. Charles, Illinois.

A Mean-looking Goshawk

Guge says that this goshawk is between one-quarter and one-third its actual size. Carved in 1985, he wanted to achieve a mean look to this bird of prey.

A Manteling Kestrel

Though Guge was commissioned to create a flying bird, he convinced his customers to accept this manteling or wing-spreading raptor, a bird and attitude he had wanted to do for some time.

One of the design problems to the piece was trying to carve it from one piece of wood. Finding that difficult, if not impossible, to do, Guge made the primary and secondary groups for one wing out of a separate piece of jelutong. This was then inserted under the

This illustrates a side view of the bird.

Here is a close-up of the side and breast of the goshawk.

Note the use of splits on the breast area.

Here can be studied the layout of the back feathers of the bird.

This is Guge's life-size kestrel underway in jelutong.

The manteling kestrel was completed in the fall of 1985. The grasses, made of copper, reflect the attitude of a bird getting its balance on a windy day. These grasses he first painted with green enamel and then gesso and green acrylics.

This manteling bird, also called a sparrow hawk, has its wings away from the body but it is not in flight. Still needed is a separately carved set of primary and secondary feathers for the right wing. Guge decided to do this when he found he could not get a piece of jelutong big enough to accommodate the body and both of the wings.

The smallest and most common hawk, the kestrel has a distinctive feather pattern on the underside of its wings.

wing coverts, which were carved with the rest of the body. No seam showed.

Its prey is a grasshopper, made out of wood, copper wire, and epoxy. Guge's explanation for the choice? "People don't want a mouse or a bird in the kestrel's talons. They're uncomfortable with that. But they don't cringe when they see a dead insect."

Guge adds that he wanted to show the bird somewhat off balance in the wind. The grass, made out of copper, emphasizes this, he explains.

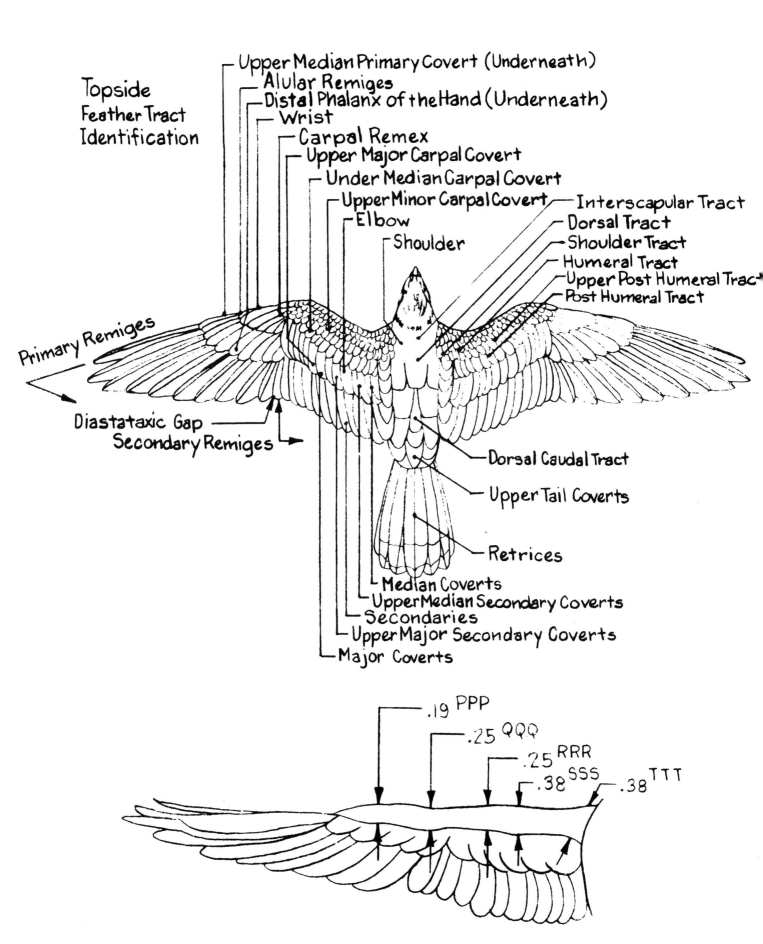

Topside
Feather Tract
Identification

Upper Median Primary Covert (Underneath)
Alular Remiges
Distal Phalanx of the Hand (Underneath)
Wrist
Carpal Remex
Upper Major Carpal Covert
Under Median Carpal Covert
Upper Minor Carpal Covert — Interscapular Tract
Elbow — Dorsal Tract
Shoulder — Shoulder Tract
— Humeral Tract
— Upper Post Humeral Tract
— Post Humeral Tract

Primary Remiges

Diastataxic Gap
Secondary Remiges

Dorsal Caudal Tract

Upper Tail Coverts

Retrices

Median Coverts
Upper Median Secondary Coverts
Secondaries
Upper Major Secondary Coverts
Major Coverts

.19 PPP
.25 QQQ
.25 RRR
.38 SSS
.38 TTT

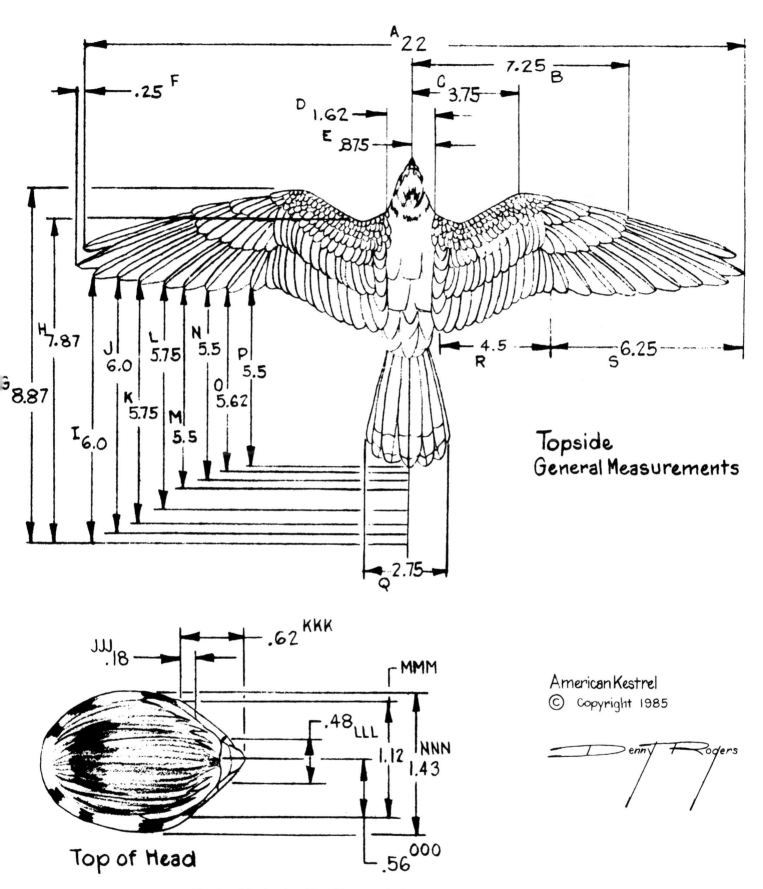

A 22
B 7.25
C 3.75
D 1.62
E .875
F .25

H 7.87
G 8.87
J 6.0
L 5.75
N 5.5
P 5.5
K 5.75
O 5.62
I 6.0
M 5.5

R 4.5
S 6.25

Q 2.75

**Topside
General Measurements**

JJJ .18
KKK .62
MMM
LLL .48
NNN 1.43
1.12
OOO .56

Top of Head

American Kestrel
© Copyright 1985

Denny Rogers

Sketches of the American Kestrel from a study chart published by Denny Rogers.

Here can be studied the face.

Note the color patterns on the back.

In its talons is a grasshopper Guge made from wood and copper.

Here one can see where Guge joined the primary and secondary feathers to the rest of the wing.

These are the tail feathers. Note the large split Guge carved into one of the feathers and how that feather does not lie symmetrically with the others.

Recognition Due

Guge believes art should be priced at a point that equals what the artist has spent a good portion of his lifetime perfecting. "Some of our best painters are getting $50,000 or more for a piece. But some of the best carvers only get a fraction of that for the same working time. The problem is that what we're doing is still so new, and it's going to take time before it's widely accepted."

He adds, "What we're doing is just as important and difficult, perhaps even more difficult, because we're working in three dimensions instead of two. We have to know all the anatomy of a bird, not just one view of it. Yet we receive far less money than the wildfowl painter."

Guge points out that art critics are in fact reluctant to accept what he and others do as art because of where they see the work exhibited. "How can the critics accept this for what it is when so many of the shows are held at Holiday Inns and even places like union halls?"

Still, Guge believes that exhibits held at such places as the Leigh Yawkey Woodson Museum will help change attitudes. Having had his work displayed at the museum each year since 1982, Guge says, "Its 'Birds in Art' exhibit is the best show in the country for displaying wildfowl art. It's a great promotion for our art form, and it's exciting to be involved."

3

Jett Brunet

Waterfowl from a Single Piece of Wood

Jett Brunet is the youngest carver ever to win Best in World in the floating decorative category of the World Championship Wildfowl Carving Competition. Here he chops away at a canvasback on what he calls a chopping block.

A Blue Ribbon Background

Despite his age, and against strong opposition, twenty-one year old Jett Brunet won Best in World in the 1985 Decorative Waterfowl Division with a pair of ruddy ducks.

His previous accomplishments were almost as impressive. He was barely a teenager when, with his first life-size carving of a bufflehead, he took a first place in a major competition. His second life-size bird took a Best in Show at that same competition, while his third took Best in Show in the novice division at the World Championships. When he was sixteen, that same competition recognized him as the most outstanding teenage carver of the year. After receiving the same award the following year, Brunet entered his carvings in the professional class and came away with a Second in Show award.

He lives in Galliano, Louisiana, a small town situated on a bayou, a lengthy waterway that leads to the Gulf of Mexico. When driving down Highway 1, signs advertise that you are in Cajun Country, where the Acadian French of Canada, traveling on boats along the East Coast and around the tip of Florida, settled two centuries ago. Even today there can be heard a mingling of French and English among the people.

Brunet points out that he has developed a style of

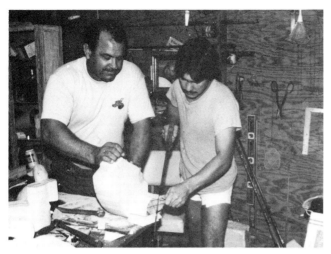

Here Brunet is seen with his father Tan, five times a world champion. He credits his father with having guided him over a decade of carving.

Fluidity and a Bird at Ease

What is the style that is typically Brunet's? He says, "I try to animate my birds to give people something a little different to look at while keeping a nice attitude, one that leaves the subject bird with a smooth attitude."

He continues that, as a judge at many competitions, he has seen too many wildfowl that looked unbalanced. "But when I twist a head or raise a wing," he says, "I try to make the bird look as though it could stay in that position for a while." Brunet calls it "keeping the bird at ease."

He adds, "My style is keeping the bird in a basically comfortable pose. The eyes are level, with no tilt. So no matter how you look at the bird, it won't look awkward. It can have an action pose, yet not one out of place."

carving waterfowl with poses and attitudes uniquely his own. But he does give credit to others who have advised and helped him with his carving, including John Scheeler (featured in *How to Carve Wildfowl*); Pat Godin, of Mount Pleasant, Ontario, Canada; Jimmy Vizier, of Galliano, Louisiana; and his father, Tan.

Brunet says, "Working with my daddy, I think I had it easier than other carvers." The elder Brunet won Best in World with his waterfowl pairs five times, more wins than any other carver. "My daddy had so much to do with developing carving here on the bayou. When he started, there were few people carving. Now it's become a community of carvers here. Today, whenever a carver has a problem, he'll come to my daddy." Brunet adds that Tan also encouraged carvers to take their work to shows, one of the first being the World Championships.

This mallard drake started from a single block of wood. There are no separate pieces on the duck, and no seams to contend with.

On Being a Cajun

Galliano and neighboring Cajun communities are not ones frequented by tourists. And many Cajuns may not even venture far from their own parishes, or counties. When asked to comment on being a Cajun, Brunet says, "People think we're living back in time in swamps where you have to get around by boat. The movies have contributed an image of a guy who can't talk English and doesn't shave and travels in a pirogue (a boat made from a hollowed-out tree trunk). But that's not true. We are proud of being Cajuns, we do live in laid back communites, but we enjoy life, we're friendly, and we're hospitable."

This canvasback drake also started from a block of wood some ten inches thick. This too has neither inserts nor seam lines.

He continues, "I carve my birds so that their heads are angled in such a way that when you focus on their profiles, you may see a wing out or open on the same side the head is turning. I believe that this keeps the bird graceful and flowing throughout."

Working from One Piece of Wood

What Brunet feels is a decided advantage to making a bird look at ease, comfortable, smooth (his adjectives), is carving from a solid block of wood. This means that there will be neither a separate head that was severed and turned or made as a separate piece, nor even inserted feathers. (Compare Habbart Dean's and Louis Kean's feather-making techniques in chapters 4 and 7 respectively.)

"Working with one piece," Brunet says, "I can make the head flow better into the breast and even pull the whole bird around in the solid block better than I can with separate pieces." He does admit that this is difficult with complicated poses, such as with his mallard drake, "but if I tried to fit a head onto the body block, I couldn't make my bird as graceful as I'd like." As he puts it quite succinctly, "I have to find the entire anatomy of my bird in a single block."

Brunet points out that this is not a widespread technique among carvers. But there are Cajun traditions for it. Carvers like his father and Jimmy Vizier made their early decoys from a single piece, and the technique continues today.

What is unique in bird carving is Brunet's lack of inserted feathers on his ducks. Instead of inserts, individual primaries are carved from the original block of wood. Brunet says, "A problem I have with inserts is that they look like inserts after I've completed them. That bothers me. I want to keep the primaries flowing into the wing and the wing flowing into the body with no breaks or seam lines. But you just can't take those primaries out to work on and put them back in."

Much of the same reasoning can be applied to the head. "It's hard to hide a seam unless you do it with a wood filler, and even that's a problem because it can melt when you're burning it. So to me, it's worth the extra time cutting out everything from one piece, though it can be hard at times putting details on the head while it's on the body."

Tupelo Gum, Wood from the Swamps

Wood, because of its circulatory system, contains water, which can amount to as much as twice the weight of the dried wood. When a tree is cut, a process of water removal begins almost immediately. But the drying-out process is rarely uniform, and splits called checks form in the wood—in part from internal stresses, in part to allow the inside of the wood to dry out. The seriousness of this depends on the species of tree. Woods such as oak can be dried without serious checking to not much more than three inches in thickness. Woods like pine can be had in thicknesses up to six inches. Basswood and jelutong, described in chapters 1 and 2, can be had in thickness of between four and five inches. But tupelo gum can be dried out without serious checking in thicknesses of eight and even ten inches. It is this advantage that allows Brunet to carve his waterfowl from a solid block of wood.

Tupelo gum, technically known as water tupelo, is also called sour gum, swamp tupelo, white gum, yellow and gray gum, and olive tree. It grows in a narrow belt about 100 miles wide from southern Illinois down through the Mississippi Valley to Texas, and back along the coast up to Virginia. And it seems to grow

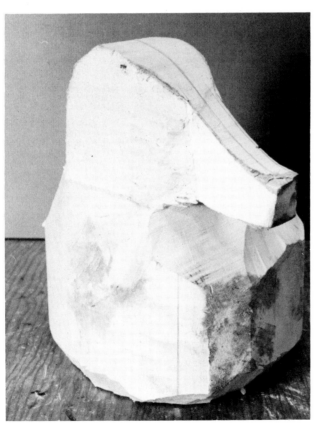

A bird roughed out with a hatchet might look like this.

Cutting tupelo gum, a wood favored for its light weight and grainless features, requires traveling deep into the Louisiana swamps. There it grows to as much as four feet in diameter. Wildfowl and alligators abound in this area.

It is really only the first four feet of the tree that is used by carvers. The rest is left in the swamps.

Growing in a foot of water, this tupelo gum tree was selected for cutting.

Sections of the lower part, or bole, of the tree are cut into sections about ten inches square.

These sections of flitches are carried out by Cajun carver Willie Badeaux. One of the reasons tupelo is used by Brunet is because it can be carved from thick blocks without having to laminate or use separate pieces.

The flitches are taken home in this mud boat. Wildfowl carvers Gary Badeaux, left, and Tim Zeringue, right, helped harvest the wood.

best in swamps. Many Cajun carvers have gone into the Louisiana swamps to harvest their own tupelo, though it is only the first four feet, botanically described as the bole of the tree, that is brought out. These trees grow in the water and can attain diameters of as much as four or five feet and reach heights of a hundred feet or more. With a chain saw, the bole is usually quartered and the chunky flitches, or sections, are brought back.

Tupelo has remarkable properties, one of which is its grain, or seeming lack of it. In most wood, grain, which indicates the direction of the cells or fibers of the tree, must be respected when carving to avoid splitting off pieces of the wood. This is not the case with tupelo. Carving, then, can be done regardless of grain direction without structural loss of strength.

Another property of tupelo is its relatively light weight. This is advantageous for the floating decorative waterfowl categories at many contests, at which the carved birds are floated in tanks and judged on how they ride in the water. Birds made from wood such as basswood invariably have to be hollowed out to lighten them. In most instances, tupelo does not need hollowing.

Yet another characteristic of the wood is that it can be worked almost immediately after being taken from the swamp. As Brunet says, "It's fun working the wood wet, and you can take off big chunks of it easily. But as you're carving it down, it will usually start checking on you because it hasn't had a chance to dry properly. This would mainly be on the breast area. So we try to

keep that area wet while the rest of the bird is drying. And even at that, we may still have to hollow the wood so it can better dry from the inside out."

Problems with Tupelo

But tupelo has other problems. Brunet says that one of them is its inconsistency. "You can get pieces of tupelo that are so hard, you can barely carve them. And you can get a good piece that came from the same tree the bad one came from." He adds, "It seems the faster tupelo dries, the better it is to work with. The slower it dries, the harder it gets and it stays heavy, as if it never really dried out." Brunet says that at times he will carve from a block of tupelo that has been drying for a few months inside his shop. Other times, he will use kiln-dried tupelo . (Kiln drying is a relatively rapid process of water removal accomplished with the use of kilns or high-heated rooms.) This he buys from Curt Fabre, owner of Curt's Waterfowl Corner. (Address in appendix.) The wood, Brunet says, "comes out light and soft."

Has Brunet worked with basswood? He has, but says, "The problem I find with it is that the grain can flake off. So you have to work with the grain, which you don't have to with tupelo." He adds, "I do think that basswood is more consistent as a wood, but you can't get it real thick to make a large, one-piece bird like my canvasback." (For more comments on basswood from Marc Schultz, see chapter 6.)

These flitches of tupelo might stand six months or more, drying out in the shop, before they are used. But the longer tupelo dries out, the harder it is to carve, Brunet points out.

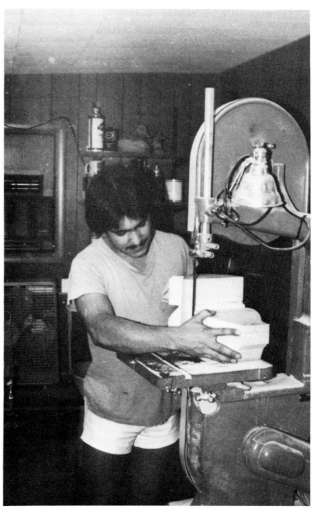

Some of the shaping of this high-necked canvasback can be done on a band saw. Photo by Jett Brunet.

Sculpting with a Hatchet

The canvasback Brunet was working on started from a block of tupelo, dried in the shop, that measured approximately 24 inches in length, 10 inches in width, and 8 inches in thickness. The finished bird would have a slightly turned head and a slightly raised wing.

The question Brunet asks rhetorically is, "How much preliminary work can be accomplished on a band saw, the tool used by nearly all carvers to achieve a rough shape?" His answer: "The problem with a one-piece bird with a turned head is that you cannot make an accurate cut. The twisted angle of the head and neck areas compared to the squareness of the band-saw blade prevents you from taking out the maximum amount of wood." What Brunet must resort to is a handsaw to cut out the width of the angled head.

But there is more shaping to be done, and for that he resorts at times to a hatchet. Once the traditional tool

The band saw cannot reach in to cut out the turn of the head. This Brunet achieves with a handsaw. Photo by Jett Brunet.

A hatchet, once used by traditional decoy carvers, is used to round off the body.

Here are the results of the hatchet work. Brunet says that most of the time he uses this chopping block in the shop.

Some shaping on the canvasback has been done with hand tools. Photo by Jett Brunet.

of decoy makers across the country, the hatchet becomes a sculpting tool for Brunet. Working outdoors on what he calls a chopping block, he can start rounding off the edges of the bird, bringing it into form. Of drawknives, also traditional tools of old-time decoy makers, Brunet says, "With those, you have to have the bird clamped down. But with the hatchet, I just hold the bird in one hand and the hatchet in the other." He will even use the hatchet on the head, bringing, he says, "everything down at the same time to keep a smooth line."

Sketching on the Block

Like Robert Guge and William Koelpin, Brunet feels confined by rigid patterns. Though he may do a sketch on paper before carving, he will definitely make sketches on the block of the top and side profiles of the bird. He says that sketching on the wood allows him to carve more spontaneously, working out a specific plan as he goes along. He states, "It keeps the work looser, unique. I call it sculpturing instead of illustrating," though he admits that a more thorough illustration will help with a complicated pose.

Still, he is not oblivious to basic measurements such as length and width of a species. "You can give or take half an inch on a species and be pretty safe with the measurements. But I tend to stay with the larger size." He notes that a slightly larger decoy appears to look better in the water. "Decoys were made that way to attract live birds. So I think it's better to look at a larger bird. It looks healthier, more mature."

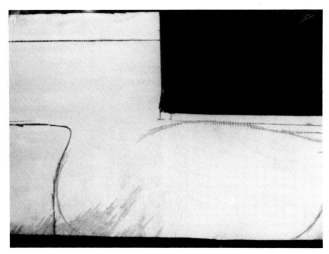

Few details are drawn on the tupelo block before Brunet starts with the hatchet. This is for the canvasback. Photo by Jett Brunet.

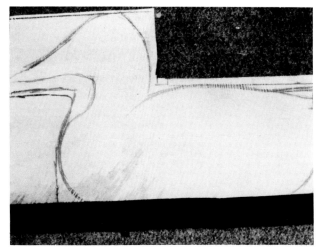

Sketching and profile changes are sometimes done. Photo by Jett Brunet.

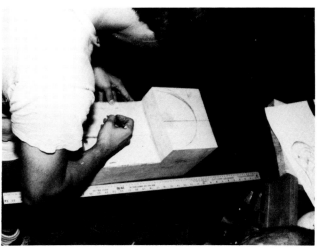

Here Brunet works on sketching the body profile after some of the head and neck areas were relieved. Photo by Jett Brunet.

Brunet does not like to confine himself to strictly rendered patterns or sketches. Still, he will bring some ideas together on a sketch pad before he goes to the block of wood. This is a sketch for the canvasback.

Here is the top profile of the canvasback drake. Photo by Jett Brunet.

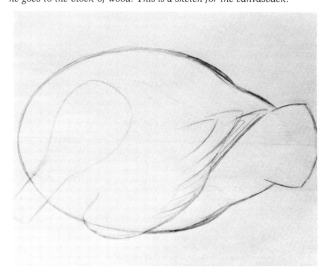

This is the top view of the canvasback. Note that one wing is raised, something Brunet says gives interest to a decorative duck carving.

This is the sketch for a mallard drake. Though this may seem rather detailed, Brunet may take license with his sculpting when he works at shaping the block.

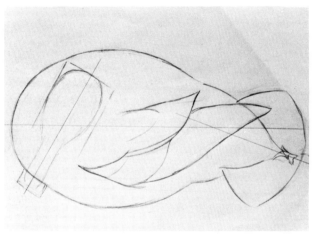

Here is the top view of the mallard drake. This, like the canvasback, has a wing slightly raised.

Perhaps more important than sketches are study mounts and photographs of the species being carved.

Has Brunet ever used clay models as Guge and Koelpin have? He answers, "I don't use one because I still enjoy working out my piece as I go along. Consequently, work may slow down when I reach an area of importance, such as an exposed wing. So I'll work closely with my references and make sure I stay accurate." These references include numerous photos and even live birds.

Scorps, Rasps, and Straight Razors

Unlike Koelpin and Guge, Brunet does not use the Foredom for shaping the block. "I don't like Foredom dust. And I hear tupelo dust is really bad for you. You should always wear a protective mask. And I don't care for the noise of the Foredom. I prefer to sit back and listen to my music as I work. However, I feel the Foredom can be a useful tool and I will use it when necessary."

One of the tools he uses instead of a grinding tool is a scorp, a hollowing tool with ancient origins. Brunet says it "scrapes wood away rather than pushing it off." Another tool is the Surform rasp, which acts much as a Foredom does with a coarse cutter.

There is yet another tool Brunet uses, one he says can remove wood quickly. It is the knife, and he prefers one with a long blade. The knives he uses are from Curt Fabre, and they are shaped from straight razor steel imbedded into wooden handles. "Razor-blade steel is the best because it holds an edge better

Brunet works with few other hand tools besides the hatchet. Here can be seen, from left to right, a scorp, two knives made from razorblade steel, and a Surform rasp.

Brunet demonstrates the use of the scorp, a hollowing tool with a long history that shaves wood away.

This long-bladed knife is one designed by Tan Brunet. It is available from Curt's Waterfowl Corner. (See appendix for address.)

Here he demonstrates the use of the Surform rasp.

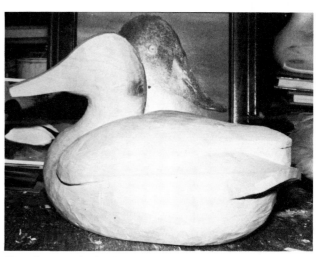

Here the canvasback takes shape, with its raised wing needing more definition. Photo by Jett Brunet.

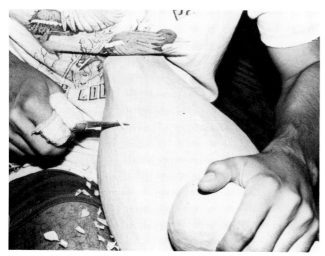

The long blade of this knife offers a great range of carving possibilities and control. Photo by Jett Brunet.

The rear of the duck shows that the wing still has to be separated from the back. Photo by Jett Brunet.

Brunet's knives were used to separate the wingtip from the back. Photo by Jett Brunet.

The knife can even separate tail feathers.

The knife is particularly useful in hard-to-reach areas because of its long blade.

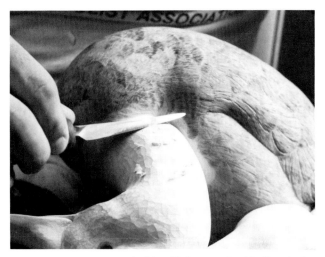

Brunet can pare away wood with a blade approximately three inches long.

than other steel, and you can get it sharper more quickly."

Brunet says that with a blade two and three inches long, he can get both reach and power. Designed by his father, the knife can turn in tight or close areas easily, while its tapered point can make sharp cuts. "But a knife can't always make a smooth cut in a round area, and that's when I go back to the scorp. It peels off wood quickly in places the knife can't get at, and it gives you a chance to rest from the knife. Otherwise, I'd have to stop working with it for a while." He explains, "It's nice to change tools as you're working. It gets tiring working a knife with the fingers, so I like to switch to another tool like a scorp."

The knife can also be used to undercut and slightly separate primaries and tail feathers. And it can separate a wing from the body.

Mirror Reflects All

"As I'm working, I'm always studying my birds in a mirror," Brunet says. "You see the bird in a different perspective. You may see something you hadn't caught before as you're shaping. For example, one shoulder may be a little too high or too far back, and you sometimes don't catch those things just looking at the bird."

He adds that even when he is not working on the bird, he will be studying it. "When I'm removing wood in a critical area such as the head and bill, I'll often stop and put my bird down so I can back off and study it. You have to make sure the bill angle is right and that the head is not tilting to one side or the other."

This pose, with the mallard's head tucked in the breast, would be nearly impossible to achieve if the head had been a separate piece. Photo by Jett Brunet.

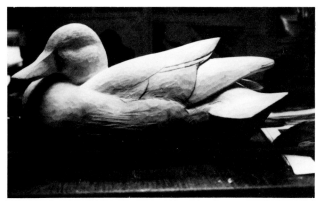

Here the mallard's basic design has been achieved. Photo by Jett Brunet.

Fingertip Sanding

"I don't sand much," Brunet says. "It seems a waste of time to smooth everything and then rough up the surface with the stoning and burning I do. But you don't want a chip-carved surface either." What sanding Brunet does do is lightly done with just his thumb and a used piece of 120-grit sandpaper. "It's just a circular motion that gets between the lumps and bumps without wearing them out. But in some areas of the bird, I still want a loose, almost rough look."

Bumping Feathers

Feather layout for Brunet starts on the side of a duck. What he calls feather patches should not be stiffly done, he advises. "You must work in graceful, sweeping lines as you sketch in the feather tracks." (Compare John Gewerth's techniques in chapter 5.)

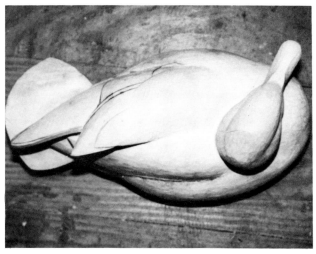

This is the mallard drake seen from above. Note the turn of the head which helps achieve what Brunet describes as "fluidity." Photo by Jett Brunet.

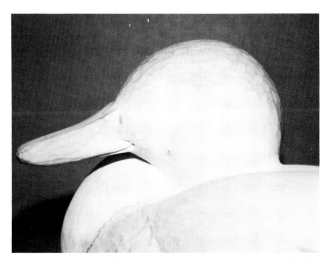

Though there are many facets, or chipped surfaces, on the mallard after knife work, they disappear with very light sanding and burning. Photo by Jett Brunet.

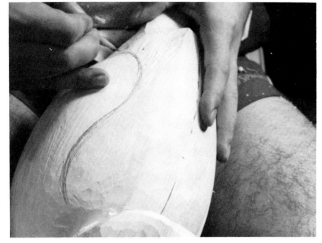

Brunet begins laying out the flank feathers on the canvasback.

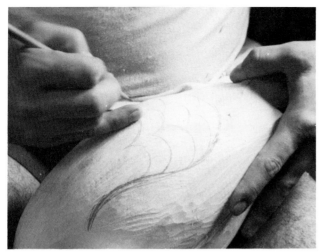

Here he lays out feather "patches" or groups.

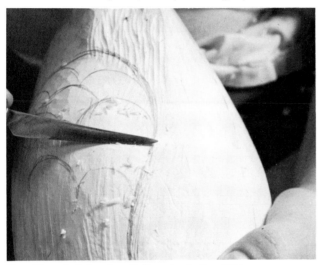

Brunet has a technique he calls "bumping feathers." This means contouring some of the patches to give "a loose, bumpy look."

A later view of the mallard shows defined primaries carved from the block. Photo by Jett Brunet.

Another view of the mallard shows an animation that is neither awkward nor unpleasing to the viewer. This is basically a bird at ease, says Brunet. Photo by Jett Brunet.

Brunet used the actual wing of a mallard drake as a study aid. Photo by Jett Brunet.

Here is the feather layout on the left side. Compare this photo with the original sketch Brunet made before carving. Photo by Jett Brunet.

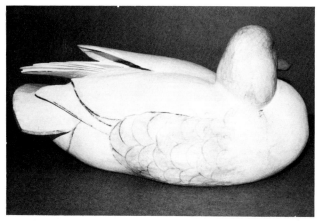

Here is the layout of feather patches on the duck's right side. Note how far the wing and primaries are undercut. Photo by Jett Brunet.

After laying out the feathers, using study mounts and photos, Brunet starts with a process he calls "bumping." He says that this begins by choosing only certain feathers that will be contoured to achieve what he calls "a loose, bumpy look on the bird." Why not all feathers? "You should stay away from carving out each feather identically to prevent a fish scale look."

He continues, "I'm adding lumps and bumps for character. With the knife, I can just chip around feather edges and lightly sand afterward. This adds another dimension, and they are something you see on a live bird."

But not all lumps and bumps can be achieved with a knife. He may resort to a ruby carver in a Dremel Moto-Tool, especially for small feathers on which the knife is too awkward to handle, or ones that are difficult to get at. Of ruby carvers, Brunet says, "They will eat a lot of wood, but will leave you with a fairly smooth finish that doesn't require a lot of sanding."

Wheeling in Splits

Once the feathers have been laid out, with lumps and bumps added to the surface, Brunet proceeds to put in feather splits. This is the separation of the barbs into groups, leaving V-shaped gaps. He points out that on a canvasback, for example, the side patches are sometimes ragged looking. "So I'll try to stay loose and exaggerate some of the splits, more so than I would on the back. It's very easy," he warns, "to get carried away with splits."

He believes, then, that splits should be put into stra-

tegic places on the duck rather than throughout. "Numerous, repetitive breaks can hurt your look."

Once he has laid out the splits, he begins grinding them in with a small, cylindrical stone and Dremel. This he calls "wheeling in splits."

Though Brunet prefers not to use a Foredom when shaping a bird, he will use this Dremel Moto-Tool for bill refining or putting in splits. Called the Moto-Flex Tool, it has a 34-inch-long flexible shaft.

When putting in feather splits, Brunet will use abrasive stones such as these.

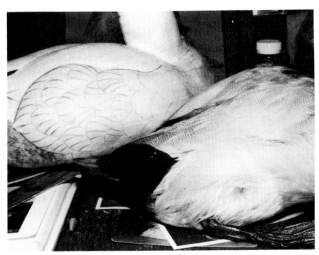

Here are the feather patches and splits on the canvasback drake. Compared to it is a mount of the actual duck. Photo by Jett Brunet.

Here is the canvasback before burning is done on the head and neck.

Burning Loose, Burning Fine

Brunet states that different areas of a bird's anatomy have different textures. He will use, then, a variety of burning strategies, as many as four different ones, on the bird's surface. On the back, for example, he will show what he describes as "fine and neat burning," while on side patches, he may exhibit what he calls a "loose and rougher type." Variations exist between these extremes.

He recalls when his father started burning in feathers. "He would use ice picks, heating them up on a stove and burning as much as he could with each before it got cool. Today, we have different tips and the finest tips imaginable."

Brunet explains that his burning strategy is not to burn at a very high temperature. "It takes too much paint to cover the burn, especially in white areas. That clogs up the burning lines. But also, the less amount of paint you have to apply, the softer the look is going to be." (Compare Marc Schultz's burning and painting techniques in chapter 6.) He adds that he does not

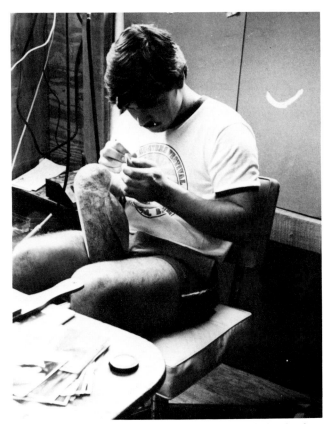

Brunet works in his shop burning on the canvasback drake's head.

burn the outlines of splits, claiming that splits will show up better with just paint.

On the canvasback, which has a black breast that borders white side patches, Brunet will burn very lightly. "Here, I'll actually paint in splits that I couldn't do if I burned real deep."

He goes on to say that he uses basically the same tip for all his burning, but he uses different temperature settings. He keeps the tip as sharp as possible, and he will frequently wear out tips with the sharpening.

Another burning strategy is that Brunet begins burning on the underside of the rump. He explains, "I start on an unimportant area so that I get a flow through my hand, and fluency for what I'm doing. And the rump area doesn't attract much attention." But he will burn most of the rest of the body before he does the head. This, he says, is to minimize hand oils

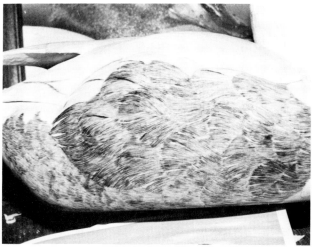

Note the almost random flow of the canvasback flank feathers. Photo by Jett Brunet.

Here is the canvasback with more burning. Note the bumped feathers.

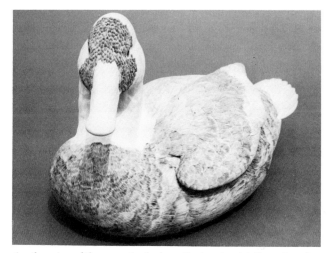

Another view of the canvasback shows the burning details on the wing and how much of the wing was relieved from the body. Also note the fine, deep burning on the face.

There is less definition of feathers and more flow on the breast of the canvasback.

Here is the back of the canvasback. Note the lumpy appearance on the neck, done with ruby carvers. (See appendix for address of supplier.)

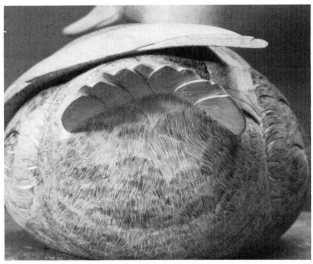

Brunet will usually start burning on the rump of a bird, building up what he describes as a "fluency" before he goes on to more important areas.

Here is the mallard drake with the layout of feather patches and some burning completed. Brunet burns from the rear forward on the flank so that the burn lines overlap as do the feathers. Photo by Jett Brunet.

Here is the feather layout for the back of the mallard. Photo by Jett Brunet.

Note the splits defined with the edge of a cylindrical grinding stone. Photo by Jett Brunet.

Brunet burns from front to back here. He says that these feathers are more important and it is easier to get exactly the right shape and texture on the tip of each feather this way. Photo by Jett Brunet.

After "wheeling in" splits, as he describes his technique, Brunet may further define splits with a burning tool. Photo by Jett Brunet.

The mallard is almost completely burned. Brunet keeps the primaries thick until all other burning is completed. This reduces the risk of breaking them while handling the bird and burning tool. Photo by Jett Brunet.

Here can be studied the burning details on the mallard's head. Photo by Jett Brunet.

Here are the burning details and feather layout on a green-winged teal drake. Photo by Jett Brunet.

The back of the green-winged teal can be studied here. Photo by Jett Brunet.

Again, the primaries and also the tail are the last parts of the anatomy to be refined and burned. Photo by Jett Brunet.

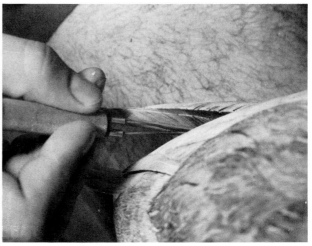

Brunet is using a spear-like burning tip designed by his father, Tan. It is used under primaries and areas hard to get at. This is needed since most of the Brunets' birds have no inserts.

Here can be seen the burning details under the primaries that are part of the original block.

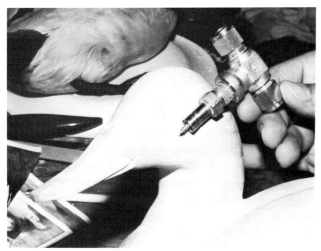

Dale Guidry of Cut Off, Louisiana, devised this device to "corkscrew" the wood out of a duck's eye sockets. It is basically a wood screw set in the middle of a piece of steel tubing. Photo by Jett Brunet.

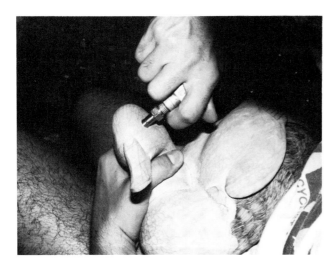

This tool removes an exact amount of wood since the screw draws the sharpened tubing only so far. Photo by Jett Brunet.

from getting on the surface, which can affect the painting.

Also, he does not bring his primary feathers down to their final thicknesses until he has finished nearly all other burning. The last part of the anatomy to be burned is the tail.

Corkscrewed Eyes

Carvers will often use some sort of rotary bit in a Foredom or Dremel to make the holes that will receive their birds' glass eyes. Brunet uses instead a sharpened piece of steel tubing with a wood screw set into its center, a device invented by his friend Dale Guidry of Cut Off, Louisiana. The wood screw actually centers the gouging device and keeps it from slipping, much as a corkscrew does. It will then pull the wood out like a corkscrew, and the device will give Brunet the exact depth and size he wants, both predetermined by the size and depth of the hole cutter.

Setting in the eyes is accomplished with plastic wood that fills the hole. When the eyes are pushed into the wood filler, some of it will squeeze out and cover the front of the eyes. This can then be worked immediately with a knife. Brunet explains that when working the Plastic Wood when it is still wet, the glass eyes will not readily be scratched, nor will the Plastic Wood be brittle enough to flake off.

Brunet says he can get different looks by opening or closing the eyes with the Plastic Wood. But he prefers to keep most of his eyes fairly open.

The glass eye is set in the hole and held in place with Plastic Wood.

Making a High Floater

"I like most of my birds to float high. Riding that way, they look stronger, livelier. This is the way I see my canvasback. I see it as just having landed. It's still dry with wings fluffed out. And a high body and head are going to make it look dominant, powerful. A sleeping attitude would have lost some of that power."

But he also wanted his mallard drake to ride somewhat high in the water. "It didn't. It was low in the back. I tried to add some weight in the front, and it brought the bird level in the water, but then the bird looked sluggish."

Not wanting to hollow the bird, Brunet opted for removing a small amount of wood from the bottom of the bird in the rear. He started with a one-inch spade bit, then removed more with a gouge. He next put the mallard into water to see how it floated with less wood. "I wrapped the bird in Saran Wrap because the bird was three-quarters burned, so I couldn't allow water to touch it."

The bird still listed slightly to one side, so Brunet drilled diminutive holes and filled these with lead-shot. But the larger hole he filled with Styrofoam pellets. "I crushed these into the hole so that in case water got in, it would have no place to go. Some birds can be in a competition tank for hours, and bottoms of hollowed birds have come off, and the birds have sunk. But with the Styrofoam, water has no place to go and Styrofoam won't sink," adding that the material will not affect the weight of the bird. He made a wooden plug and joined it to the bottom of the mallard with boatbuilder's glue.

Many decorative waterfowl are floated in competitions and are judged on how well they float. This is a tradition that goes back to hunting decoys. Photo by Jett Brunet.

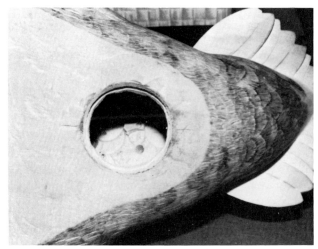

Though tupelo is light in weight and floats well, Brunet still had to lighten the back of the mallard drake by removing some wood. Photo by Jett Brunet.

To keep water off the bird when it is floated to test its balance, Brunet covers it with Saran Wrap. Photo by Jett Brunet.

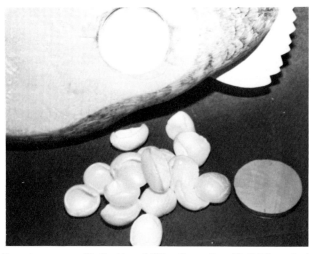

Brunet came up with the idea of filling the cavity with tightly packed Styrofoam pellets. Floating birds have been known to take in water and list or even sink. Photo by Jett Brunet.

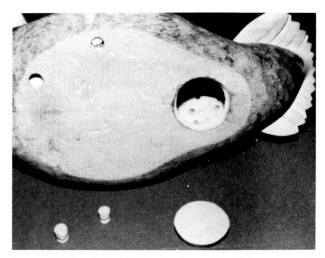

Some weight had to be added to the front of the bird to counter the weight removed from the rear. Brunet used lead shot and wood plugs. Photo by Jett Brunet.

Painting with Oils

"I consider oils to come off so rich," Brunet says, "giving a soft look. Acrylics have the advantage of drying so much quicker, but I feel more comfortable with oils and have become used to the slow process of painting.

"Some oil colors you have to give two or three days to before they dry. And with the blacks and whites you may have to wait even longer. White out of the tube seems to be the worst. But the browns and siennas dry in a day or two."

He continues that he has started working with gesso as a replacement for white. "But since I find that gesso bulges out the wood owing to its water base, I use a sanding sealer first. But both acrylics and oils adhere very well to gesso."

He adds that he is starting to learn about the value of acrylics and will perhaps learn the best advantages of both acrylics and oils on a bird. "But for now, I'm happy with oils, especially with the blending."

Blending Oils

"When I'm blending two colors, I'll first use a firm brush to apply each, then stipple them together with a nice soft brush, working one color into another." How does Brunet define stippling? He says it is bridging two colors together with a soft brush using rapid up and down strokes.

Brunet's mixing techniques are not dissimilar to Robert Guge's (chapter 2). He will mix up two or three values of light and dark variations of a color. "I'll make them nice and wet and thin them with Number One Art Thinner." He notes that this medium has little oil and reduces shine considerably.

"It's hard to stay neat and clean with oils. You have to select one area and do that and not work on another area that day. (Compare Marc Schultz's painting schedule in chapter 6.) A beginner will try to do too much in one day, end up touching the bird, and messing it up."

Keeping a Duck Pen

Brunet is not the only one of the eight carvers featured in this book to keep live birds as a reference. (Manfred Scheel, chapter 8, is the other.) But Brunet restricts his birds to ducks.

"It's important to study live birds as they are, especially in water, because all the birds I make are competition grade floating decoys. So I study them as they act on the water, even how they float.

"Looking at pictures is a great help, but live birds show you things you won't see in a photo. Sitting there and studying gives you a better view." Brunet will have not one but two birds of a species. He gets all his birds from Curt Fabre.

While other carvers will call their outside cages aviaries, Brunet calls his simply a duck pen. "I have anywhere from six to twelve birds at one time. And for a championship carving, I'll get birds a year in advance." Each year the World Championship Carving Competition requires a different species to be carved for the

The Brunets keep a duck pen that measures approximately 20 x 20 feet. Here they can study birds in and out of water.

He keeps only the type of bird he is working on at the time. In the pen are cinnamon teal, mallard, and canvasbacks, all borrowed from Curt Fabre of Curt's Waterfowl Corner.

Brunet says he cannot have too many references. In addition to live birds, he studies photos. (See appendix for suppliers.) These are particularly important to him when planning how a bird will be posed.

decorative floating pair category. In 1985, the species was ruddy ducks. In 1986, cinnamon teal will be required.

Brunet's duck pen measures 20 x 20 feet and is about four feet high. "Ducks don't need anything bigger than that," he says, "but make sure the ducks always have clear, clean water. It keeps the birds happy and in the water where you want them for study."

The enclosure is basically made of building lumber and chicken wire. But the top is fashioned from a plastic mesh. Brunet says this is more flexible and has more give than chicken wire so that should the ducks decide to fly, they will not be injured.

Has he had problems with predators? He says, "I used to have trouble with rats. But I put rat poison around the pen where the ducks couldn't reach it, and I haven't had trouble since. I used to feed them at night, but that's when the rats would come. Now I feed the birds only in the morning."

How secure are the ducks in this enclosure? Brunet recalls that someone once left the door of the pen open. Though the ducks got out, they did not fly away. "I guess they felt safe there and they knew they could get food."

The Dominant Canvasback

Brunet has definite ideas on the personalities of the birds he carves and how he translates personality into wood. The canvasback, for example, he sees as "a powerful, dominant-looking bird. So I'll make a bull neck and high head that help project that dominance.

And leaving more wood over the eyes will help get some of that look."

Brunet adds that he favors doing canvasbacks over many other species. "It's one of the largest and most popular of the diving ducks that carvers like to do. And it's for those reasons I feel that in a competition, the canvasback has a better impact on a judge than say a bufflehead when you're trying to win the ribbon for best diving duck."

A Preening Mallard

Another bird Brunet enjoys doing is a marsh duck. Not meant to look dominant, his mallard is simply getting ready to preen. "I had to open up the wing for that, but having the head and bill picking at feathers

Brunet designed his canvasback to have a high, thick neck, giving it a dominant look. Note the way the head turns to the side on which the wing is raised.

Here Brunet has compared his mallard drake to photos in a book. Photo by Jett Brunet.

Here can be studied the painted flank of the mallard, done with oil paints and light burning.

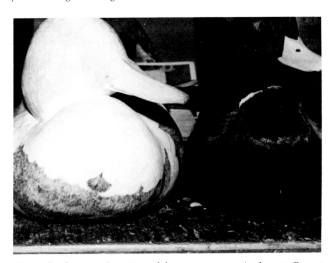

The mallard mount Brunet used has a crease on its breast. Brunet created the same crease or separation on his carving. Photo by Jett Brunet.

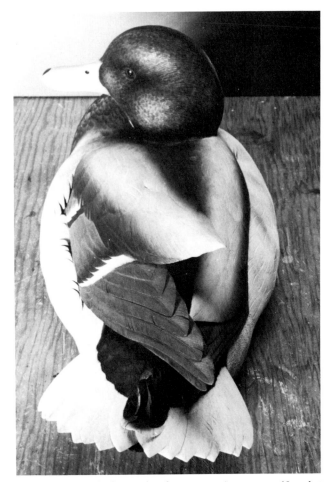

Brunet has his mallard in a relaxed pose, preparing to preen. Note that the head is turned to the side on which the wing is raised. This is a typical pose Brunet incorporates into his carvings.

Here is the crease on the nearly finished mallard.

would have made a pose that was too active." What he was interested in was achieving a relaxed look.

Still, he says, "I wanted the bird to look like it's moving around, that there's some action. This gives the judge more to look at and think about than if you have a bird in a tank just sitting there. It won't attract the judge's attention." Brunet adds, however, that very simple poses will do well in competitions because judges will find little to criticize.

Is a judge looking for other attributes in the carving? Brunet answers, "The final judging, when other birds have been eliminated because of anatomy or coloring or other inaccuracies, is often done from the tip of the bill to the back of the head. This is especially true when you have birds real close in a competition. So the bird with the best facial expression seems to come off well and do well."

A Beautiful Speculum and an Iridescent Head

Color also has a strong role, not only in contributing to the appearance, but also to the pose of a bird. The mallard, he says, "has a beautiful blue speculum. But nine times out of ten you won't see it on a live bird. So if I can put that mallard into a position where you can see the speculum, it's to my advantage."

But the strong colors of the mallard's head are not lost on Brunet. "I wanted the bird to be seen as having this powerful green head fading into the blue violet color of its speculum. The colors echo each other without anything jumping out at you." He adds, however, "If you put the colors on just exactly the way you see them on the bird, they would come out a little flat. So I work them out to look as if the sun is hitting them." Using Pearlescence, a powder additive that will contribute an iridescent color, Brunet says, "The mallard's colors should look good under any light."

Inserted Curls

Mallards have distinctive, curling feathers on their rumps above the tail feathers. The tupelo curls on Brunet's duck are the only insertions. Brunet explains the reason for the insertions: "It's virtually impossible to do it any other way. But I still had to make them flow with the rest of the body. You see, the whole bird is in a twisting position, with the head and tail coming toward each other with the open wing almost joining the two. So I had one curl going one way, the other the

Brunet opened the wing of the mallard to expose a blue speculum, adding color to the carving.

The double curls on the mallard had to be carved and inserted on the rump. Photo by Jett Brunet.

Here are the finished curls.

This is the first black duck Brunet carved. It was done in 1984. Note that the blue speculum is exposed. It is in the collection of Richard Stephens.

Here can be studied the feather patterns on the side of the bird. Note the implied sense of motion in the carving. Brunet describes this as "an action pose with a relaxed attitude."

Here can be studied the head of the black duck.

opposite way, while keeping the same attitude of twisting and turning. I also believe that the curls, which I exaggerated a little, are more noticeable this way. And everything on the bird works together." (Compare John Gewerth's curl insertions in chapter 5.)

The First Black Duck

As on the mallard, Brunet made use of the speculum colors on the first black duck he carved. "It's a brilliant, blue violet when the sun hits it," he describes. "It adds so much color to the bird that I opened up the wing and fanned it out. I also threw up the tertials over the back and put a twist and cock in the neck and head to give it an attitude of motion and action. He adds that the piece, like the canvasback, comes across as a large and powerful bird.

A Teal in the Cold

When designing his green-winged teal drake, Brunet was looking to give the duck the attitude of being

The breast can be studied here for details. The carving was done from a block of tupelo 7½ inches thick.

Brunet sees this green-winged teal he carved in 1985 as being in very cold weather. It is from the collection of Fausto Yturria, Jr.

Brunet has the back feathers puffed up as if the wing were catching them.

Another view of the black duck can be studied.

The primaries for the black duck were carved from the block.

Note how low the head of the teal rests on the breast.

Here can be studied details on the back.

Here are the teal's tertials.

A profile of the teal's head can be studied here. Note the alert, attentive look Brunet captured in the eyes. Judges, he says, look particularly at this part of the anatomy.

Here are the teal's primaries he thinned down last after shaping and burning the rest of the bird.

in cold weather. "The head I squashed down as if a cold, north wind had just passed through. So he's all puffed up as if the wind is catching some of the feathers on the back and tail. He looks as if he's sitting there trying to stay warm."

Best-in-World Ruddy Ducks

The ruddy ducks that won Brunet the Best-in-World title in the 1985 World Championships were the first he had ever carved. He recalls the preparation for the pair. "I knew I had to follow my live pair and photos closely, not putting anything into them I wasn't sure was there. I wanted to stay accurate, and I think that's what helped pull me through to the end."

But there were other aspects that contributed to the win. Though he sees ruddies as "just quiet little birds that just sit around," he did carve the drake of the pair with its head up and the hen's head down and to one side.

A Heavy Foot

What made his pair unique (and competitive) was nothing more than the addition of a foot. Brunet explains, "I did show one leg of the hen showing through a side pocket. It's something I saw frequently when studying her in the duck pen. When the hen was resting in the water, she would put her foot inside her side pocket. Then after a half an hour or so I would

Brunet's ruddy pair won Best in World in the 1985 World Championship Wildfowl Carving Competition. They are in the collection of the North American Wildfowl Art Museum, the Ward Foundation, Salisbury, Maryland.

Here can be studied feather patches or groups and feather splits on the ruddy drake.

Here can be studied details on the ruddy drake.

Note the look of lumpy feathers on the drake's head. Also note the bill details.

Here is the layout of the ruddy hen's back. Note the position of the head, the primaries, and the slight tilt of the tail.

Brunet feels that what helped him win Best in World was capturing this partially concealed foot on the ruddy hen. It was something he observed on a live bird in his duck pen.

The Hungry Artist

"I have a competitive attitude and I juggle my work between the collectors who buy it and the judges who judge it," Brunet says. But he admits, "I put my heart and work into making a bird to win a competition. The shows keep me hungry to try to be the best, and that shows up in my work. And I believe the collectors know it too."

He goes on to say, "Someday I want people to say, 'That guy is the best carver there is.' But it's just as good having people admire your work, and listening to their praise." He also hopes that people twenty years down the road will look at his waterfowl and marvel at their construction. "Maybe someone will see what work went into a decorative decoy that was made all in one piece."

see the leg get heavy and start falling through the feathers. I said to myself, 'That's something no one else has tried, and that's what I'm looking for after two months of study.' "

Still in keeping with his philosophy of poses, Brunet says, "The birds still look comfortable and not awkward. And I keep them simple, even though I put in that little touch with the leg. It's a fine line between going too far and staying within the boundaries of what judges will accept."

The Perfect Bird and Artistic License

Though Brunet believes that carvers are getting very close to the live bird in terms of accuracy, "We have to look beyond that and put more artistic license into the carvings." Yet, he admits that for the competitions accuracy is still an important criterion. "Stay within the bounds of reason and don't get too abstract," he suggests. He adds, "I hope someday we'll be recognized as true artists."

4

Habbart Dean
Expression Through Heads and Wings

Tie Tacks, Fat Ducks, and Carver of the Year

Though his father was a bayman, and though he never lived more than 65 miles from Ocean City, Maryland, home of the Ward Foundation's World Championships for wildfowl carvers, Habbart Dean started carving only in his early fifties. But the "delay" apparently had little effect on the quality of his work. Only six years after carving his first full-size piece, he was named Carver of the Year by the Southeastern Wildlife Exposition for 1986. In 1985, he received an award of excellence for a black skimmer from the Academy of Natural Sciences in Philadelphia, Pennsylvania.

Whereas most carvers began with serviceable or decorative hunting decoys, Dean's carving career began with a tie tack. He explains, "I had been going for years to bird carving shows such as the Easton (Maryland) Waterfowl Festival and the Ward Foundation's World Championships and Wildfowl Carving and Art Exhibition, but I wasn't entering or even carving. It was in 1978 that I was looking for a tie tack, and couldn't find what I wanted. So I went home, took a little piece of wood and a coping saw and cut out a duck profile. Then I whittled it, painted it, attached jewelry hardware, and wore it."

Habbart Dean, a carver of mainly shore birds and waterfowl, is shown here working on a least tern.

He continues that he made a few more, which he sold. He carved still more and rented a table at the 1979 World Championship Competition and sold out. Adding primitive decoys and stickup shore birds to his table, he was soon having no trouble selling a variety of items at shows and exhibits.

"Soon I wanted to find out what more there was to carving," he says. In 1980, at the encouragement of Dan Brown, a noted Maryland carver, he entered his

An award of excellence was given Dean for this black skimmer by the Academy of National Sciences in Philadelphia, Pennsylvania.

first competition with a hooded merganser drake. Three months later he won a Best in Show in a novice class. But he soon entered the open class where he would have to compete with professional carvers. In 1981 he won his first blue ribbon in the open class of the World Championships. This early move, he believes, taught him a great deal about carving, "being able to compare one on one with the established carvers," he says. Since that time, he has won his share of Best-in-Species and Best-in-Show awards.

During that time of recognition and advancement, Dean also produced a series of miniature collectible decoys cast in resinwood. Other hand-carved and hand-painted pieces have been made into tie tacks and stick pins and have been marketed nationally. All have exacting detail.

The Influential Critics

Dean says that when he first started carving, he was reluctant to ask questions of those he calls "the leaders. By that I mean such people as John Scheeler, Jim Sprankle, Ernie Muehlmatt, and others. But when they realized I was serious about carving, not doing this for a lark, they were extremely helpful and influential, making suggestions when I asked." He adds, "If you ask a legitimate question of a top carver, there's rarely a problem getting an answer."

He recalls asking John Scheeler to critique the first bird he entered in the World Championships. "I remember how tactful he was. He didn't say there was anything wrong with the piece, but suggested things I might do to improve. He really gave me a boost. Several years later he gave me my first piece of tupelo."

He goes on to say that Scheeler has been a tremendous influence. Of Scheeler's work, he says, "John's carvings excel in so many ways. It's not just his technique. The whole bird projects." He adds, "It's difficult enough to project into wood what a bird is doing, let alone what every feather or group of feathers is doing. Yet, this is what John does."

The time he spent with Lem Ward of Crisfield, Maryland, was of tremendous value and inspiration, Dean says. The Ward Foundation was named for Lem and his brother Steve, two decoy makers who captured the essence of a bird with paint and pose as few have been able to do. They made thousands of decoys that once sold for thirty dollars a dozen, while one was recently purchased for thirty-eight thousand dollars. Steve died in 1969, and Lemuel passed away in 1984.

The Meaning of Best in Show

Dean was asked what winning Best in Show means to a carver. "There are seven categories in the decorative life-size class. They are for waterfowl, shorebirds, upland game birds, birds of prey, seabirds, songbirds, and stained or natural carvings. The best of each of those categories receives a blue ribbon. And the best of those blue-ribbon winners wins a Best in Show."

For the floating decorative decoy category, there are three divisions, he says: one for marsh ducks such as mallards and pintails; one for diving ducks such as canvasbacks and mergansers, and the other for geese and confidence decoys. "A blue ribbon represents the best in a species. Then that duck is compared to all other diving duck species that won blue ribbons. And last, the best diving duck, the best marsh duck, and the best goose or confidence decoy are chosen. From these three entries, the Best in Show is selected."

Describing a Best-in-Show award as a high level of accomplishment, Dean says, "It therefore means that you have done your research and have translated that research into a piece of work more accurately than anyone else at that point in competition.

"If you have won, you are looked upon as a carver who has excelled, has made innovations on the presentation of a piece, and that you should be able to improve and expand upon that which you have learned."

Dean also compares winning a Best in Show to a degree received upon graduation from college. "But it's also a mandate to improve, to go on for a masters or doctorate."

Expressions in Art Form

What has helped Dean achieve his own "level of accomplishment" has been his particular presentation of a piece that can be put into a competition or an art exhibit. He explains, "I do not think some of what we are doing can attain its proper place in the art world by leaving almost nothing to the viewer's imagination. In a great painting, for example, you continue to see something of interest. This is what we have to do in our work – project something in the piece by not making it necessarily complete in detail or absolutely realistic." (Compare William Koelpin's comments on abstract art in chapter 1.)

He admits, though, that competitions do not readily allow a bird to be interpretive or without exacting detail. Still, "Who are we to say that there are absolutes with the live bird, which is used as the ultimate criterion by competition rules? Every bird has differences with regard to anatomical sizes and even coloration."

In order to reconcile the conflicts of art and competition, Dean decided to do compositions with more action than is usually seen in his carvings, concentrating on the wings and heads of his wildfowl. He says, "I can express movement with open wings, or the shape of the eyes, positioning of the tail feathers, or the flow of the crest feathers on a head. There should be an interplay which translates into an expression of the whole bird."

A Black Skimmer

There are only three species of skimmers in the world, with the black of North and South America being the largest. All three are characterized by long, knife-like mandibles, with the lower mandible longer than the upper one.

With wingspans of up to 40 inches, the black skimmer can be found from Massachusetts to Florida to Texas. Why did Dean choose a black skimmer to carve, and what expressions was he able to achieve with its head and wings?

First, Dean says, "It is the gracefulness with which it flies that attracted me to it. It has an unusual feeding habit that leads to the manner in which it flies. A skimmer will come in at a very low altitude and maintain a constant speed and elevation with that lower mandible in the water. When it strikes a small fish, it will clamp down on it, pull its head up, and swallow it without changing speed."

Dean's skimmer, with a wingspan of nearly 40 inches, literally skims the water in search of food.

Only the lower mandible of the skimmer cuts through the water. A steel file laminated between thin strips of walnut provides the suspension.

A good view of the tail and the flow of the wings from the body.

All the primary feathers for the skimmer's wings are inserted.

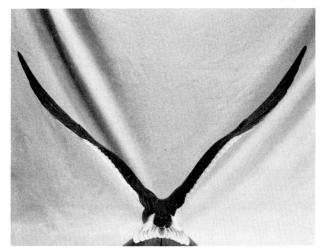

Most of the motion of a feeding skimmer is in the wingtips.

A view of the underbelly and feet can be studied here.

He also points out that much of the flight action is in the wingtips. "After a skimmer starts making its run, a lot of action is in those wingtips, done with a wrist action to maintain the elevation and speed. That's one of the reasons it has such a large wingspan."

A Wake in Walnut

"A skimmer can work long stretches without having to vary its flight," Dean says. "The wingbeat is very slow compared to a gull or tern, but it still will leave a wake." To capture the look of a wake or track of waves left by that searching lower mandible, Dean used a solid piece of walnut. Why didn't he use a more realistic base of a fiberglass resin that, when tinted and solidified, would look like water? Dean answers, "I feel the simplicity of the base enhances the carving of the bird and permits the viewer to come to his own conclusion as to what he is seeing. If everything is laid out with resin, this detracts from the subject. The indication in the base is that there is water created by the carved wake and the lower mandible inserted into

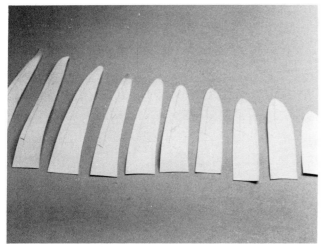

Note the paper patterns for the skimmer's primaries.

Because of how he shaped the opening and for the pupil and the size of the pupil itself, Dean gave his skimmer an intense look. Note also the unusually small tongue of the bird.

the wood." (Compare Louis Kean's techniques in chapter 7.)

He adds that with too much habitat on a base like this one, the viewer tends to look for small details, thus taking away from the bird or the subject matter.

One of the pleasures of doing the skimmer was its placement, he states. "Too far forward," he says, "and it would have given the feeling of running out of water. Too far back and it would have looked stern heavy." How was he able to decide on the correct placement? He answers, "I used a piece of plywood the same size as the walnut base and put a large nail into the head where the bill was going and started trying it on various spots on the plywood."

A Suspension System

Dean points out that when the skimmer's lower mandible strikes a stationary object or something larger than it can pick up, it will go back parallel with the head. "The lower mandible can be compared to an oyster knife, it's so thin."

To recreate that mandible, which alone holds the skimmer above the surface of the walnut water, Dean used a small, flat file only one-sixteenth of an inch thick. He laminated this between pieces of walnut, chosen because of its hardness and because it can be cut almost paper thin.

He then recessed a small hole into the base and put a two-part epoxy into that. Just before the epoxy set, he slipped a grease-covered file-mandible into it. He explains that the grease allowed the mandible to be

removed after the epoxy had set. The socket that was formed became an asset when transporting the piece, and the epoxy strengthened the slot.

Eyes Like a Cat's

Dean believes that this is the only bird that has a slit pupil, not unlike a cat's. "This is probably because of the tremendous amount of glare off the water that it is confronted with." He says he designed "an attitude" indicating "it is ready and intent upon striking a fish at any moment." He had to be careful, then, with the eyes. "Changing the eyes even slightly by lifting the lids or closing them, or bringing the pupils forward, can dramatically change the expression."

Sculpting Tupelo

"My skimmer would have been difficult to do in basswood without hollowing it out," Dean says. "With tupelo, it is much lighter, and therefore there is less strain on the supporting mandible."

Aside from its light weight, Dean feels tupelo can be shaped better than another wood like basswood. "With tupelo, it feels like you're sculpting it, especially when you're working with a knife."

Does tupelo have disadvantages? Dean would agree with Jett Brunet (chapter 3) that it is not as uniform in density as basswood. He does feel that a key to working tupelo is obtaining a piece that is uniform throughout and not too hard.

Here is a willet roughed out in tupelo gum, a wood that Dean says he can sculpt nicely.

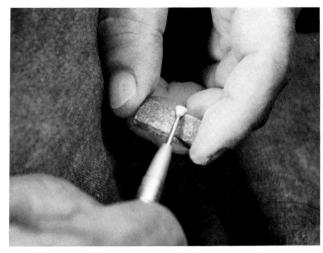
Sharpening of the texturing stone is done on a dressing stone.

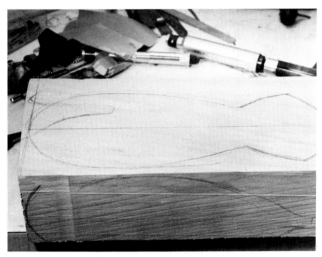
Here is the tupelo block with the side and top profiles for a hooded merganser hen.

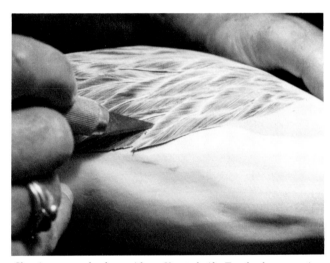
Cleaning up can be done with an X-acto knife. Tupelo shapes particularly well with knives if they are extremely sharp.

Tupelo takes details well, says Dean. Here he textures the side of a pintail drake with a texturing stone.

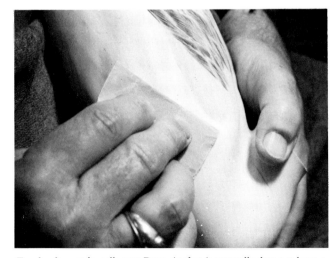
Tupelo also sands well, says Dean, in that it generally does not leave a fuzz or raised grain.

Here is seen the flow of the tertial feathers on the pintail body.

He works on the pintail in his Piney Island, Maryland, home.

Dean has burned the feathers on the back of the pintail.

The least tern Dean carved is suspended over a painted block of tupelo gum. The bird and its inserted wings and primaries are all tupelo. When feeding its young, as this bird might be doing, it may well remain in the air. The bird is in the collection of Dicky Trotter, Charleston, South Carolina.

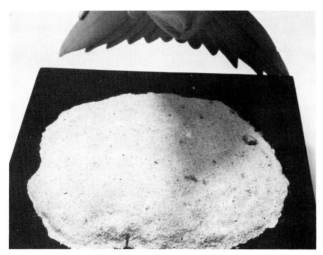

The habitat for the least tern is simple. It comprises a mixture of Tuf Carv, Carpenter's Glue, sand, and gesso.

Only one point on an outer tail feather touches the tupelo block.

Here is the tern with the brass support projecting out of a tail feather. This part is inserted into the tupelo base.

A Least Tern

Another piece Dean carved from tupelo and even mounted on a tupelo base is a least tern. The smallest of the terns, it has neither the extremely forked tail nor the length of other terns. This shore bird, which is found on either coast, has a rapid wingbeat and utters excitable cries.

Dean says he got the idea for his piece while sitting in a physician's office and browsing through a magazine. "Actually, the bird was feeding its young, but the bird will not necessarily land when doing that. In fact, it may not even touch down."

He realized that the problem was going to be one of presentation. "I didn't want the diorama effect of grasses and shells. I wanted the piece to be suggestive and interpretive." He explains further, "I wanted the composition to be suggestive as to what the tern might be doing, and interpretive from the viewer's point of view; that is, is the bird feeding its young or landing or preparing to pick up something?"

Dean feels that the challenge of doing the piece was not confined to carving a flying tern. There was also the problem of choosing a suitable base. He finally squared up a block of tupelo and applied no fewer than ten coats of a flat black paint to it. The patch of sand on the base started as a polyester resin called Tuf Carv. Applied over that was a mixture of sand and carpenter's glue, then gesso, and more sand.

Supporting the Tern

The contact point between the least tern and the base is only one small point on one tail feather. To begin to make the support, Dean took a length of small, square brass tubing, flattened the longer length of it, and bent it at a right angle. The flattened part he recessed into an outermost tail feather. Dean continues, "It goes all the way up the feather and a short way into the body. There it is held with epoxy. I then applied small pieces of tupelo on top of the brass, laminating the three parts together, using epoxy, and clamping them with hand spring clamps." This veneering permitted Dean to texture the feather as he did the others instead of having to grind on steel; the still-square brass end now projected at a right angle from that tail feather.

The next step was to put a slightly larger piece of square brass tubing into the base block to act as a

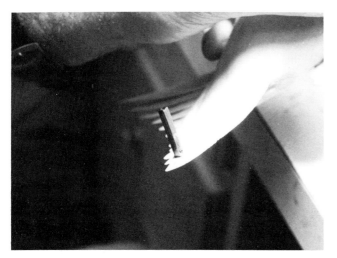

This brass tubing is bent at a right angle. What can't be seen is the flattened end which goes up into the body.

While a piece of brass tubing in the base hardened in epoxy, Dean supported the bird with this wooden lever. The lever also allowed him to position the tern just where he wanted it.

sleeve that would accept the piece projecting from the tail feather. This Dean describes as a slip joint.

Reducing Torque

But that sleeve or female end was not casually fitted into the block. It had to be positioned in a fill of two-part epoxy before the epoxy hardened. Dean says, "I had to be concerned with the torque or tendency of the piece to twist, owing to the weight of the bird, especially from a point opposite the slip joint. I had to experiment while the female end was in the epoxy and still prevent torque while the epoxy was drying." To accomplish this, Dean used a length of scrap wood as a lever between the block and the tail feathers, one that could push the bird up or lower it, but still keep the bird steady when he found the position he wanted.

What also helped position the tern is this clay and sheet metal model of the bird.

A Clay Model

However, positioning the tern required more planning than just designing a slip joint and a lever. The bird also had to be located over its base so it did not appear to be too far forward or too far back. This could in part be determined by the curvature of the tail feathers, which were not inserted but carved from the block. But what also helped solve the problem was modeling the bird in clay with sheet metal wings and tail. Mounted on a quarter-inch diameter dowel, the clay tern could then be trial-fitted on a scrap block of

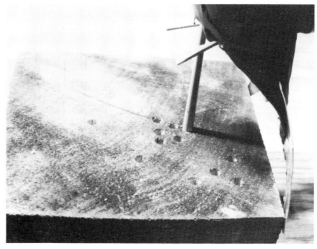

Dean experimented with different placements of the tern on a piece of scrap wood.

The metal tail could be bent to help determine how the wood tail would be shaped.

Here is the tern attached to the base. Dean carved the tail feathers and axillars from the original body block.

The head was made from a separate piece of tupelo to give strength to the beak by having the wood's grain run with it.

wood and the metal tail positioned until it touched the edge of the block.

Avoiding a Seam

Was there an advantage to using tupelo for the piece? The tern, he says, was done in that wood because of its lightness. Yet he did not hollow this bird. "I did not want to fight with a seam that would be too noticeable, especially since the bird is exposed to the viewer all around."

Axillars and a Separate Head

Though the wings and their primary feathers are carved from separate pieces of wood, the tern's axillar feathers are not. He carved these feathers as part of the body. He explains, "This makes for a natural joint and a stronger one. It disguises the joint by putting sets of feathers both above and below the joint." (Compare Louis Kean's technique in chapter 7.)

Dean did the head separately so the fragile beak of the tern would have the slight grain of the tupelo running along the length of the beak rather than through its cross section. He also coated the beak with Krazy Glue. "It hardens it tremendously, thus enabling it to be worked to a nice smooth satin finish." But he warns that the glue may also make the wood more brittle. "And tupelo is notorious for breaking at points where you least expect it," he says.

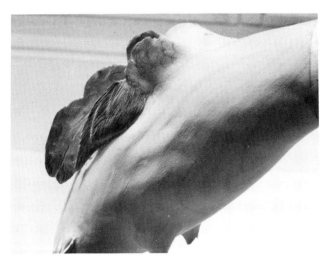

What helps create a smooth transition between the body and inserted wings are these axillar feathers.

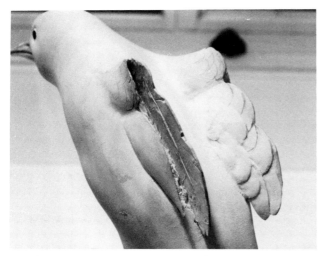

To make this cavity for the wings, Dean used a metal disc coated with diamonds, which enabled him to use it as a circular saw. Available from P.C. English Enterprises, Inc. (See appendix for address.)

Inserted Feathers

Unlike the preceding carvers, Dean inserts feathers such as the bird's primaries, though he will carve the tail feathers from the body block. There are usually ten such feathers on each wing of a bird, and each must be traced onto thin pieces of wood, usually tupelo because of its bending properties. After being cut out with a knife, they are detailed and burned with barb lines and quills in preparation for insertion.

If Dean wants the feathers to be curved slightly, he will burn one side of each on a flat surface and then the other while it is pressed into a concavely shaped piece of wood. He will then insert them into slots he made in the wings, spray a light mist of water on them, press the feathers together on a flat surface to get what he calls "the right sweep," and dry them with a hair dryer.

Landing, Not Landing, or Feeding Its Young?

Dean points out that the tern's wings on his carving are fairly parallel, "expressing that there is a lot of forward movement. Also, I thrust the feet out in the event the bird has to land. And the tail is fanned out to indicate breaking. All this will let the viewer wonder whether the bird is landing, or feeding its young, or getting ready to pick up something without landing."

As for an expression in the face and head of the tern, Dean notes that he tried to capture an intensity, "not

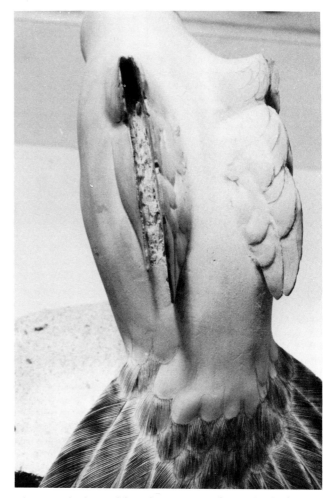

After using the diamond disc, cleaning up was done with a knife and a series of grinding tool cutters.

Note the slot in the nearer wing. This accepts the primary feathers.

Here are the burning details on the wings.

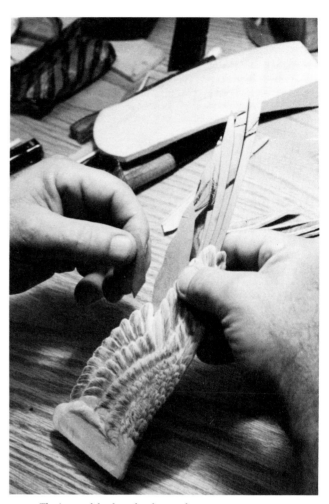

The inserted feathers for the tern began as paper patterns.

Once the wings are inserted, what seam line remains can be disguised with a wood filler.

A closer view shows the slot and underwing burning.

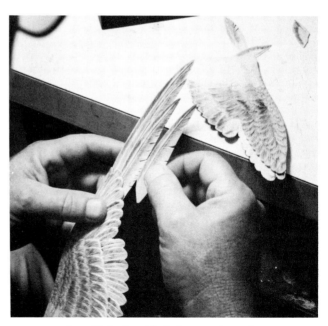

Assembly begins with the longest primary first.

Here all the primaries have been inserted.

A rear view of the least tern shows a completed bird.

Note the details, including feather splits, on the primaries.

Here the tern has all its inserts temporarily in place.

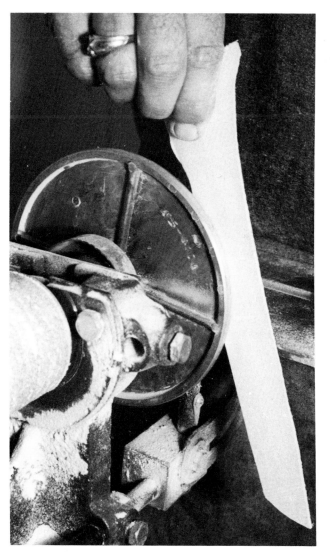

To ensure a uniform thickness for feathers, Dean will run wood strips between a sanding disc face plate and table edge.

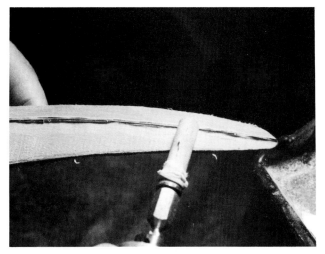

The shaft of a feather can be raised with the aid of a sanding roll.

He demonstrates how heat and a concave piece of wood can make a bent feather.

The barbs, which are burned in, radiate from the shaft.

Dean demonstrates the flexibility of tupelo as opposed to basswood. The tupelo feather is in Dean's left hand.

What also helps bend feathers as a group is to first lightly wet them and then press them together on a flat surface. Then they are dried with a hair dryer.

Dean says his tern might be intent on feeding its young, landing, or getting ready to pick something up.

necessarily one of aggression but just intensity. The head is thrust forward, and the eyes are looking straight ahead. It's very intent upon doing something."

Painting Tips

Dean used basically the same combination of acrylic colors on the least tern as he did on the black skimmer. Only three were different: ultramarine blue, burnt sienna, and titanium white. But he used different values of the combination to give variations. (Compare John Gewerth's use of color values in chapter 5.)

The black for both birds was a combination of ultramarine blue and burnt sienna. However, he may use Mars black on another species to enhance a certain set of feathers.

Unlike the tern, the skimmer has distinctive red, orange, and black mandibles. The colors, Dean says, are intense, and the combination for these was cadmium orange, napthol crimson, and a small amount of yellow ochre. He also added a small amount of burnt umber to decrease the intensity of the napthol crimson and blended the colors to water. This means that one area is painted and, after drying, is wetted with water. An adjoining area is painted and the water helps bring the areas together without a sharp line.

Tension Breaker

Dean uses a liquid additive called Tension Breaker with the acrylics. He explains that it helps relieve what he describes as a tension between water-based

When making washes of acrylics and water, Dean uses a simple straw to control the amount of water used.

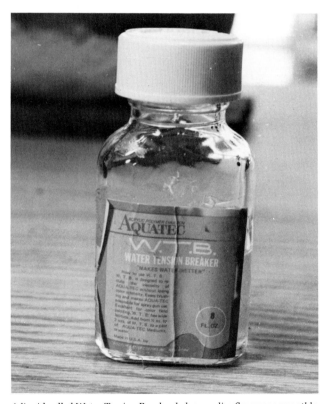

A liquid called Water Tension Breaker helps acrylics flow more smoothly or evenly on wood, especially where there is fine burning or texturing. This is available from Christian J. Hummul Company. (See appendix for address.)

paint (like acrylics) and the wood. "This is especially helpful where there is very fine texturing. The additive allows the paint to flow more evenly."

Graceful Birds

Why does Dean do shore or sea birds, unlike most of the other carvers featured in this book? He answers, "I find there are challenges with them that I do not find with most waterfowl. There is a gracefulness that can be expressed or observed that I do not see as much in ducks."

He adds, "I don't have the desire at this point to do birds of prey, though I enjoy watching a bald eagle or an osprey that sits on an oak tree by the river behind my house. Rather, I like to do birds that relate more to the relaxed part of life."

He goes on to say that wildfowl carving is as acceptable to the public as it is because "it portrays that part of nature many people cannot get close to. And when we see a bird, we relate to it as a soft, friendly creature, both graceful and beautiful."

Hooded Merganser Hens

Dean does, however, carve waterfowl, and among those are hooded merganser hens. Two of these are quite different from each other. One is flat-bottomed in the decoy tradition, the other is full-bodied, complete with individually carved feet and legs.

Dean says he likes to do the females of the species because of the size and subtle coloring. "I see femininity expressed in their smallness and gracefulness. They're fantastic to watch because they are so quick."

With the flat-bottomed hen, he has the crest "whipping around as if a puff of wind were catching it." But perhaps most expressive on this bird are its eyes and face. "I see that she is simply swimming along, saying perhaps, 'I think I'm pretty good looking' in a very subtle way. She's content, then, but alert."

The eyes, Dean says, are open but not wide-eyed. "Yet opening the eyes ever so slightly more would have given a different expression. And for that, I would have chosen a different pupil," he says, noting that glass eyes are available with a variety of pupil sizes.

"The crest is expressive by being up and out. If she were frightened, it would come up even more. And if she were less alert, or at rest, I would not have had much neck showing, the crest would be down, and the eyes would be closed even more. So my merganser hen is very aware of what's going on around her."

This hooded merganser hen, says Dean, is in a semi-relaxed pose. It's from the collection of Reid Newcomb, Salisbury, Maryland.

This full-bodied hooded merganser hen is hollow to allow it to float. The legs are added, but the raised wing is part of the original block. It took First in Species at the 1984 World Championship Wildfowl Carving Competition. It's in the collection of Marvin Betz, Stouffville, Ontario, Canada. Photo by George Ross.

Here is another view of one of Dean's hooded merganser hens. Note the sweep of the crest feathers and the low-lying tail feathers.

A Preening Hooded Merganser Hen

The idea for the full-bodied hooded merganser hen, says Dean, came from watching one on the St. Martin River, on which his home is located.

"I wanted to do one without inserts, and with one wing raised up. But with the twisting of her body and the position of the head and neck, I knew there was going to be a problem floating it correctly. The challenge, then, was getting the proper flow with that raised wing, getting the attitude of preening, and floating it properly."

Dean feels the piece expresses concentration. "She's definitely concentrating on what she's doing. Her crest shows no relaxation, and the eyes are intent upon her shoulder. I used a pupil larger than usual to reflect that intensity of concentration."

Note the slightly different flow of the crest feathers from the previous hen.

The opened eye of this hen shows an alert look, though it is not startled or frightened.

He says that the hen is exhibiting some "self-indulgence." Note the flow of the crest feathers, as if the wind had caught hold of them.

A hooded merganser hen from the collection of John Lerch, Salisbury, Maryland.

The full-bodied hen is intent on preening itself, says Dean. Photo by George Ross.

Dean burns in the teeth, which are characteristic of mergansers. Photo by George Ross.

A difficulty in doing this bird is the twisted body. Photo by George Ross.

Pupil size and eye opening can dictate a great deal about the look and intent of a bird, says Dean. Photo by George Ross.

Note the flow of the leg and tail. Photo by George Ross.

Note the detailing of the crest feathers. Photo by George Ross.

Dean carved the foot for this bird from a separate piece of tupelo gum. Photo by George Ross.

To help achieve a good flow in the wing from the shoulder on back, Dean had a hooded merganser hen mounted in that position.

To help achieve the correct balance, Dean hollowed the tupelo unevenly and placed weights on its inside.

A Racy Red-breasted Merganser Drake

Dean wanted to express a racy look to his red-breasted merganser drake, and an intensity of movement. A diving duck, this bird is particularly recognizable by its black and white body, rusty coral breast coloration, and a long, ragged-looking crest. It is the crest, then, that most carvers use to imply motion, but find difficult to carve.

Bamboo Crest Feathers

What Dean did was insert these ragged crest feathers. Rather than use a wood like basswood or tupelo, he opted for bamboo. "I pulled tines off a bamboo rake I had and split each tine as finely as I could. The very fine slivers I inserted into a slot I cut in the back of the merganser's head."

Shaping a Head

When shaping a head, Dean draws a top and side profile on a piece of tupelo. First the side profile is cut to shape, the waste wood then held or nailed back into place, and the top profile is cut out on the band saw.

Here can be studied a shoulder patch of the bird. Photo by George Ross.

Here is the red-breasted merganser drake's vermiculated flank. Photo by George Ross.

One of the difficulties in painting the red-breasted merganser drake, says Dean, is the pattern and coloration of the breast feathers. Photo by George Ross.

This red-breasted merganser drake, carved by Dean, is a racy bird. It took First in Species and Second in Diving Ducks at the 1985 World Championships. This is in the collection of Marvin Betz, Stouffville, Ontario, Canada. Photo by George Ross.

Note the detailing on the tail of the bird. Photo by George Ross.

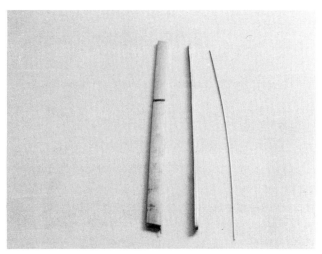

The bamboo "feathers" came from rake tines. Bamboo splits into very thin slivers, says Dean.

A red-breasted merganser has distinctive, stringy crest feathers. This is a mount Dean uses for reference.

Cutting of the hooded merganser hen's head begins on the side profile. Dean made the pattern from a two-and-one-half-inch-thick piece of tupelo.

Instead of carving the stringy crest feathers from the block for the red-breasted merganser's head, Dean inserted slivers of bamboo into a slot.

Holding the wood cutaway against the side profile, Dean cuts out the top view of the hen's head.

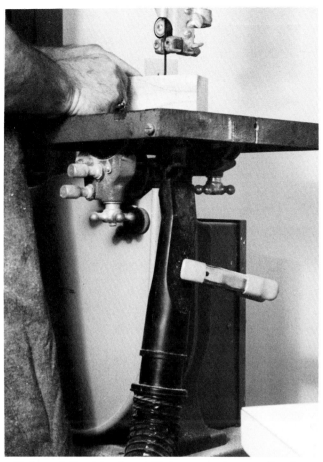

Underneath Dean's band-saw table is a vacuum hose to collect dust.

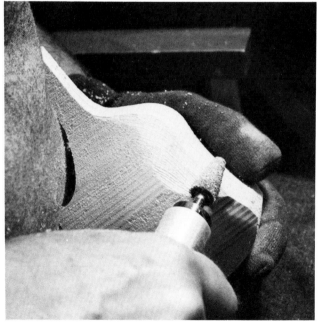

Shaping the head begins with this conical-shaped, carbide-impregnated cutter. It is one-half-inch in diameter at its base.

Another dust collecting system is right under Dean's work table. The dust is collected in a space beneath the floor.

The same cutter can make quick depressions for the eye channels.

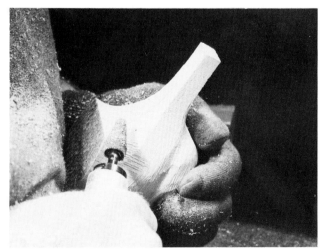

Shaping continues by rounding the neck.

The same carbide cutter defines the curving crest feathers.

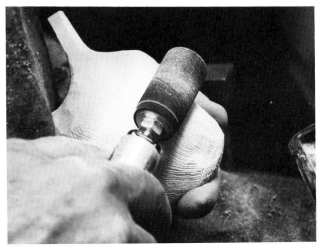

The merganser's bill must also be rounded.

A one-inch-diameter rubber-cushioned sanding drum removes the coarse marks left by the carbide cutter.

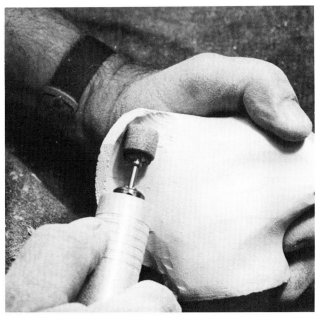

A smaller sanding drum removes the coarse grinding marks left on the crest curvature.

With a basic shape to work with, Dean then goes to a variety of sanding and grinding bits and his Foredom Tool. A coarse, conical stone and a one-inch diameter sanding drum will do most of the wood removal and refining for the time being.

Using a Study Bill

With the crest shaped and the area of the eyes defined, Dean starts working on the bill. An indispensable aid for him and most other carvers is the waterfowl study bill. (See appendix for suppliers.) Cast from a freshly killed duck in materials such as epoxies or resins, they hold exacting details and do not change shape. The problem with using mounted ducks is that their bills are fleshy and start to shrink as soon as the duck dies. No amount of taxidermy can halt that shrinkage.

Measurements such as the length and thickness of the mandibles or jaws can be taken from the study bills, as well as determinations made of how the lower mandible fits within the upper. Once established, Dean will use a burning pen to define the projecting V-shaped base of the bill and the mandible separation.

Dean cautions, "If you don't get the area where the lower mandible goes into the head just right, you'll come off with a completely different look or expression to the bird."

Here on a window ledge above Dean's work table are a few of the many study bills available to wildfowl carvers.

Most carvers, as does Dean, use a study bill for determining dimensions on the wood. The overall length is one such measurement. The study bill is cast from a freshly killed duck and acts as a fixed reference. This one is made by Bob Bolle. (See appendix for address.)

Here the bill length taken from the study bill is transferred to the wood. Dean leaves ample wood from which to carve later the nostrils and the tip or "nail."

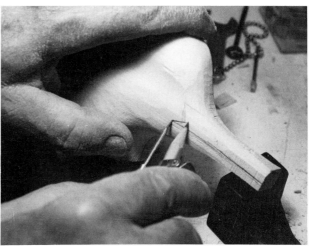

Another dimension is the length of the legs of the V-shaped profiles defining where the bill meets the forehead.

The height of the V profile is taken with dividers.

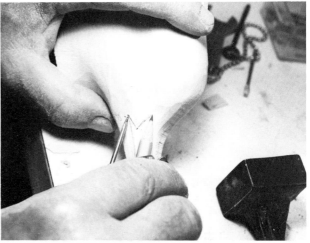

Here that dimension is transferred to the wood.

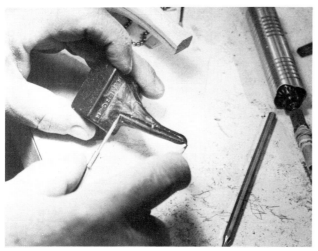

The length of the study bill is again taken.

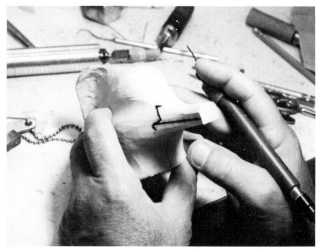

Here Dean checks the symmetry of the burn lines on either side of the bill.

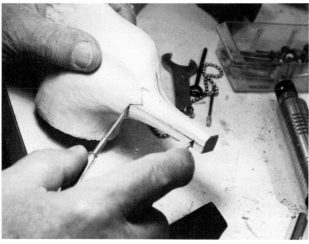

The length is again transferred to the wood to make sure it measures from the lower point of the V profile. The bill must be exact, and all other dimensions and preparations will relate to this part of the anatomy.

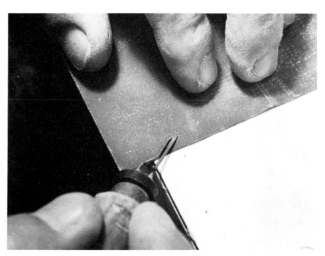

Dean sharpens the tip of the burning pen on a piece of fine sandpaper. This ensures sharply defined burn lines.

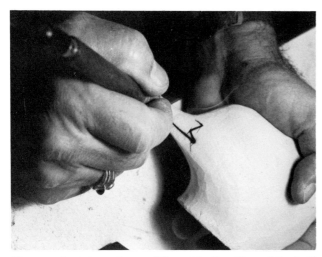

The separation between the mandibles and the V profile are defined with a burning tool.

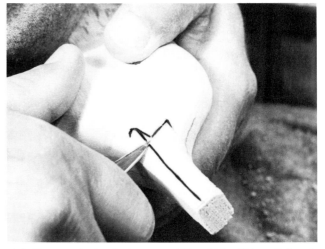

A knife starts shaping the lower mandible, which will later fit into the upper one.

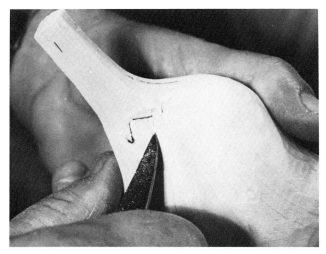

Here the knife does shaping where the bill meets the forehead.

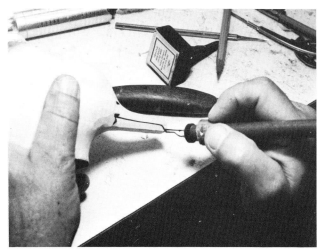

Note that the upper mandible tip overlaps the end of the lower mandible on this merganser.

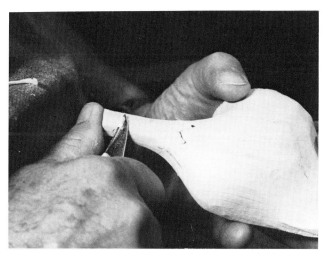

Shaping continues on the tip of the bill. Note that Dean removed the burn line separation, feeling it was not quite right.

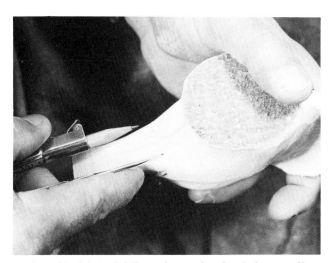

The width of the study bill must be transferred to the lower profile.

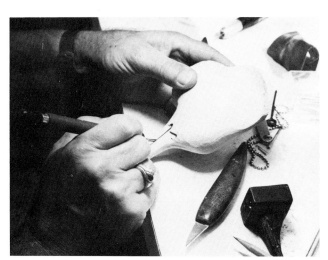

Dean redefines the mandible separation.

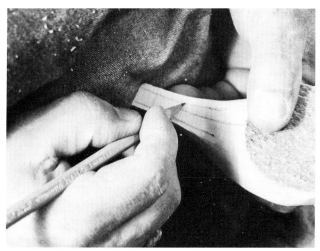

Here Dean outlines the general width and shape of the bill.

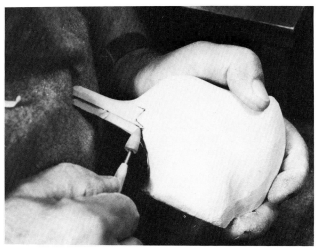

The lower mandible must be reduced now in width so that it rests inside the upper one. Dean uses a fine grinding stone.

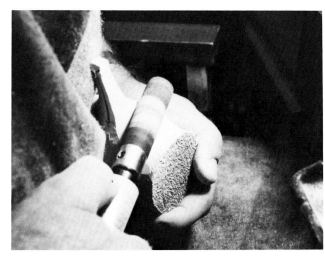

The same drum is used to smooth the neck area.

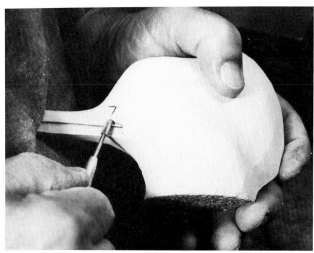

A small fluted cutter helps define the V-shaped profile of where the bill meets the forehead.

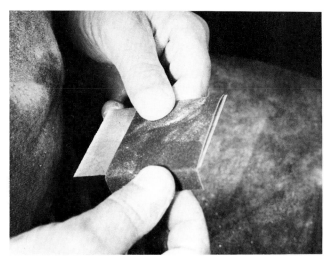

Dean demonstrates how the sanding drum attachment is assembled. He uses a piece of sandpaper 2¼ x 3¼ inches and puts a crease on each end.

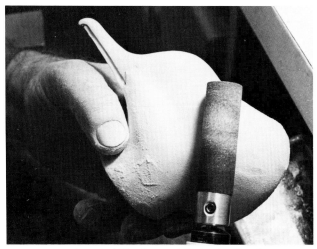

Dean stops work on the bill to fine-sand the head with a three-quarter-inch-diameter sanding drum.

The sandpaper is then wrapped around the rubber-cushioned armature.

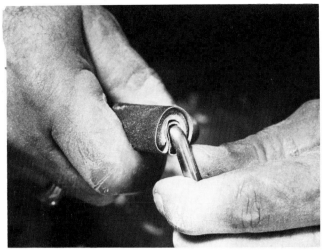

The last step is tightening the drum with a key.

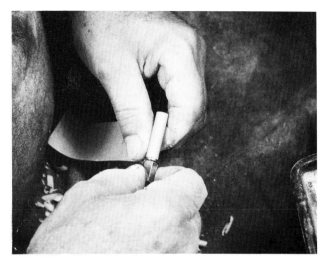

The armature, or mandril, has a slot that holds one end of the sandpaper strip. Dean made this from the core of a worn-out sanding flap wheel.

Seen here is an assortment of sanding drums and grinding tool handpieces.

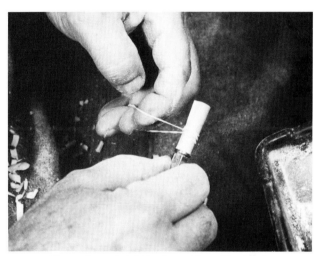

The sandpaper is held in place with a rubber band.

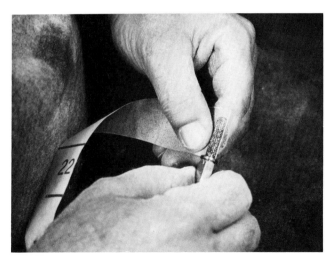

A smaller replacement for the large sanding drums is a simple steel armature and a strip of sandpaper.

For fine sanding that does not gouge the wood, the tip of this sanding roll is used.

Here can be compared Dean's progress on the bill and head and the study bill for this hooded merganser hen.

Another study bill measurement that is taken is from a point where the bill meets the forehead and the center of the nostril.

The location of the nostril can also be taken from the origin of the mandibles to the center of the nostril.

Making a Nostril

Study bills will also provide an accurate reference for the duck's nostrils. Dean says he takes a measurement for its location from the base and not the tip of the bill. "It is possible," he says, "that the tip may still need some shortening. If that were the case, the nostril would not be accurately located."

Some carvers build up the nostrils with epoxy or wood filler, but Dean defines his from the available wood, having made sure, as he shaped the bill, that he left enough extra wood in that area. Forming them can be done with small rotary stones or fluted cutters, and the nostril holes, which form a continuous channel through the upper mandible, are done with a small dental drill in a Foredom Tool.

Knotts' Knives

Once the burning pen establishes guidelines, a knife can do much of the rough shaping on the bill. Dean uses knives made by Cheston Knotts. (See appendix for address.) Of them he says, "They hold an edge and are comfortable to handle." He adds, "Chet will do anything for the carver. If you want a special knife, he'll make it for you. He is very willing to accommodate."

Still, the knife must be very sharp, Dean points out, especially when working with dry tupelo. What helps keep a knife sharp is a felt buffing wheel that does not grind the steel but hones it.

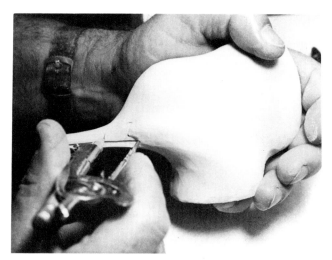

Here Dean locates the nostril center on the bill.

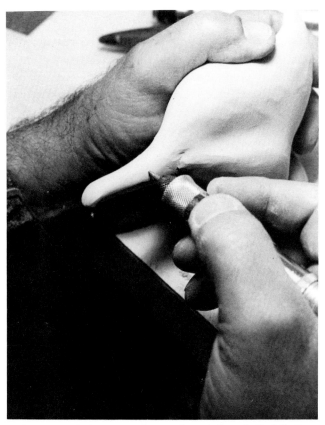

A way to clean cutters is by running them in crepe rubber.

A duck's nostrils form a continuous channel through the bill. Dean works a tapered diamond cutter through both sides, followed by larger dental bits.

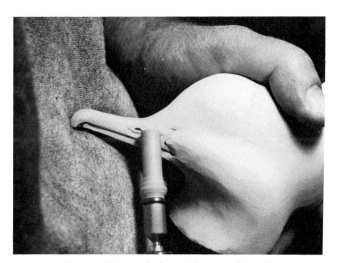

The nostril is smoothed out with the sanding roll.

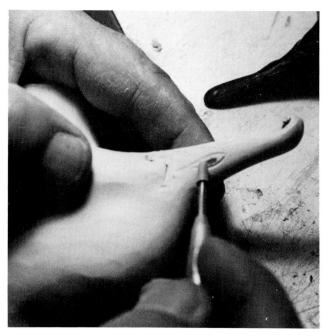

Though some carvers build up the nostrils using a wood filler or epoxy putty, Dean carves his from the original wood. Here he uses a round-ended diamond cutter.

A way to keep an edge on a steel knife is by touching it up on a felt buffing wheel.

Dean uses Cheston Knotts' knives. This one he designed and had custom-made by Knotts. (See appendix for address.)

More Refining

Small cylindrical rotary files and stones do more refining on the bill, and a knife removes wood underneath the bill where there is a long, V-like depression in the lower mandible. Here too a burning pen is used to define the area to be removed.

Also used for refining areas on the bill are sanding boards devised by Dean. Describing them as large emery boards, Dean explains that they are thin pieces of mahogany plywood with wet/dry sandpaper glued to one side. Grits range from 300 to 500. These thin boards can also be cut to any shape required.

Other sanding is achieved with a sanding roll. This is a slotted mandible with a piece of sandpaper wrapped around it, held with a rubber band.

Mergansers have definite teeth that facilitate their catching fish. Dean burns an area between the mandibles so that he can later put in those teeth.

A fluted steel cutter does some more shaping on the upper mandible.

The burning pen also gives definition to the underside of the nail, which is on the tips of all ducks' bills.

That same cutter reduces the width of the lower mandible. Here can be seen the recess on the upper mandible where the teeth will be formed.

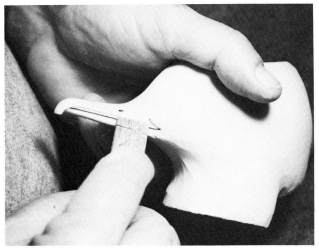

Here Dean demonstrates the use of a homemade sanding stick.

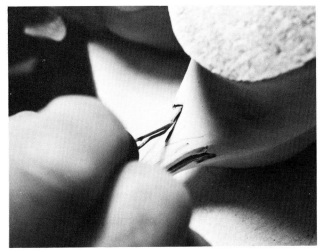

Back to the burning pen, Dean begins to give definition to the underside of the lower mandible.

These sanding sticks comprise sandpaper of different grits glued to thin pieces of mahogany plywood.

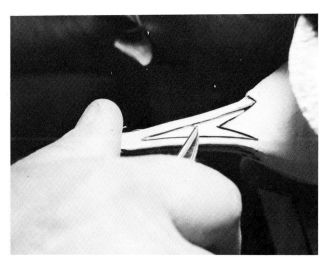

There is a distinctive V-shaped depression in the lower mandible from which wood must be removed.

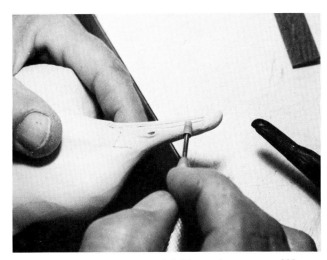

A diamond cutter gives more definition to the upper mandible.

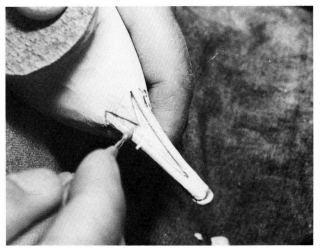

A pointed ruby carver gives definition to that area and removes sharp lines left by the knife. (See appendix for address of supplier.)

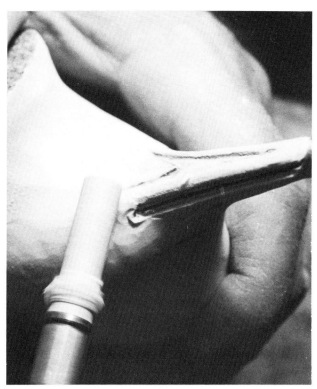

The sanding roll is used on the underside of the head for fine finishing.

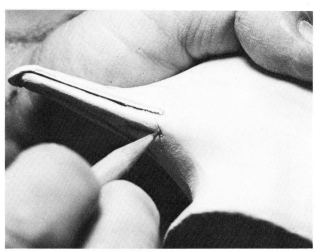

Dean indicates that the location where the lower mandible joins the cheek area is critical. Too far in or too far out will change the look of the bird.

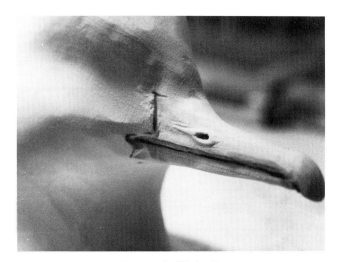

Here are the bill details.

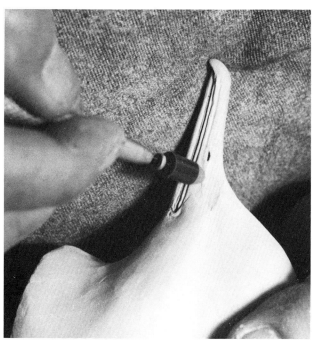

This rubber-tipped accessory is impregnated with small bits of abrasive. Dean uses it for smoothing around the nostrils. It is available from P.C. English Enterprises, Inc. (See appendix for address.)

Here can be studied the shape of the head.

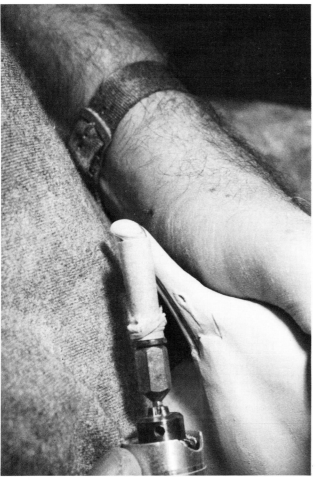

The sanding roll is used to help shape and define the nail.

Locating the Eyes

"I like to get the bill fairly well finished before I do the rest of the head, especially the eyes. If you drill for the eyes early and need to change the bill even a little bit, you run into trouble with proportions and expression."

Dean says that, in most cases, the center of a duck's eye can be located by first taking a measurement from the top point of the upper mandible to the lower point of the lower mandible. This distance will determine the space between the center of the eye and the origin of the upper mandible. If a compass is used, the pointed leg can then be placed at the upper mandible point and a line is drawn to locate the center of the eye socket. (For setting in the eyes, read about John Gewerth's techniques in chapter 5.)

Saw-like Teeth

Mergansers have distinctive, saw-like teeth, adaptations that facilitate their catching small fish for food. After recessing an area between the mandibles for the teeth, Dean will define them with a burning tip, one made for him by Colwood Electronics. (See appendix for address.)

After spraying the nearly finished bill with alcohol to raise the grain for final sanding, Dean uses a hair dryer to hasten the drying. (The teeth have yet to be put in.)

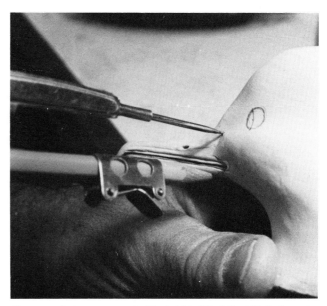

Dean says that measurement of the height of the bill will help determine the placement of the eyes. Note where the points of the compass are.

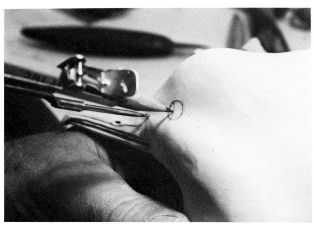

That same compass marks off a distance from the upper point of the V profile to where the front portion of the pupil will be.

Note the flow and direction of the stoning lines on the back of the head.

Final details on a duck's head are accomplished with a grinding stone and a burning pen. This is the head of a pintail drake.

Here is another view of the pintail's head with more fine burning.

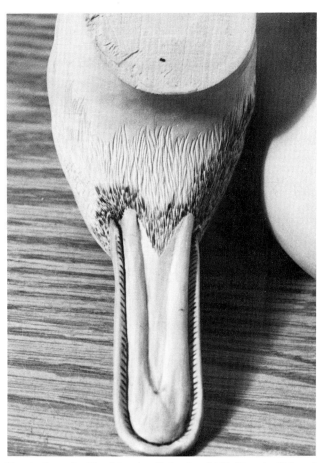

Here is the underside of the pintail's head and bill. Note the V-shaped depression in the lower mandible.

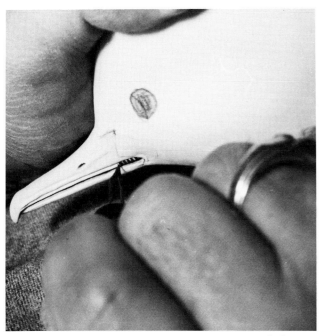

The final step on the bill is defining the teeth with the tip of a burning tool.

Dean's home is on the St. Martin River, not far from Ocean City, Maryland, where the World Championship Wildfowl Carving Competition takes place. This is the view from his studio.

Dean had a special tip made by Colwood Electronics to burn in mergansers' teeth. (See appendix for address.)

He keeps one of his feeders filled throughout the year to attract songbirds.

On the St. Martin River

Dean is fortunate to live where a variety of wildfowl can be seen. On the St. Martin River behind his home and studio, he has observed osprey, skimmers, great blue herons, egrets, clapper rails, and numerous ducks: from ring-necked to blue bills, from ruddy ducks to widgeons.

Keeping two feeders going all year round, Dean attracts untold numbers of song birds that will return with their young.

To observe ducks better, Dean will go out in a canoe and spread corn and milo, a grain sorghum, to draw birds in closer to shore. But, he says, "I have to be careful because I don't want game wardens thinking I'm illegally hunting them."

Is Dean a hunter, or has he hunted wildfowl? He says that shortly after World War II he bought a shotgun. "I went out once and then sold my gun. I'm not sure why. I enjoy eating wildfowl, but I guess I can't bring myself to kill them."

Mourning Doves, *William J. Koelpin*
Courtesy of William J. Koelpin

Saw-whet Owl, William J. Koelpin
Courtesy of William J. Koelpin

Willow Ptarmigans, William J. Koelpin
Courtesy of William J. Koelpin

Long-eared Owl, William J. Koelpin
Courtesy of William J. Koelpin

Goshawk, *Robert Guge*

Bluejay, *Robert Guge*

Indigo Bunting, *Robert Guge*

Bluebird, *Robert Guge*

Mallard Drake, *Jett Brunet*
Courtesy of Jett Brunet

Black Duck, *Jett Brunet*

Green-winged Teal, *Jett Brunet*

Ruddy Pair, *Jett Brunet*
Courtesy of the North American Wildfowl Art Museum, The Ward Foundation

Hooded Merganser Hen, *Habbart Dean*
Photo by George Ross

Hooded Merganser Hen, *Habbart Dean*

Red-breasted Merganser Drake, *Habbart Dean*
Photo by George Ross

Black Skimmer, *Habbart Dean*

Widgeon Pair, *John Gewerth*

Springtime Ruddies, *John Gewerth*

Red-breasted Merganser, *John Gewerth*

Mallard Hen, *John Gewerth*

Black-bellied Plover, *Marc Schultz*
Photo by Michael Diorio

Widgeon Hen, *Marc Schultz*

Canvasback Drake, *Marc Schultz*

Wood Duck Hen, *Marc Schultz*

Bobwhite Quail, *Louis Kean, Jr.*

Widgeon Pair, *Louis Kean, Jr.*

Mourning Dove, *Louis Kean, Jr.*

Redwinged Blackbirds, *Louis Kean, Jr.*

Winter Wren, *Manfred Scheel*

Wood Duck Drake, *Manfred Scheel*

Condors, *Manfred Scheel*

Great Blue Heron, *Manfred Scheel*

5

John Gewerth
Sculpturing and Animation

An Artist Finds His Medium

Since he started carving in 1975, John Gewerth has become one of the finest carvers of waterfowl in the country. In that year, he entered his first duck, a ringnecked hen, in the U.S. National Decoy Show, held on Long Island, New York. He won an honorable mention as a novice. The following year, he entered shows as an intermediate carver and won a Best in Show with a mallard hen at the Midwest Decoy Contest held in Michigan. With this he began competition in the open class. By 1981, he won Best in Show in all of the four open class competitions he entered, including the World Championship Wildfowl Carving Competition.

How did Gewerth get started as a carver? He sees several influences as having been important to his carving career. He credits a close friend, Jim O'Neill, with having introduced him to duck hunting and decoy carving. Another friend, an old time decoy carver of the Mississippi River School, Don Zeug, was also an early influence. After he became initiated, however, eminent carvers such as Randy Tull of Wisconsin, Pat Godin of Ontario, Canada, and Larry Hayden of Michigan helped shape Gewerth's techniques.

Carvers and friends were not the only influences.

A champion carver, John Gewerth is shown here shaping the head of a mallard drake.

Gewerth had studied commercial art for a year, worked as a draftsman, and taught himself taxidermy. He says, "Perhaps all along I have been a frustrated artist who needed a medium to express myself in, which I have since found in wildfowl carving." But he does not carve full-time, which has been a limiting factor on how much time he can devote to his art. And although Gewerth has no trouble selling his work, he admits that making little or no money would not deter him from continuing what he is currently doing.

New Reference Material

In addition to his background and friends, Gewerth gives much credit to the innovative tools and reference material made available over the last few years. "When I started," he says, "carvers didn't have all the reference material you have today. You can accumulate knowledge and become relatively skilled at such a fast rate.

"Seven, eight years ago, there were a handful of carvers in this area [of Illinois]. No one was really any better than the other. I guess we were all on the same level. So we stumbled around looking for new techniques and sharing whatever little discoveries we made."

Gewerth also sees seminars and workshops as giving carvers a decided advantage. "If a new carver attends a seminar, he can find out things it would otherwise take years to discover on his own. And this is owing to top carvers being willing to share what they know."

How much has carving evolved during the past decade? Gewerth says he revisited the Ward Foundation Museum (in Salisbury, Maryland) in 1984 after a few years absence. "I realized that championship birds carved ten years ago, which were fantastic then, wouldn't even get an honorable mention today."

An Artist's Story Board

Gewerth does not rely only on the reference material supplied by others. Using a Nikon camera with a 70–210 zoom lens and multipliers, he takes many of his own reference photos at sloughs and refuges near his home. What he looks for, he says, "is a shape, a form, an attitude, or pose to work out my patterns, though I do little detail work from a photograph."

Still, the photographs get put up on a cork board in his carving room, making what he describes as "an artist's story board." He explains, "I'll put up all the pictures of a species that interest me and work a pat-

An important reference for Gewerth are photos he himself has taken. Mounted where he works, he calls the collection of photographs "a story board."

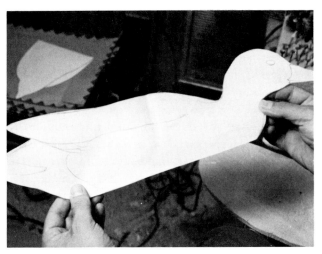

Though photos are useful, Gewerth does not generate a pattern from any particular one. Rather, he makes what might be called a composite. This pattern is for a mallard drake.

The result of the pattern is shown above. What is important for him is what he describes as attitude, character, and personality.

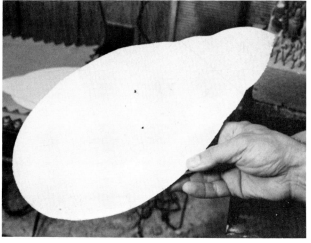

Here is a wood pattern for a mallard drake Gewerth has kept for a future reference.

tern out from them, though not directly from any one photograph."

He warns that no bird looks quite the same when reduced to two dimensions. "So what I end up with is a very simple pattern, basically a profile. On it, I may define flank feathers, where the tail comes in, where the tertials and primaries lie." He adds that he never uses the same pattern twice, but will use his old patterns as general references for new ones.

Casting a Study Bill

Since the advent of study bills, carvers have had a fixed reference, particularly in terms of length of the bill. (For more on their use, see chapter 3 with Habbart Dean.) Given that length, other dimensions of the bird could be determined by using photographs and proportional comparisons. He says, however, that the sizes of birds vary. "Not all mallards are 13½ inches long." What he aims for are "good proportions and a good attitude."

Interestingly, Gewerth has cast his own study bills from freshly killed ducks, especially bills he is unable to buy. Using a dental-impression compound that is mixed with water and put into a container, Gewerth can then push the duck's bill into the material. He says it is important to have holes in the sides of the container to allow air to escape. The compound takes only five minutes to set, and then the bill can be eased out.

He adds that he will even push the head in past where the eyes are located. "It gives a good reference for eye location and width," he explains. "Some of the commercial suppliers do that as well, but when I first did it, it was by accident."

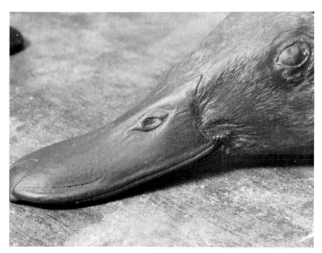

Gewerth has cast his own study bills, using a dental compound into which the head of a freshly killed duck is pushed.

Here can be compared a commercial study bill, left, Gewerth's homemade bill, center, and a nearly finished carved head, right. All represent a mallard drake.

Mounted Birds

Gewerth will also use mounted birds, some of which he has done himself, to gain anatomical knowledge of waterfowl. When he started carving, he discovered that many birds, especially waterfowl, were not properly mounted. Anatomy can easily be distorted because a skin will actually stretch beyond its original size. Not only that, Gewerth notes, a study mount may be greasy. He explains, "If a skin is not properly washed, the oils in the skin will start bleeding through the feathers. This will affect the colors you're trying to copy. So a taxidermist has to scrape off as much fat from the inside of the skin as he can."

Stating that a carving will only be as good as the available references, Gewerth says that a taxidermist's mount makes up much of that reference, so it is important to find a good taxidermist. Gewerth praises Jeff Cooper for his taxidermy work. (See appendix for his address.)

Why is a good mount so important to Gewerth besides its value as a color reference? He answers, "You need it to get the right relationship between feather groups."

Sculpturing Feather Groups

"When I look at the real bird, I don't see every feather. I see dividing lines between feather groups and the way they flow. I try to duplicate that using a process I call sculpturing."

Sculpturing, then, refers to defining feather groups. "I don't particularly like to see every feather carved. That results in a scaly effect," he says. He begins work on the shaped and sanded wood by drawing nearly every feather, but that, he says, is only a guide.

"I've noticed that when you pull out a feather from a bird, it has a natural tendency to cup. Feather groups will also cup, so I look for these natural divisions, exaggerating or intensifying them. The basis of my sculpturing, then, is to try to find these natural breaks."

Roadmapping Feather Flow

"Though I'll draw on every feather, doing that is just a guide for my feather texturing and feather splits. You have to have some kind of road map or guide to begin with."

But while he is determining the flow, he is also working out variations. "You want variety in your feather groups," Gewerth says. "A common mistake I find in some carvings is every back feather radiating out from a single point, and having each row very regularly increase in size. That makes for a boring composition that doesn't give any life to the piece." How is he able to vary feather flow? He answers, "Just by varying the direction of a quill I can vary the flow of a feather." He adds that he will sketch in and erase feathers and quills many times before finding a pattern that satisfies him. He adds that having feathers blend together is important.

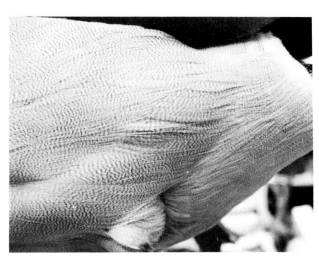

One of his techniques is capturing not individual feathers but groups of them. Here is the side of a mallard drake mount Gewerth uses to find these feather groups.

Note the flow of the feathers on that same mount, a significant aspect of what Gewerth calls sculpturing feather groups.

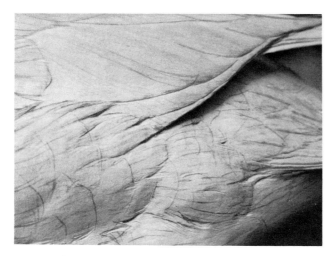

An interesting feature of a mallard is its large tertial feathers. Note how the flank feathers split and slightly overlap the tertials.

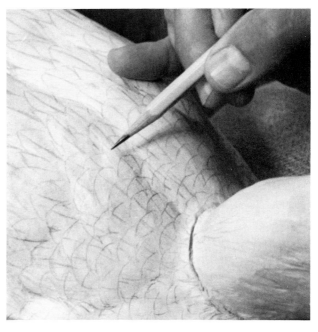

One thing to avoid is not having the back feathers uniformly radiating out from some central point. This is something Gewerth has seen on many carvers' waterfowl.

"I tell beginners that you have to over-exaggerate this feather sculpturing. If you don't, it will virtually disappear when you texture it and then paint over it. And though you might be able to feel it when you run your hand over it, you won't be able to see the results."

Gewerth states that sculpturing also includes how a feather is textured and burned. "I rough-texture with grinding bits toward the base of a feather. I then let the tip of that feather flow into the next feather without any delineation, making it lay flat on the following feather," though definition can be added with burning and paints. When burning, he says, "I lighten up the burning pen as I near the end of a feather. This creates

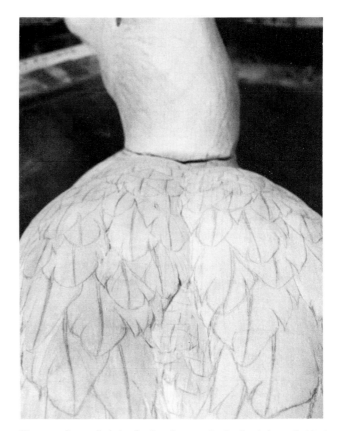

Here can be studied the feather flow on the back of the unfinished mallard drake. Note that quill lines help establish that flow.

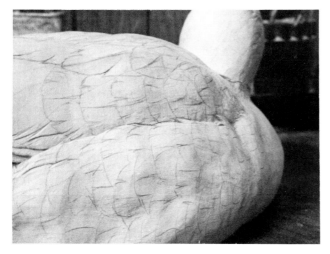

A great deal of detailing and pencil work is done before burning and sculpturing are begun. Gewerth describes this as roadmapping feather flow. Note that early on he established major feather splits.

Shown above is the back of a widgeon hen. Note how effectively he uses splits; though Gewerth says there is some artistic license involved here.

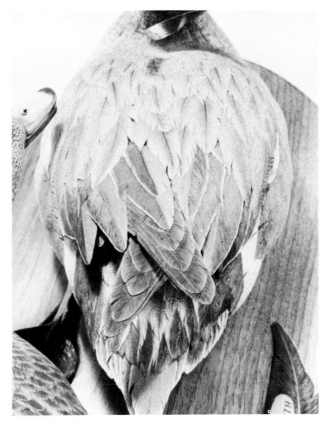

Shown here is the back of a widgeon drake.

Here is the back of a mallard hen. Note that there is some variety to the feather patterns, though on first sight they would seem symmetrical.

a shadowing effect. So I texture each feather, then burn more finely. This gives more variation to a feather."

Splits and Artistic License

Gewerth, as he is roadmapping feathers, will often put in numerous feather splits or separations. He says that some critics might argue that a bird with many splits is an unhealthy bird because it can't preen itself well. He defends what he does, saying, "This is artistic license, but I am not sacrificing accuracy in terms of shape, color, and detail."

He points out that splits can open up light and dark areas on a bird and have them blend together, while allowing the viewer to see portions of feathers, thus creating interest in the composition. "I'll even sketch in light and dark areas while I'm roadmapping because you have to think about where these areas will fall when carving, even in the early stages." When he has finally decided where splits will be located, he will either carve in what he calls major splits with a knife, or use a fine grit grinding stone for minor splits.

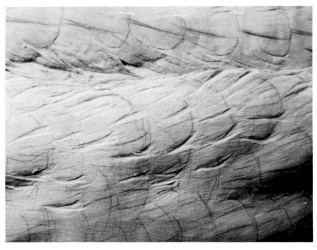

Note the number of splits Gewerth has carved into the flank of his mallard drake.

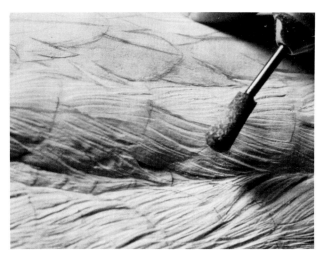

A larger grinding stone or ruby carver with a rounded end can create high and low areas of feather flow.

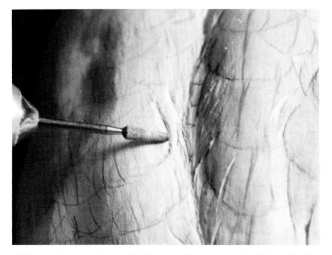

Splits can be carved using this fine grinding stone with a blunt, flat tip.

The side of Gewerth's widgeon drake can be seen here. Observe how splits have a definitive flow, which contributes to an animated look.

A Burning Strategy

As Gewerth already pointed out, he burns his feather flow lines deeper at the base of the feather and lighter as he gets to its end. He adds that he follows the flow of the stoning marks, sometimes burning between them, sometimes within them. "If you don't follow those lines," he says, "you'll end up with a mess."

He notes that he burns in the quills first. He can create these by laying the burning pen over to one side of the quill and then the other, thus smoothing the surface of the quill with the heat of the burning pen. As for splits, some of these he will burn in, though many will simply be accented with paint.

Here can be studied the sculptured feather flow on the side of a ruddy duck.

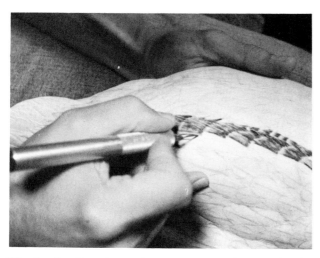

When burning, Gewerth starts from the rear and works forward so that that burn lines overlap as feathers do.

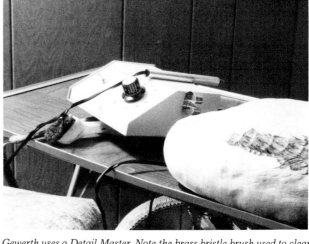

Gewerth uses a Detail Master. Note the brass bristle brush used to clean carbon deposits from the burning tool tip.

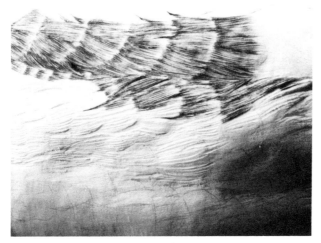

Note the flow of the burning lines that define feather separations. But note that individual feathers are not sculptured. Also, small splits can be achieved with just burning.

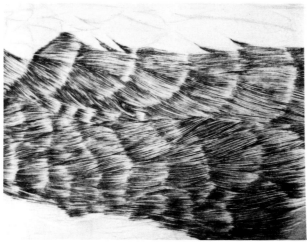

More burning can be seen above. Note the splits in the upper portion of the photo. These will take advantage of color changes in the feathers and will add interest to the piece. Also, Gewerth will carve in large splits with a knife.

Is there any particular place he starts burning on the bird? Gewerth says he starts at the tail area and works forward so that the burn lines will overlap naturally.

A Temporary Head Attachment

Besides sculpturing feather groups, Gewerth must also contend with other areas of the bird's anatomy. One of them is joining a head to its body.

Though Robert Guge and Jett Brunet (chapters 2 and 3) work from a solid block of wood without attaching heads as separate pieces, Gewerth prefers working on his heads separately. He claims he can achieve more control and detail with his tools, especially when working on the bill.

"With a detached head, I feel I have more freedom to carve, say, the lower mandible if the head is low and over the breast.

"The other thing is, I like to move the bird around a lot in my hands when I carve. That can be very cumbersome sometimes if the head is attached early on to the body."

Still, for what Gewerth calls the roughing stage, he temporarily secures the head to the body. He explains, "I never shape the head fully until it's on the body. Then I shape the head and breast and body at once."

To accomplish this temporary bond, Gewerth uses a combination of Tuf·Carv (a two-part, quick-setting, polyester resin) and then cardboard between the head and body. "It makes a good strong bond when rough carving," he says, "but it pops right off when I'm ready to carve the head. And when I'm prepared to attach

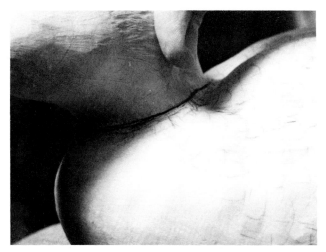

Gewerth prefers to work with a separate head, one that can be temporarily attached so that breast and neck can be carved together. A piece of lightweight cardboard and a bonding resin called Tuf Carv allow the head and breast to be carved as a unit. For fine detail work, the head separates from the body between the layers of the cardboard.

Before gluing the head in place, he scallops the neck with a grinding tool. This, when covered with Plastic Wood, will help disguise the seam line.

As an early reference, Gewerth locates the eyes of a bird and carves them to shape before glass eyes are inserted.

the head permanently, I'll grind off the Tuf Carv and use an epoxy to bond the parts together."

Before he did this, he would find that he had a tendency to carve the head too much or the breast too much and not have enough stock left to do the detailing he wanted.

A Scalloped Seam

Having decided to work on his heads as separate pieces, how then does Gewerth deal with the seam line? He first bevels or chamfers the bottom edge of the head and neck. Then, with a conical cutter, he scallops first that edge, then the corresponding area on the neck where the head will be glued. This leaves two scalloped edges that will be covered with Plastic Wood. Gewerth explains, "What I've done is broken up the two mating surfaces and covered them with a wood filler. (Compare Louis Kean's technique for dealing with seams in chapter 7.) The line becomes not straight, but irregular. So when I texture and paint over that, the line should have disappeared."

Carved Eyes

Gewerth, like most carvers, waits until a fairly exact head has been shaped before the eye sockets are drilled and glass eyes are inserted. But he is unique in that he first carves the eyes into the wood as a reference.

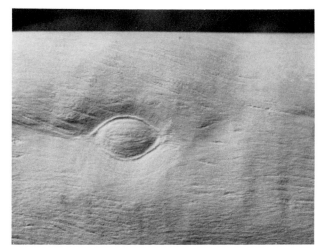

Here is the close-up of a carved eye, complete with lids.

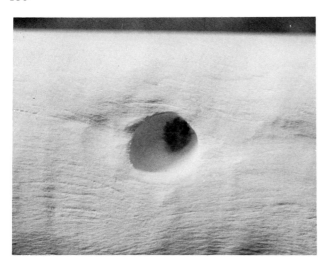

Insetting an eye begins by grinding out an opening larger than the eye.

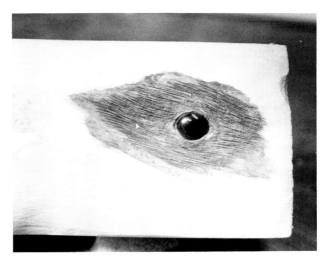

The eyelids are then shaped with a knife and a burning pen set at low heat. Plastic Wood, Gewerth says, can be burned and shaped to form the eyelids and even the tear ducts.

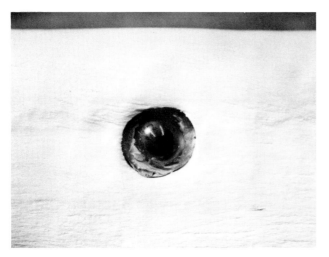

Gewerth sets the eye in clay, a soft substance that allows him to position or reposition it.

When he is ready to put the glass eyes into place, Gewerth bores holes where the eyes will be placed and fills the eye sockets with clay. The reason for this? "With clay, I can get a good relationship of the eyes to each other without affixing them into something that will harden. So if they're crooked or not at the correct angle, I can always adjust them."

Once he has the eyes located correctly, he will fill in around the eyes with Plastic Wood. The wood filler is burnable, Gewerth says, "and I can form the eyelids with my burner by turning it down to a very low setting. Otherwise Plastic Wood, being a cellulose material, will melt. But because it melts, I can also reposition some of it with low heat, forming the tear ducts in front of the eyes."

Flexible Rulers, Dental Probes, and Modeling Tools

While working on the head, and especially the bill, Gewerth feels that there are critical measurements that have to be met. He explains, "The head is at least fifty percent of a good carving. And a bill, unlike feather dimensions, has no latitude for changes."

One of the critical dimensions Gewerth refers to is the distance from where the lower edge of the upper mandible joins the face to the tip of the bill. To facilitate taking that one from a study bill, he uses a flexible ruler, one only five inches long, a handy tool for taking other bill measurements.

Gewerth also points out the importance of maintaining a centerline. "If I grind it off, I'll redraw it," he says.

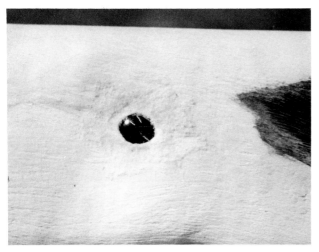

The next step is filling the eye cavity with Plastic Wood.

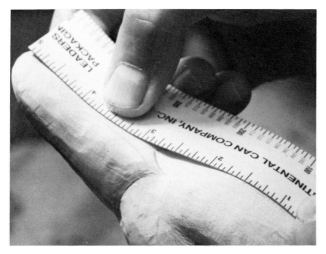

A typical tool he uses is a flexible ruler to establish critical dimensions taken from a study bill. Gewerth also likes to maintain a centerline to help keep the bill symmetrical when carving.

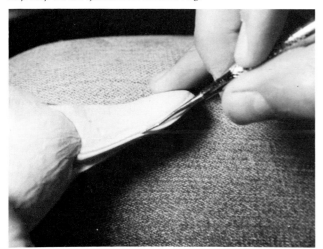

Another useful tool for defining bill anatomy is a dental probe.

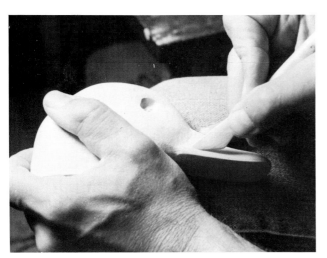

This boxwood tool can press details into a bill. Boxwood is harder than the tupelo he uses for his waterfowl.

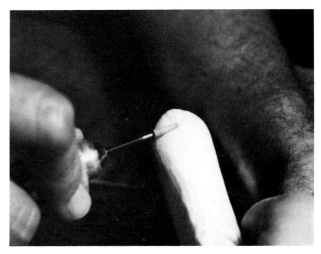

This stone is used to define the nail or raised tip on the end of a duck's bill.

This small, blunt-ended red oxide stone Gewerth uses a great deal for shaping and sculpturing. It tapers to five-sixteenths of an inch at its tip.

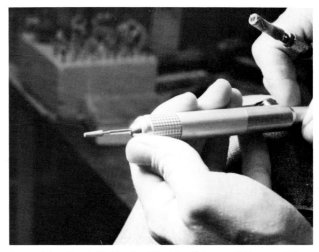

Gewerth has found this Foredom No. 8 handpiece useful because it has a quick release mechanism that facilitates changing bits. Available from Woodcraft Supply. (See appendix for address.)

"It's a way of keeping the bill from being twisted or high on one side. With that centerline, you'll pick up a high spot right away."

When it comes to finely detailing the bill, Gewerth uses dental probes and clay modeling tools. "You can push a lot of detail into a bill with these tools," he says. Also, "You can define an edge by pushing it down, not gouging it out," adding that wood, especially tupelo, has the characteristic of accepting pushed-in details.

Flexible Tupelo and Fuzzy Basswood

For Gewerth, tupelo gum is a more flexible wood than the two others he has tried, basswood and jelutong. Noting that he started with jelutong, Gewerth eventually found that it wasn't as stable as other woods, and he was limited in how much detail he could put into the wood, especially in the bill area.

But he also found that at times jelutong has a tendency to crumble, while basswood, the next wood he went to, did not. Still, he says, "With basswood, the fuzziness of the grain has to be dealt with. The only way I could get rid of it was to burn the whole bird." Why is fuzziness or a slight raising of the grain a problem? Gewerth answers, "If you have fuzziness between your texture lines, you don't have a neat, clean carving."

He also experienced other problems with jelutong, such as when burning an area such as on the breast. He found that when burning perpendicular to the grain, the wood crystallized and fell out, leaving fine lines that did not look attractive. "These show up as scratch marks," he says. "But you do get a nice, clean texture when stoning the wood."

Drying and Repairing Tupelo

Gewerth keeps a sizable supply of tupelo on hand. He points out that he will not carve the wood until it is thoroughly dry, even if it takes a year for that to occur. To aid in the drying, he seals the ends of his tupelo with paraffin wax, which allows evaporation to take place more slowly with less checking or splitting.

If he should get splits, he will vee out the area, getting a straight-sided cut. He can then pound in a wedge of tupelo and grind it down flush to the surface. Then the wedge is held in place with carpenter's glue.

Yet, he admits he has had some exceptionally difficult-to-carve pieces of tupelo. This may be the result of what part of the tree the wood was taken from or its degree of hardness, he explains. But unlike some carvers who work tupelo when it is freshly cut, Gewerth says that would mean, for him, working on a wet surface. "Because I draw so many pencil lines on my bird, that won't work."

Inserting Primaries

Many carvers will insert primary feathers rather than carve them from the block. This is usually ac-

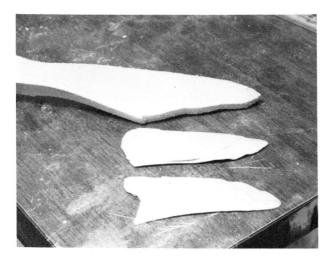

To achieve a unified contour to primary feathers, Gewerth carves a primary group from a solid piece of wood.

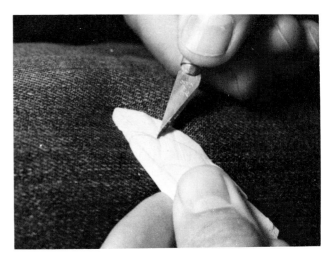

Defining feather separations can be achieved with an X-acto knife.

complished by gluing together veneer-thin pieces of wood to build up as many as ten feathers and then glue them underneath the tertial feathers. But Gewerth has a different approach. He will carve his primary grouping from a single piece of wood, saying, "I can get some arc and bend to the feathers this way. With that extra thickness to begin with, I can give the feathers more definition and character."

This is not unique, but what might be is the way he inserts them on the body. Instead of simply gluing them underneath the tertials, he relieves an area on the top of the primary grouping so that the tertials appear to rest slightly within them. This way, he says, "I maintain the unified flow of the two sets of feathers." Plastic Wood can then help disguise the joint.

Also, he reminds beginning carvers that one side of a duck has to be slightly lower than the other to allow the primaries to overlap as they naturally do.

Rippled and Splayed Feathers

Using a grinding bit, Gewerth will grind in ripples on the surface of such feathers as the primaries. He explains, "It will offer some interesting irregularity because nature is not that regular."

Another interesting treatment of feathers is how he splays them from one distinctively colored area to another. A good area to illustrate this, he says, is the rump and tail. On his mallard drake, Gewerth points out the transition from the dark to light feathers. Instead of leaving a dark line there with his paints, he

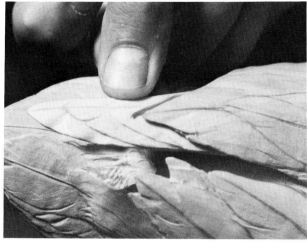

Gewerth recesses an area in the primary group so that the tertials will be within them, creating a unified flow.

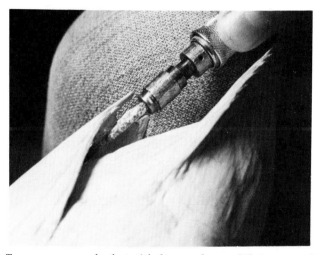

To recess an area under the tertials, he uses a long, carbide-impregnated cutter.

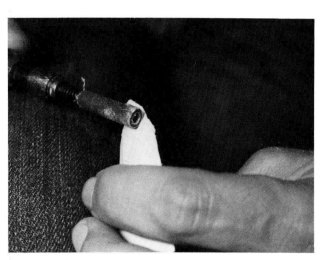

Shaping can also be done with a sanding roll.

Note the ripples on the primaries of a widgeon hen Gewerth carved. He says to pay close attention to how the primaries originate from under the tertials.

Slight ripples and folds can be noticed on the primaries, as can be seen on a mallard mount.

Note how the dark color on this widgeon drake carved by Gewerth splays into the light area.

Splaying feathers from one area to another is a technique Gewerth says is important. Here, dark feathers on a mallard mount's rump splay out slightly into the light tertial feathers.

There are even splayed feathers on the underside of the carved mallard. Splays like this, by bringing one color into another, add interest, say Gewerth.

Here can be observed how Gewerth carves in the same splayed feathers on his mallard drake.

Gewerth makes separate inserts to represent a mallard's distinctive curls. These he made from chicken tree wood, a scrub tree of Louisiana. Real curls are in the background.

carves tiny feather edges or ends from one area to the other. This splaying, he says, "promotes some interest, bringing dark feathers into light ones, and light feathers into dark ones. This can be overdone with too much regularity, but I don't think this technique is done enough by some carvers."

Chicken Tree Wood and a Mallard's Curls

As did Jett Brunet (chapter 3), Gewerth had to insert the distinctive curls found on the rump of a mallard. But instead of using tupelo, the primary wood for the duck, he used what he was told was called chicken tree wood. He says it came from a Louisiana carver, and is probably from a scrub tree or vine. "It's a very hard, very dense, very resilient wood, and it has good flexibility. But whatever wood you use, it's got to be something that's very tough because you can't orient the grain to the curls. A softer wood will break as you're working on it."

He says that rather than carving two individual feathers, or making veneer-thin pieces and bending them, he chose to carve them into a shape to simulate the curls. "There are two feathers that you see, but actually each curl is made up of two feathers, lying inside each other.

"I just sketched the pattern on a block of this wood. The trick will then be trying to texture it since the barbs radiate out from the curls, and to get it to look ragged, yet soft."

Hollowing and Balancing

Though Gewerth uses tupelo, he has found that not all pieces can be left unhollowed and still ride properly in a competition tank of water. What he will do, as he did on his mallard drake, is drill out the wood using a Forstner bit in a drill press or even use a large cutter and Foredom Tool. He says he will take away as much wood as possible, even in the rump area. He states, "I'd rather add weight to it than try to take out more after the outside of the bird has been finished."

The next step is making a bottom or plug for the bird. This can be done with one-half-inch-thick tupelo with a beveled edge that corresponds to a bevel made on the edge of the hollow. He will then smear Tuf Carv on the edges, vee out the bond line when it hardens, and then cover that void with epoxy. This process, Gewerth explains, makes the wood as water

Here can be seen the placement of the mallard mount's curls.

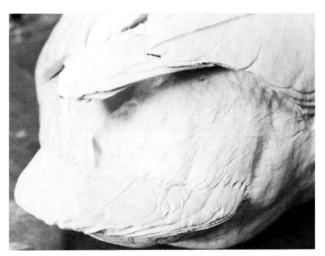

Gewerth carves a slight recess in his mallard to accept the wooden curls.

Here are the carved curls fitted into the recess made in the rump.

resistant as possible. Any water entering through the bottom of the bird can cause it to list or capsize, disqualifying it from a floating competition.

Overcoming Future Mistakes

"When I finish a carving," says Gewerth, "I take photographs of it from every angle possible, including feather patterns, under the rump, the bill, every place I can." What is his reasoning behind this? "This is not because I think the carving is great, but it is because it allows me to remember areas that I was not totally happy with so I do not duplicate them on the next bird."

He adds that six months after completing a bird, he will see what he calls obvious mistakes. "With photographs you can overcome them," he explains, "if you can look at your work objectively."

Animation

By 1983, Gewerth felt he was ready for a change in his style. He says that a red-breasted merganser drake done that year was his first attempt at a more animated look. "I saw a trend developing back then which was going away from the classic decoy pose. So I decided to change my style. Since then, most of my birds have exhibited some motion, usually being caught in the act of doing something." But, he adds, "Animation just for the sake of animation can lead to an unnatural pose, so the trick is to catch them doing something flattering." (Compare Marc Schultz's remarks in chapter 6.)

He points out that animation can be affected significantly by how feathers are sculptured and by their flow.

With grinding tools or bits in a drill press, he removes as much wood as he can to lighten a floating bird. Weights can always be added after all carving and texturing is completed.

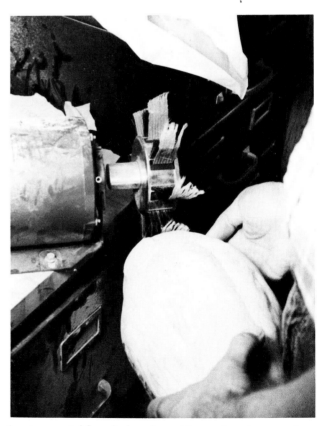

A motor-mounted flap wheel can be used to smooth contours on a large bird.

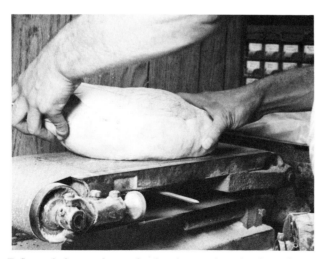

To flatten the bottom plate or plug that closes up the cavity, Gewerth uses a stationary belt sander.

A Streamlined Red-breasted Merganser Drake

"To me, a red-breasted merganser is a racy bird. So you want the illusion of one that is streamlined," says Gewerth. What achieves that look are the long, narrow bill and ragged-looking crest feathers. But instead of inserting crest feathers as others have done, Gewerth elected to carve them from the head block. After sketching the raggedness on the wood, he carved in openings to give the impression of individual feather strands.

Gewerth says that these feathers are difficult to duplicate because they are so ragged and hairy. "I didn't believe for this composition that inserts would be the best way to portray this area. And since I see this bird as just having come out of the water with a fish, I wanted to give the impression of wetness to the crest, with both joined and separate strands."

A Separate Mandible and Making Teeth

To get what is a diminutive large-mouth bass into the merganser's mandibles, Gewerth carved the lower one separately, and glued it into place.

To make the teeth characteristic of this fish eater, Gewerth used a burning tool instead of a knife. "If you use a knife, you have a tendency to break off some teeth. But the burner will give you the sharpness you want by burning back the wood from the teeth."

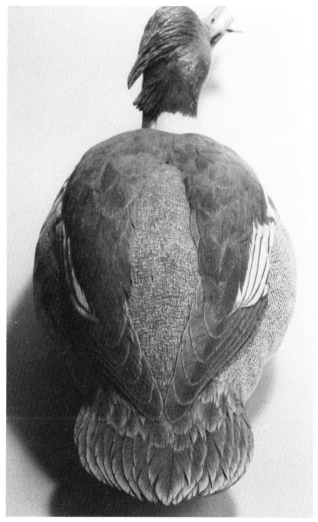

Here are details on the back of the merganser. Note the separations of the crest feathers, which might look that way after the bird comes out of the water.

Gewerth sees his red-breasted merganser drake, carved in 1983, as a racy bird.

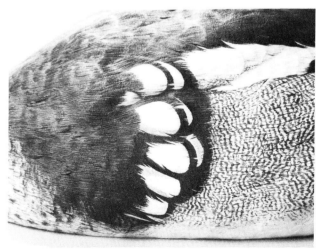

Here can be studied details on the flank of the merganser.

Another view shows flank feathers overlapping tertials.

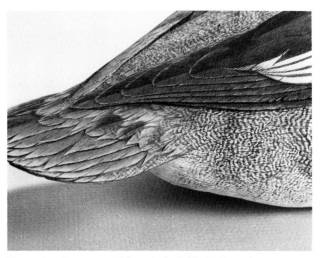

These primaries are carved from the body block. Gewerth says a carver can do this on diving ducks, which typically carry their wings on their backs.

The diminutive large-mouth bass is carved separately. The lower mandible or jaw is also carved separately to allow for the insertion of the fish. Note the teeth that are shaped with a burning tool.

Aggressive Widgeons

Gewerth feels that the natural aggressiveness of a widgeon lends itself to animation. He says that is probably the most aggressive duck to be found. "Widgeons are constantly threatening and charging one another. If another bird comes too close to a widgeon's territory, there's a challenge."

When Gewerth carved his widgeon pair for the 1984 World Championships, he was particularly concerned with having both birds animated. To achieve this, he made the male of the species with a piece of shoal grass from the Texas Gulf in its bill and the hen partially behind the drake, reaching for the grass. "The composition goes from a low point, the hen, to a high point where the drake has the grass in its bill. It gives a pleasing illusion or impression of motion and action."

A Unified Composition

A problem Gewerth also considered was how to keep the composition together, even when it was to be removed from its base and floated in a tank of water. "I felt that as soon as these individual birds would be taken off their base and floated separately in the water, the composition of the two would be lost. Their proximity is gone. So I thought at first of having the grass in both ducks' mouths to join them. But if the grass were to be proportioned correctly, it would not have offered enough support. It was then that I got the

Gewerth's widgeon pair was carved for the 1984 World Championship Wildfowl Carving Competition.

The marsh grass held in the widgeon drake's mouth is made out of copper.

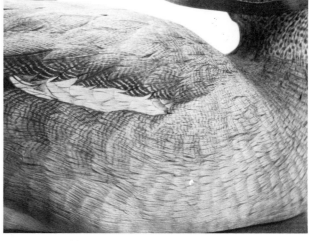

Note the flow of feather groups on the flank of the widgeon drake. This contributes to an animated look, says Gewerth.

idea of using a leg as a means of tying the ducks together with the leg and foot as a spacer."

A Steel Leg and Screen Webs

"I needed strength to bind these birds together, a rigid armature to support two birds since you are likely to pick up the pair by only one of them. Deciding on a steel armature for the unifying leg, Gewerth took a three-sixteenth-inch-diameter rod and ground flat areas, where the foot flattens out, to diminish its thickness. He then coated the steel with two-part epoxy paste. The material gave him about an hour to build up the knuckles on the leg. The toes were shaped and ground from copper and added to the steel armature with epoxy.

The webs between the toes were done with pieces of screening material. This was then coated with a thin layer of epoxy putty that was worked around the toes. Gewerth says the putty can be shaped with a brush and water because it is water soluble before it hardens. Then it can be ground with a slow-speed grinder and a ruby carver or a red oxide stone. The crosshatching lines of the webs can also be done with a grinding stone.

Springtime Ruddies

Gewerth says the drake ruddy for this composition, Springtime Ruddies, is a "semi-display position. I saw a similar pose in a book by Paul Johnsgaard. (See appendix for books by this ornithologist.) The hen was in

Here are the widgeon drake's primaries, the top set having a slight recess to allow the tertials to lie in them.

Note the steel core foot and leg that connects the widgeon drake to the hen. This is a means of unifying the composition when removed and floated in a competition tank.

A closer view shows a three-sixteenth-inch-diameter steel armature covered with epoxy paste.

Here can be studied the details on the bill and parts of the breast. Note the use of splits even there.

This ruddy duck pair, titled Springtime Ruddies, was carved for the 1985 World Championship Wildfowl Carving Competition.

Gewerth has his ducks looking at each other. Note that there is an upward flow from the hen to the drake.

Note the fine detailing on the rear of the tail, which is usually upright during a courtship display.

John Gewerth

A side view of the hen shows a great deal of animation.

Details on the back of the hen can be studied here.

close proximity to the drake, but the back of the hen was high up. I modified the pose a little bit to make it more pleasing."

He adds, "I wanted the hen to look up at the drake and the drake to look back at the hen. I was trying to convey the idea of each bird trying to catch the other's eye."

Gewerth also says that this composition portrays what he calls an "Audubon style." He says, "It's typical of that because the necks are stretched out and the tails and wings are extended. (Compare William Koelpin's "Audubon Doves" in chapter 1.) I have an animated flow leading from the back of the piece which culminates in the head of the drake, similar to the widgeon composition."

What also makes Springtime Ruddies similar to the widgeon pair is a steel armature that connects and unifies the two birds. The problem he found with the ruddies, however, was that the steel leg tended to drag the pair down in the water. For these birds, hollowing was necessary. The hen, he found, had to be hollowed more than the drake, to which he had to add some lead for counterbalancing.

Painting a Hen

Gewerth offers tips on painting a typical hen or brown-toned bird. "I'll start with burnt umber to get my earth tones, plus raw umber, black, white, and, if there is yellow or an orangey cast to the light tones, I'll add raw sienna, yellow ochre, or azo yellow orange Liquitex paint.

"The black I can tone down with raw umber and a speck of white or gesso to warm it up or give it a

To achieve the gray-brown look of this bird, Gewerth uses raw and burnt umber, raw sienna, yellow ochre, white, black and azo yellow orange. The last color he used, sparingly, to brighten certain light areas around the breast.

The body for the hen is carved from one piece of tupelo, as are the primaries and tertials.

Here can be seen the steel-cored foot that connects the ruddy hen to the drake. The webbing between the copper toes is a screening material coated with an epoxy paste. When hardened, it is textured to simulate a webbed foot.

When painting a waterfowl hen such as a green-winged teal, Gewerth puts down a light base coat of white, raw sienna, and raw umber.

The first coat of dark is a "roadmap" to establish feather patterns for subsequent coats, says Gewerth. He uses here a brown tone of burnt umber, raw umber, and a touch of Mars black.

Here Gewerth goes over the dark spots with a lighter base coat to promote a shadowy effect, which will project dark feathers showing through lighter ones.

Finer and finer brush strokes refine light and dark tones. Little brush strokes bring the composition together using many thin washes.

Here is similar coloration work on Gewerth's widgeon hen.

lighter tone. When I use black, I put both Mars black, which is an opaque black, and ivory black, which is a translucent black, on my palette." He says that he will mix both these blacks together to temper the gloss of the ivory black.

Multitudes of Colors

Gewerth says that he does not mix a large amount of paint together, and that when he begins again it is with fresh, unmixed colors. But, he says, "I'll keep my previous palette to get close to the last mix as a guide. With acrylics, I find it no great difficulty to change the color value or intensity of the paint by adding other thin coats.

"I find by this method that I introduce onto the surface a lot of different colors and a variety of tones. On the breast of a mallard hen I did, there are probably dozens of different color values put on a stroke at a time to create the feather pattern."

Is this a typical procedure for bird carvers? Gewerth answers, "Some carvers paint with only three basic values, a light tone, a dark tone, and an intermediate tone. But this can lead to a very monotone bird. I can vary color just by wash-coating a different tone over a previous one, warming it up, increasing or lessening the intensity." He compares his painting technique to using a highlighter that leaves a thin color over lettering. "I'm blending light washes to build a variety and a multitude of colors." He adds that since a carver cannot duplicate the absolute color pattern of a bird, "He has to put in his own impressions of them."

To paint a typical hen puddle duck flank feather, Gewerth lays out the feather pattern with a light wash of raw sienna and gesso. The light middle feather markings define the flow.

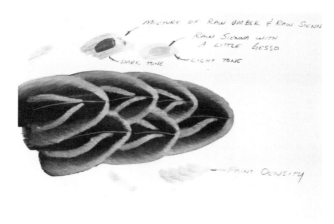

An intensity of the light tones is built up with many thin coats of the same color.

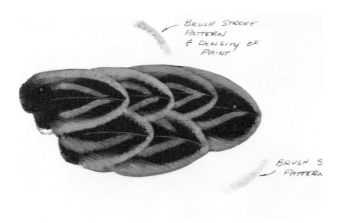

Gewerth softens the transition between light and dark tones at the base of each feather with an intermediate tone, which is between the light and dark colors.

Shown here is a mallard hen. Gewerth will apply dozens of different intensities of color, a stroke at a time, to achieve variety and interest.

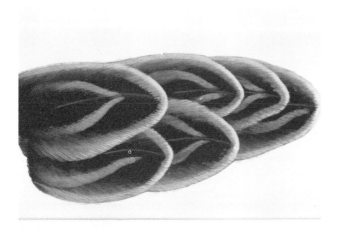

Here he highlights the trailing edges of each feather with a white tone of gesso and raw umber. The feathers should be lightest at their tips.

Note the transitions of colors at the edges of the feathers.

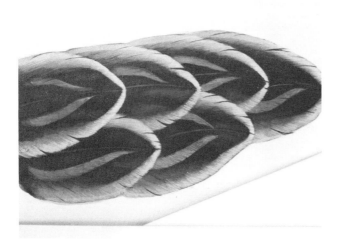

The feathers are finished with a mix of Mars black and raw umber to sharpen the definition between light and dark tones. The splits are painted in.

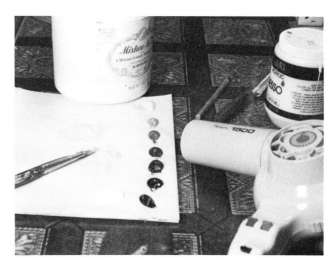

Gewerth prepares to demonstrate the painting of the side vermiculation of a green-winged teal drake.

Vermiculating

Gewerth describes how he would recreate the side vermiculation for a green-winged teal drake. "Normally, when I vermiculate, I'll base-coat my bird with a light color. For the teal, it is unbleached titanium, raw umber, and gesso. But the base coat color is not that important in this case because it will eventually be covered up with subsequent coats."

He explains that his vermiculating technique suggests not individual feathers but overlapping ones. "On vermiculated birds I cannot pick up a separate feather on the flank or side of a bird; I can only pick up pieces of feathers. So what I'm trying to achieve is the look of overlapping vermiculation patterns."

To establish the pattern of the vermiculation for this duck, Gewerth starts with a mix of black, raw umber, and a small amount of gesso to achieve a gray tone. Letting the tip of a brush splay out, he applies this mix as light washes of vermiculation. "Some of it will look blotchy in spots," he says, "but you can lighten these up afterward to give the impression of a darker tone of vermiculation coming through lighter ones."

With acrylics, Gewerth says, "You can change almost immediately what you've just painted. If you don't like the pattern, you can change it. But you still need to fix on the surface a road map or basic pattern for succeeding coats."

Once a pattern has been established, Gewerth says, "You then have to intensify your darker colors and brighten the lighter ones. The green-winged teal has dark vermiculation. So you want to darken your previous coat. I'll use more raw umber with black in my mix to achieve more of an earthy, dark tone. The same procedure with light paint is done to lighter areas."

And how does he achieve the look of overlapping vermiculation? He explains, "I splay out the brush so that there are four or five peaks and hit the brush with a dark tone over the previously done vermiculation. Some of the lighter gray tones will show through, giving the illusion of depth."

Joining the Vermiculation

There is a final step Gewerth follows when vermiculating to bring the vermiculation together. "I use a finely pointed brush to put down many hairline strokes that may bridge four or five lines of vermiculation. These lines will bring it all together and will give the illusion of splits in the feathers."

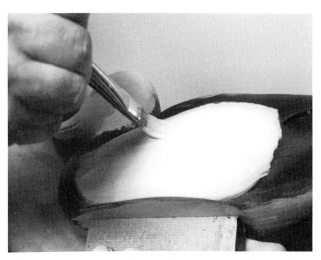

He uses a base coat of unbleached titanium, gesso, and raw umber.

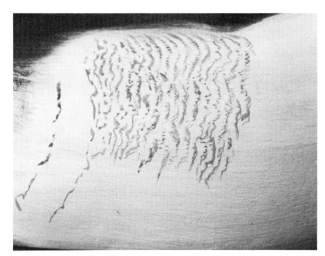

In this simplified sequence, Gewerth starts with a kind of roadmap of vermiculation. The mix comprises black, raw umber, and a small amount of gesso.

To create a vermiculated look, Gewerth has the brush splayed out.

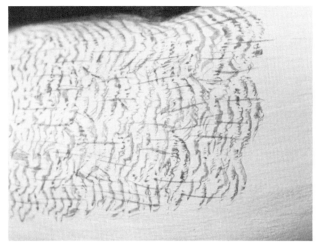

These hairline strokes, says Gewerth, bring the vermiculation together.

With vermiculation, Gewerth says he wants to vary three things—the size or thickness, the intensity, and the color.

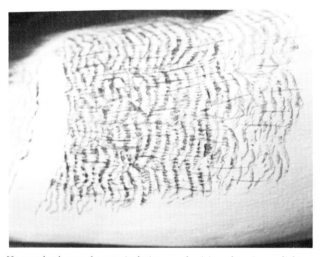

He goes back over the vermiculation, emphasizing, changing, or lightening areas as he sees fit.

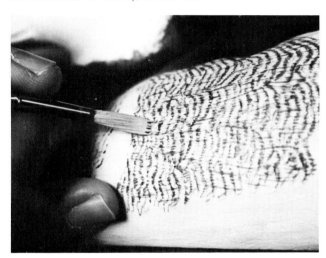

Gewerth demonstrates what he calls "bouncing splits" across the vermiculation to bring it all together and give the illusion of splits. The brush itself will have four or five splits.

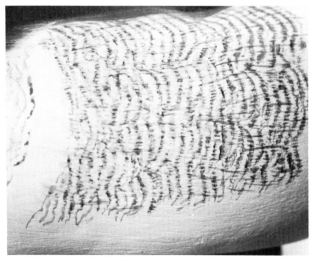

He says some of the vermiculation may look blotchy in spots, but these can be lightened up later to give the impression of darker vermiculation showing through lighter feathers.

Here is the actual vermiculation of a green-winged teal drake.

For comparison, shown here is the vermiculation on Gewerth's red-breasted merganser drake.

Realism and Interpretation

Many carvers feel that their work should be recognized as an art form. Gewerth agrees, saying, "We're trying to recreate nature by striving for realism in our work. Realism, however, is not always accepted in the art world. But if the definition of art is to interject style, imagination, and expression into our work, then wildfowl carvers, even though they are paying attention to detail and realism, are incorporating art into what they create."

Gewerth continues, "If we were to introduce total impressionism into our carvings, I'm afraid we would be creating caricatures. And as long as we continue to judge our carvings, we need the real bird as our criterion." Gewerth believes that the competitions should continue, saying, "They offer the participants as well as the art form the opportunity to gain exposure and recognition. I've gained much from being a part of them."

6

Marc Schultz
Avian Personality

Working on a black-bellied plover, Marc Schultz, a virtuoso carver, is shown here applying oil paints, a medium he has well mastered.

The Analytical Carver

Perhaps more consciously than other carvers, Marc Schultz has synthesized theory with technique. When he speaks of his art form, it is of poses and personalities, of "baleful stares," "argumentative stances," and "vigilance in the eyes." But be assured that these are not anecdotes, for Schultz is highly analytical, engaging the listener with keen observations of avian behavior.

Just as significantly, Schultz has also overcome the habit of burning and painting wood with the hope that real feathers can be recreated. Burning for him is done only as a component of his painting application. What he arrives at is a bird that shimmers and radiates softness under light. Paint is no longer a cover-up, but a medium that enhances burning lines.

The judges seem to be impressed with Schultz's attention to such details. Over the span of two years and fourteen competitions, he won eleven Best-in-Show awards. In four of the contests, his waterfowl took Best and Second in Show.

A Genealogy of Genius

Schultz, though college-trained in wildlife management, took to metals as an ironworker long before he handled carving tools. What initiated the change for him?

Like Jett Brunet, Schultz comes from a distinguished carving background. William Schultz, a pioneer in the field of decorative bird carving, was his father. (See William Koelpin's comments on him in chapter 1.) In a span of two decades, the older Schultz carved a remarkable array of wildfowl, winning perhaps 500 blue ribbons, more than any other carver. He died in 1983.

In spite of his father's work, Marc Schultz did not start carving seriously until 1979, and he had never really tried it until three years before that. He explains, "I grew up with my father carving, and I would sit with him while he worked. And though I helped him sand some of his birds, I had no real interest in carving, and I was quite sure I couldn't do it." He continues that his father attempted to talk him into carving, "and perhaps I reacted negatively to it. But I was always interested in the living bird."

But the older Schultz did have an important impact on his son, and it manifested itself in hunting. The two hunted together nearly every fall weekend for years in the lakes, marshes, stream bottoms, and ridges of Wisconsin for ducks, deer, and upland game birds.

But what of the carving? Schultz, still recalling those years of watching his father make wildfowl, says, perhaps not conscious of the irony, "I'd watch him burning the texture and I'd say 'There's no way I can do that.' But I recall, it was back in 1979, a pair of service bluebills he had done that were sitting around in his house that really excited me. Perhaps it was the simple contours and stylized paint that came together at the right time that got me to go home and do some serious carving."

William Schultz Remembered

The elder Schultz began his own carving by making himself service birds, ones to be used as hunting decoys. "But he too," the son explains, "decided to make them a little more elaborate. In fact, that was during the years that other carvers and contests were making the transition from the smooth working bird to the decorative life-size carving."

Interestingly, the father at the time was employed by the Milwaukee Public Museum, where, for 27 years, he painted background dioramas. But those years also took him on collecting trips to Africa and South America. What he saw on those visits were

This canvasback drake is in what Schultz describes as a "quiet pose," one he often imparts to a carving. He says it well portrays the character of a duck.

Capturing the essence of this black-bellied plover, Schultz describes its stance as "argumentative."

This widgeon hen has been attracted to a forgotten decoy, part of the composition. Schultz says she is "curious but apprehensive."

exotic birds that fascinated him. "My father," explains Marc, "had done all the native species of waterfowl so many times that he became intrigued with exotic wading birds and birds of prey. He would, then, bring to shows carvings of species that few people were familiar with. But they were well done, and he'd win a blue ribbon or a Best in Show."

How does Marc remember his father? He talks of their hunting trips together, and how the father would describe fall colors in terms of siennas, russets, and burnt umbers. As a carver, Schultz says, "My father unquestionably has to be remembered as the most prolific carver and the carver who did the widest variety of birds ever." He adds that his father occupied the same time frame as John Scheeler, who survived him and carries on. He and John were the leading pioneers of the transition from decoys to the fully decorative sculptures of today. Theirs was a time of experimentation and discovery, an exciting time, though I think we still are in the early stages of wildfowl carving."

Red-breasted Geese and a Harpy Eagle

Were there memorable pieces done by William Schultz? What the son feels is not only a memorable piece, but also a highly successful one, is a pair of red-breasted geese. "The animation is so typical of what my father tried to do," he explains. "Individually, each bird is carved in a preening pose, frozen in time, as it were. It is not until the birds are seen together in the context of the whole composition that the real extent of my father's imagination is evidenced. Suddenly, the viewer realizes that the position of each individual bird complements the other in such a way that, together, they perfectly describe the preening process, and the piece becomes a moving picture."

Another dramatic piece, says Schultz, is his father's harpy eagle and macaw composition, a sculpture of predator and prey. "This was a monumental piece. The harpy eagle [a native of South America] stands nearly four feet high. But with its half-opened wingspan of 52 inches, when assembled, my father could not remove it from his shop."

In spite of large and dramatic pieces of native and exotic birds, Schultz feels his father was also highly competent with paints. "He understood the properties of color," the son says, "and the integrity of paint components. He had, then, a good sound knowledge of what color can do. Beyond that, he also knew how to

make paints behave on a textured surface that behaves so much differently from a canvas. So he discovered that you must at times fool the eye, and to do that sometimes involves using some unlikely formulas."

Looking for an Avian Essence

But the son says there is yet another accomplishment of his father's to be mentioned. "He also had that ability to animate his pieces in a way that was characteristic of the bird.

"I only recently discovered that I share the objective my father had, though he didn't tell me what objective to pursue, and that is to try to capture the personality or essence of a bird." Schultz adds, "My father once said that he was excited by competent plumage rendering and workmanship, but what further excited him was a portrait of the character or essence of a bird."

Schultz states that, in the early and critical stages of defining that essence, he must force himself to understand what he is looking at. "Observation of the living bird is the most important place to begin," he explains, "but at times that is not always available. So the next available source material is study skins and, especially for the character of the bird, photographs. The latter then becomes the most abundant and usable source material. So perhaps the most practical training in wildfowl carving is learning to read a photograph.

"You must force yourself to figure out what you are looking at and to recognize the lack of character in your carving, or the successful capturing of it. This only comes with time. But I am so adamant about it that I consider it my basic approach to what I am doing."

In Search of a Baleful Stare

Schultz compares bird carving to a discipline that can only start to take shape when certain physical components are recognized in any particular bird of a species. He uses a redhead drake as an example for analysis. Pointing out that what on the surface defines a redhead is the color of that part of the anatomy, he says, "Redheads have this characteristically aloof and baleful stare. Now you can recognize that in the live bird or in photographs, but that doesn't mean you can duplicate it. A carver must be able to translate the

This is Schultz's pair of redheads on "water" carved from walnut. Note the baleful or menacing stare of the drake in the background.

adjectives describing the bird into mechanical components that can be transferred into wood."

He continues, "When a redhead assumes a certain pose, it looks to be very tall above the eyes and flat below the eyes. It has a slight supraorbital ridge that suggests a Neanderthal crown. If you can get the wood to reflect light in just the bottom half of the eyes together with a tall forehead and a hollow, flat cheek, then you can get that characteristic look." But he warns that at times a redhead might be nervous and have its head slicked back, resulting in what Schultz describes as the look of a garter snake.

Quiet Poses

"Each bird seems to have one or two characteristic poses," says Schultz. "It's in those positions that the personality of the bird seems to be best defined." Is this an arbitrary choice? He answers that it sounds like one, "But almost anything has its definitive association for a wide range of people, so that certain associations are going to be accurate and at the same time pretty generally agreed upon."

He continues, "It becomes a matter of being familiar enough with a bird to decide what that characteristic look is, and then in what position you can best portray that. But there is a lot of research and study that must go on first to ascertain what that characteristic look is going to be. And this is what should be portrayed in the carving so that you let the carving speak for itself, as if to say, I am a pintail, or I am a ruffed grouse."

Schultz notes that a bird assumes hundreds of different positions, but nearly all of them are not going to be positions that the bird habitually assumes for periods of time, positions that best typify the essence of that bird. There are only one, or two, or even three, says Schultz, that are definitive for a species. But one of them seems to typify nearly all species, and that is what he calls "a quiet pose."

Schultz explains, "If a bird is in a quiet pose, it is what I call a strong pose. It is saying what it ought to say. My best judgment tells me that that position best typifies the essence of a bird."

The Problems with Complexity

He does admit that some birds are querulous, or aggressive, or get agitated, "and really should be done that way because it's in their nature. What I object to is seeing a bird done in a position that, while it may be completely accurate, may not be typical for it. That's doing complexity for its own sake.

"If you're going to do a bird in a very animated pose, you should incorporate that in a strong design function. Yet, the pose ought to be pleasing for a variety of reasons. One, it might be typical of the bird. Or two, the animation should be a component of a well-designed composition. To do a bird in a grotesque pose I find unsettling, uncomfortable. It isn't something you're going to look at for years. If it's not appealing, it won't endure. And that too is a criterion for choosing a pose. Is the bird going to be looked at for a long period of time? So to freeze arbitrarily a moment in time and stop the bird in mid stroke in some awkward position, even though accurately done, is not good judgment. The majority of my pieces will, then, be in a quiet posture because so often it's the resting bird that is most appealing."

A Resting Wood Duck Hen

Typical of what Schultz has carved in a quiet, restful pose is a wood duck hen. He says, repeating his position on poses, that there are a couple of positions a wood duck hen might be in, each of which would be typical. The one Schultz chose, "is a pose I often see a wood duck in on a quiet pond." He admits, however, that "wood ducks are nervous, excitable birds, and hens often scold and harass the drakes. So a person might do an argumentative little hen and there you could put more action and excitement in that duck, which would be quite a departure from the pose I chose."

Though wood ducks can be aggressive, Schultz preferred to carve this hen in a relaxed, quiet pose. It is a way of expressing the character of the bird which he has often seen on ponds and lakes.

The head tucked down low on the breast contributes to the relaxed look. This, Schultz says, creates an appeal and best describes the essence of this and many other birds.

Aesthetic and Design Considerations

There is more to Schultz's choice of poses than quietude, though the resting pose lends itself to other considerations. He states that one reason he chose a resting pose for the wood duck hen instead of an argumentative one was to enhance the fullness of the cheeks and cape. "I don't think there would be much argument that a nervous bird would be an unattractive bird. It slicks its head feathers back, and bulges its eyes out. So by making the wood duck hen relaxed, I could also enhance the fullness of its cheeks and its cape. This is what I call the element of aesthetics."

Schultz believes, then, in incorporating into a pose and its design an element he describes as "something

Schultz has his plover running up a basswood rock. The shape of the rock complements the attitude of the plover.

pleasing." It is this emphasis on anatomical features that would seem strongly to affect the choice of the quiet pose. Of the wood duck hen, he says that it possesses large, iridescently colored, secondary converts. In certain positions, they are nearly hidden. When the sides are dropped low to reveal secondaries and coverts, these are exposed. On Schultz's wood duck hen, there are five secondary feathers of the speculum exposed. "That occurs when the bird is very relaxed," he says.

An Excitable Plover

The black-bellied plover Schultz decided to carve is an Arctic nester, residing in a narrow, latitudinal band. He describes it as large for its size, even for a plover, and almost gull-like, with a wide square head and downward-looking eyes.

But what intrigued him about the bird "is its striking plumage patterns and its excitable, aggressive nature. and that excitable nature complements its gull-like physiology."

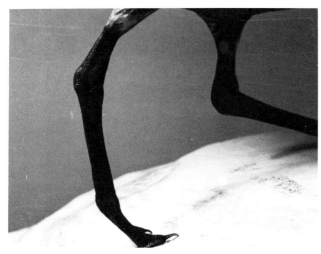

To emphasize the bend in the legs, Schultz has the plover walking up an incline. These legs are made of steel and covered with a two-part epoxy putty. Here the bent legs suggest an argumentative stance, and the inclining rock complements their shapes.

A tundra nester, the plover is chattering at an intruder, says Schultz. What goes on in the eyes and cheeks makes this a plover and no other bird, he says.

Schultz has his black-bellied plover running up a rock. Why this choice of stance? He explains, "It's an argumentative or aggressive one. It's running up an incline and chattering at an intruder." He adds that he is pleased with the position of its legs with one being at a different height from the other. "In order to have the bends and staggered heights of the legs, I had it going up an incline."

The base of the plover is a carved-from-wood, weather-worn rock typically found on the tundra where the bird nests. Schultz says, "The idea is to get a complementary line so that the line of motion of the bird complements the face of the rock, each suggesting motion."

Why a rock and not sand? He answers that not only is sand difficult to render, but the grey-green rock color will better complement the colors of the plover.

Perhaps the most striking feature of the piece is its head and face. "There's a nervous vigilance and wariness in the eyes," Schultz says. "Plovers have a characteristic shape to the eyes that distinguishes them from other birds. I tried to get that."

Also notable with the bird is its open beak and projecting tongue. Schultz says that black-bellied plovers have "a conspicuous voice," adding that other tundra nesters interact with this plover for protection.

A Widgeon Intruder

For the 1984 World Championships, Schultz carved a widgeon pair. What was unusual about the composi-

This widgeon hen is one of a pair which, when on their base, is confronted by an old widgeon decoy.

The widgeon drake of the pair is challenging the old decoy which has drawn the attention of his mate. This bird's wings and tail are being repaired. The block underneath the carving is a holding fixture that enables Schultz to put the piece in a vise.

tion was the presence of another bird, a widgeon decoy. Of the widgeon drake, he says, "It just wants to be done in an argumentative pose, which is so typical. But I had to find an interesting way to justify that pose with the hen. So I incorporated an old widgeon decoy (one that he carved) that the hen had been attracted to. Still, there is an uncertainness, a wariness that the hen has."

Thousands of Little Reflections

Characteristic poses are not the only design elements in Schultz's vocabulary of techniques. There are still feathers to be dealt with. (Compare John Gewerth's feather rendering in chapter 5.) Schultz says he can achieve "the feeling of looking through depths of feathers, with light coming down deep in

the dimensional depth of the bird," adding that, as the bird is turned or walked around, different areas will light up while others will fall into shadow. How is this achieved? It is done not with burning or paints alone. For Schultz, it is the interaction of both that will create what he describes as "a satiny look with thousands of little lines throwing back reflections."

Schultz says he will burn and stone with two objectives in mind—the type of feather and the color it is going to be. Basically, he says, "I have to use a more open texturing in the pale or lightly colored areas and a fine burn in the darker areas." Referring to the black-bellied plover, he says, "In white rump areas, for example, I only stone, which lends to a nice, pure white. But in a black area, I will burn very fine to achieve a good reflective surface for the intense dark tones."

Satiny and Lacy Feathers

Schultz states that fine burning can be used to achieve other effects as well. When satiny feathers are called for, he will employ very close burning, while carving in folds in the feathers to enhance the effect.

The scolding drake is asserting his rightful position over the interloper.

Another view of the widgeon drake shows Schultz's attention to details of bill, eye position, and patterns of coloration.

Fine burning was done on the breast of the black-bellied plover, which, when combined with oil paints, will create a shimmering of color.

It would be difficult, says Schultz, to achieve a depth and purity of white if this area were burned. The rump of the plover is stoned, allowing a purity of white to be applied.

If he wants what he calls a lacy effect on an area such as the scapulars, he may still burn finely, but with more emphasis at the edge of the feather. "There I'll burn a little deeper as opposed to tertials and secondaries where I burn almost not at all at the end of each feather."

How Fine Can Burning Be?

"John Scheeler asked me a couple of times how closely I burn," Schultz says. "The inch mark is the only reference you can use, so I counted, and found I was burning, when I started, about 85 lines to an inch. Then I started pulling in a little bit more because I liked the effect, and I got it up to 100 lines per inch; then up to 120. But since I felt there was still room for that effect in certain areas such as iridescent feathers, I pulled in even farther to where I was doing 185 or 220 lines per inch on the wood duck hen."

Schultz wishes to point out, however, that when he burns, it is not for the appeal of burning itself, but for the effect that will enhance the properties of a particu-

This area of the black feathers on the side of the plover allowed for the use of fine burning to give a satiny, lacy texture.

These secondary coverts are burned very fine, about 220 lines per inch, to provide a favorable surface for painting the wood duck hen's iridescence. The feathers of the side are not burned as closely, and are burned a little deeper at the edges to impart a little looseness, he says.

He emphasizes that burning is not done for its own sake, but to enhance the character and look of a bird. But more specifically, burning is done with both the type of feather and its color in mind. Fine burning helps achieve a purity of color, Schultz adds. This is another area on the wood duck hen.

These tertial feathers on the wood duck hen are burned finely because they are satiny in appearance on the live bird and are somewhat iridescent. The fine burning provides a good reflective surface, Schultz points out.

This is a typical scapular-type feather, burned slightly deeper at the edges to give a lacy look when done alongside other feathers.

These tertials on the widgeon hen are burned slightly deeper along the shaft than near the edge, allowing for the painting of the white margin.

Schultz's burning is done as finely as is needed to enhance an area or achieve a purity of color. Though he does not use a special tip, he keeps what he does use finely sharpened.

The flank feathers of the widgeon hen are both stoned and burned, since they are more loosely structured feathers than tertials and secondaries are.

Fine burning creates a multi-beveled, reflective surface, which will reflect light, shadow, and color, all combining to achieve a liveliness to the carving.

lar type and color of feather and hence an important part of the character of the bird.

"It's irrelevent that I burn 185 or 220 lines to an inch. What is relevant is how the burning reflects the light and plays with the paint. In black areas, I don't have to take two different shades of black to define margins and origins of feathers. The texturing will do that on its own." The texturing he describes as "many little V grooves, that, when closely allied, make beveled surfaces. So since light is usually unidirectional, coming from one side or another, it will light up one side of the burns and the other will fall into shadow." He adds that when burning lines are far apart, there results flat surfaces between them, which become "the dominant reflective surface."

On the breast of a canvasback, for example, he sees a velvety appearance. There he will not burn individual feathers, but instead what he calls "a flow of texture." He says, "Such texture lights up as you turn a bird, revealing depth."

Burning Hot, Burning Cool

Schultz is careful to prepare the wood before burning it, saying he likes to "polish it" with 600-grit wet/dry sandpaper. When burning, he says, "I will use a high setting of heat where I do general texturing, just to achieve the flow with a lot of lines done rapidly. But where I'm burning carefully such as on individual secondary or iridescent feathers, I'll go slowly and precisely, using very little heat. In fact, I do a lot of burning with the tool set on zero." But after burning, he will clean up the surface with a natural bristle brush, removing as much of the carbon as he can.

The burning tool Schultz uses is The Detailer, made by Colwood Electronics. (See appendix for address.) Does he use a special tip for his fine burning? He says he owns all the interchangeable tips that range from rounded to spear-pointed, but he sharpens each one on a hard Arkansas stone to get as sharp a tip as possible.

Painting Without a Primer

Schultz reiterates that the depth of his feathers is achieved by deep and close-together burning lines. It is important, then, that these not be filled, especially with gesso.

Still, he does seal the wood before painting with a sanding sealer. But doesn't the burning itself seal the

The breast of the canvasback drake, being only black, can come to life with burning and little paint applied. But, Schultz says, it must "glow" without being shiny.

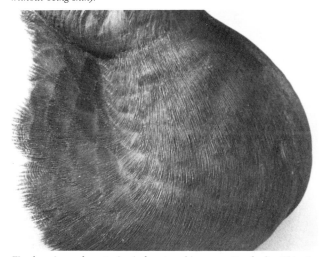

Fine burning and no stoning is done to achieve a purity of color. This also achieves what Schultz describes as a velvety look. Note the absence of individual feathers. This too enhances a soft, velvety appearance.

Note the absence of gesso on the side of the black-bellied plover. Also note that the burn lines are deeper at their ends on the shoulder feathers.

wood? Schultz responds, "I have serious reservations with the school that promotes not sealing the bird on the basis that burning does it for you. On the microscopic scale, at which the chemistry of the paint is operating, burning a line on that wood is not sealing the porosity, though it would seem to under the eye.

"As for not sealing the bird with a chemical, the danger is that the wood is still porous enough to absorb the oil and resin out of my painting solution and leave just the unfortified pigment on top, which will not be durable. And any successive coats of paint are only as good as the first coat."

In Defense of Oil Paints

What allows Schultz to achieve a lacy look, a reflective surface, or a variety of sheen, is the deep burning, the lack of a gesso primer, and the application of oil paints. Yet, other carvers such as Jett Brunet (chapter 3) cite the lengthy drying time as a problem with using oil paints.

Schultz works with oil paints combined with the mediums of added oils, resins, and turpentine. Here he is using a burnt umber and an alkyd white for the patterns on the plover.

Schultz argues that though the technique of painting with oils is very different from painting with acrylics, there is not much more total elapsed time for painting.

He begins his argument by explaining that an acrylic painting schedule comprises building up the intensities of color with successive washes of paint in a particular area. "You can achieve the same effect with oils, only with a different procedure. With acrylics, you can achieve a range of tones with successive applications of the same paint rather than making a new mix. With oils, you premix exactly the color you ultimately want the area to be."

How does this affect the time schedule for the drying of oil paints? Schultz states, "Where a typical schedule of acrylic painting is to finish completely an area as you go, with oils the typical formula is to do one stage of the painting completely for the entire bird. Then do the next stage for the entire bird. By the end of three days with acrylics, you could have part of the bird completely painted. With the oils, you would have the entire bird partially painted. I think then, that the total schedule for a finished job is probably pretty similar."

Blending and Building Up Colors

Schultz discusses the application of oils to his black-bellied plover. For it, "I came through the first time with basic underpainted patterns. Then I came back a second time over those basic patterns and purified them with the same colors and subtly blended the colors to soften their edges. The third time I came through to do the detail painting of shadows or patterns that show through the pale areas of overlaying feathers, and then perhaps painted in some splits." (Compare John Gewerth's techniques in chapter 5.) He adds, "With blending oils, there are no abrupt transitions and no buildup of paint."

Instead of applying washes and seeing what the effects of the succeeding washes will be, he will mix the exact colors he wants on his palette and blend them together.

Schultz says he has some twenty minutes during which he can blend two colors together, "subtly breaking off the edge of one to leave a distinct color band, yet not a hard painted edge. I can blend one color into the next so that you cannot tell where one color stops and the other begins."

He says that, using oils, if he has a feather with a soft margin and a dark center, he would paint the two

Here can be studied the transitions between the various colors on the plover. Also notice what Schultz describes as a purity of color on the breast.

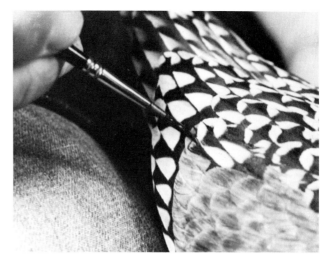

Here he paints in the dark pattern using burnt umber oil paint. These patterns describe an arrowhead figure, he says.

The alkyd white is applied here.

colors involved on the appropriate areas with one touching the other. Then he will come back with a clean brush and blend one color into the other. "You can pull the light into the dark, or the dark into the light. However, if it's a softly blended area where the transition of color from the deep value to the light is very gradual, then you continue to pull your lighter band into the darker band." He says that this amounts to mixing a large number of color values right on the bird. He adds this can be done to the point where there is no visible differentiation of color.

In addition, Schultz says he can regulate the amount of luster from a sheen to a chalky flatness by "alternating the components of my medium."

Mediums for Oil Paints

Schultz notes that turpentine is a basic thinning agent for oil paints. He advises using the best grade of turpentine that can be purchased. He explains, "Oil pigments are ground earth pigments or oxides of metallic substances suspended in purified linseed oil. When you thin to the extent that you must paint a textured surface, you are washing out most of the durable medium, which is the linseed oil. The turpentine, on the other hand, disappears completely with evaporation, leaving a hardened linseed oil and pigment suspension clinging to the surface. But too much turpentine can spread the oil film too thin."

How can this be prevented? He says that a variety of resins and oils must be added to the oil pigments that,

Schultz says that instead of mixing washes as one would with acrylics, he mixes an exact color on his palette and applies that.

Blending is done with a clean brush, pulling the light into the dark color or vice versa. Schultz says that blending is a decided advantage to using oil paints.

when dry, will leave a hard and durable paint film. "If you thin colors just with turpentine, you'd have a watery substance that will not have any real purity. It won't be paintable. So you have to replace the original vehicle with some resin or oil or a combination of the two to get your paintability and durability."

Schultz points out that the old masters experimented with resinous and oil-based mediums "to impart paintability and to give their pigments durability." He says his "own concoction" is "super permanent. I end up with a surface that is flexible yet entirely insoluble."

The Unity of Burning and Oil Paints

Schultz summarizes his union of burning and painting techniques. "My depth of burning is done so I can apply enough paint to get a pure tone while winding up with no flat areas on my birds. So not just light but also color is reflected from those thousands of little beveled edges produced by the burning. And by not priming with gesso, I can paint right down into the depth of my burning lines. That is why my painting and texturing are not mutually exclusive."

Eccentricities of Details

Though paint and burning can do much to enhance the surface of a bird, still more can be done with the planning of feather patterns.

Here can be studied the feather patterns on the back of the plover, all established with oils and done with as few steps as possible.

Schultz has many of these feathers on his canvasback drake clumped together to give the idea of wet plumage. This is work done with hand tools and not grinders.

While defining feather patterns, he also creates some irregularity. He would describe this as "casual rows that fall off at their margins."

Schultz is meticulous in his study of feather patterns as he was on the widgeon hen.

Irregularities in the breast feather patterns can only be achieved after the carver is totally familiar with their patterns, says Schultz. Putting in irregularities and not regimented rows creates interest, he adds, as can be seen on the wood duck hen.

But an aspect of this planning is making patterns irregular or clumping feathers together. On a canvasback drake he carved, for example, Schultz says that the plumage, when saturated, groups into clumps and orients to one another. "It's a way to get some liveliness and interest into a relatively blank area without being highly stylized or inventing something that can't happen, though it is an exaggeration of something that can." But, he cautions, "You have to learn them first before you can mess them up, that is, how do feather patterns behave in stock positions before they take on odd appearances."

Schultz says he must first establish patterns and then be comfortable enough to impart irregularities. "In an area where I'm endeavoring to show wet plumage, there should be the appearance of randomness but at the same time a uniform, definite pattern."

He continues that he searches for "converging sets or groups so that they look casual. This is the elusive part but most advantageous when you capture it. It suggests life and softness. It is something that has to be painstakingly done."

Unlike most of the other carvers featured, Schultz does not use a grinder and bits to achieve feather patterns, be they uniform or random. Instead, he uses traditional carving tools, not unlike those used by William Koelpin in chapter 1. Especially with these groups, Schultz says, "I have to carve them in. With a grinder, the results are vague, ambiguous, fuzzy. But with the chisel, I'll get a precise cut."

A Surface Like Glass

Unlike the other carvers who have opted for jelutong or tupelo, Schultz finds basswood works best with his carving techniques. Saying that it both burns

Schultz prefers basswood over other species owing to its consistent grain and carvability with hand tools. The only power tools he uses is a die grinder, and that is for the initial rough-shaping of the wood. A well-sharpened chisel, he says, leaves a glass-like surface.

All of this exacting detail on a wood duck hen was accomplished with a few chisels and gouges. This piece started from a 4¾-inch-thick piece of basswood. Grinding tools and bits, he says, would make many of these details "fuzzy." Photo by Marc Schultz.

Schultz was able to obtain a piece of basswood big enough that he did not have to carve a separate head. Note the detailing on the cheek patches. This helps project a quiet pose. Photo by Marc Schultz.

The wood duck hen has been burned and is ready for painting. Note that the feathers appear to lift up slightly, something Schultz describes as an interesting feature. He also points out that basswood burns well. Photo by Marc Schultz.

and carves well, Schultz admits that he does some grinding in the initial stages, but with a die grinder, not a Foredom. "Those who do much more work with the grinder object how basswood fuzzes up. I only grind in the initial stages to achieve a contour." But with a gouge or chisel, "a cut surface on basswood is like glass," he says.

Lively Basswood and Brash Tupelo

Are there other benefits to basswood? Schultz responds that it is very strong, even in small dimensions, "and it stays lively. Tupelo, in contrast, is a won-

The back of the finished wood duck hen's head can be studied here for details. This flow of feathers also enhances the quiet pose, one he says is definitive for many species.

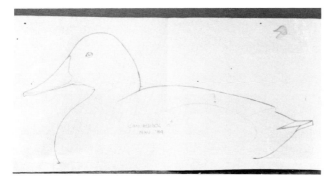

Designing a head-to-body joint is begun on the pattern.

Notice that Schultz has located the seam line horizontally in line with the top of the back of the canvasback drake.

derfully homogenous, grain-free wood, but it can get hard and brash when it's fully dry. And you get more breakage with dry tupelo."

Adding that good blanks of basswood are nearly as grain-free as tupelo, Schultz prefers to use air-dried basswood, wood that is readily available to him in Wisconsin. His supplier goes to the forest and selects trees big enough for his use and cuts them in November or December. "He saws the blocks out of logs and into appropriate lengths right away and starts to dry them," he says, "usually in January. Air-dried to seven or nine percent moisture content, basswood carves best. If drier, it tends to tear when carved."

Designing a Neck Joint

Schultz does admit that basswood is not readily available in thicknesses greater than five inches. But many of the ducks he carves, even at rest, are higher than that dimension. He must, then, design a bird to have a separate head.

When designing a head joint, Schultz begins with his pattern. He explains that he tries to make a design that has the head joint as parallel as possible to the body of the bird to facilitate clamping. Also, if possible "I try to align the neck joint with a natural break in color. With a wood duck drake, it was where there is a transition between a white bar and the dark breast to camouflage it."

Yet, despite the placement, Schultz claims his neck joints are nearly always invisible. What is his technique? He answers that he prepares the glue joints on a disc sander, which, he says, "creates an absolutely, mathematically flat surface, so that when I clamp the pieces together, there are no irregularities." He notes, however, that he does not prepare the glue joint until he is ready to glue, citing the fact that there are subtle

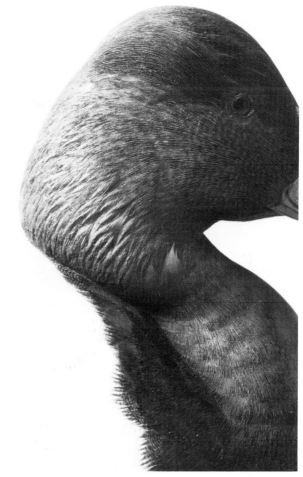

To make the head joint invisible, the two mating surfaces must be absolutely and mathematically flat. This can be accomplished on a sanding disc plate. Schultz is also careful when applying glue that it does not coagulate thickly at the outer perimeter of the joint. He uses, then, a thin film of glue near the outer edges.

Schultz says he likes to "fuss with a bill," using no grinding bits except to create the nostril channel. Also note the interaction of the breast and head feathers, something that could not be achieved if the head were a separate piece.

changes in the dimensions of the wood that would be reflected in a prematurely-made glue joint.

But, he points out, the glue is not casually spread on the wood. "I apply the glue uniformly to the mating surfaces, but more heavily to the middle and only a film of glue to the perimeter."

Working the Head and Body Together

Though he often must deal with a separate head, Schultz says he prefers to work both pieces together. "I like to carve the birds out of one piece when possible, and if not, I glue the pieces together before I do too much carving. On the canvasback, all I did was carve the bill and front one-third of the head with the body carved just to the point where I could determine where the neck joint would be. The rest was left over-sized and blocky."

The wood duck hen was more challenging, however. In fact, he says it is in a position that a beginner should never attempt. He explains, "Starting with the head, you have to consider the cheek and breast contours that all have to interact, not just the bill itself. Plus, it was difficult to work underneath the bill, which took a lot of fussing. But doing this as if it were one piece was the only way I could get the interaction of the contours."

Fussing with a Bill

Schultz's favorite carving tools are limited to about ten chisels and gouges. With them he will carve rip-

pling feathers, separate primaries, define tail feathers, or shape a bill. The contours of the bill he will carve and sand, with the wrinkles either carved or pressed in.

These techniques are not unique. But what may be is his early treatment of the bill shortly after it is carved. He seals the bill immediately with lacquer sanding sealer, explaining that there will be no swelling or changes in dimension in relation to the rest of the bird. Sometimes, he says, "I will even paint the bill right away, simply because it is one stage that's done. Plus, the bill gets four or five coats of flat varnish over the completed paint."

Interestingly, he discovered that, with the wood duck hen resting its chin on its breast, the breast feathers lifted and pulled away from each other, making an interesting feature.

Avoiding Primaries as an Afterthought

The strategy of working a bird as a single piece of wood extends to feathers as well. Schultz says candidly, "A pet peeve of mine is that primaries are invariably treated as an afterthought. You often see where the space was allowed for the inserting with the enthusiasm going into the rest of the bird while at the end of the entire process the carver 'remembers' that he still has to do the primaries." This he describes as "rapping out a little set of veneers and stabbing them in that space. There's no life, no curvature, nothing going on."

Schultz seals a bill immediately after carving, and sometimes paints it right away. This prevents dimensional changes, he says. Also, he applies four or five coats of a flat varnish as a last step.

What Schultz does, then, is meticulously carve the whole set of primaries out of a single piece of wood and insert them into the rear of the bird. (Compare John Gewerth's similar technique in chapter 5.)

When to Carve Feathers

Schultz has definite opinions on what kind of feathers should be carved from the block and why some should not be. He says, "While some feather carving techniques may prove exciting by themselves, they may not work well because they are not consistent with the rest of the carving, or they may not do what they are supposed to do."

He uses the case of plumed birds to continue his reasoning. "There's no way you can get that lacy or elongated pluminess flowing in the wind because wood is not feathers. You can achieve the look much better in pencil or on art paper. Any attempt will look stiff because you have to treat those feathers in less than a spectacular way. So whatever you do, they will still look like wood." He does say, though, that a carver might want to "lay them right down tight on the back without undercutting them just to suggest feathers."

Schultz adds, "Choosing a subject and attempting its plumage is a time for humility. Experimentation and imagination are vital to the production of a lively carving, but certain techniques do not work out in wood, and a carver must be able to recognize this."

Simplicity and a Future Project

Schultz says simplicity is a real strength when designing a composition. "A piece can be quiet, dignified, yet still imply a tremendous amount of action and animation."

Here can be studied the back and primary inserts for the widgeon hen.

Note the careful separation and layering of the tail feathers of the widgeon hen.

Notice the ripples that were carved with chisels and polished with sand-paper in these primaries for the widgeon hen.

Note the curvature of the primaries for the wood duck hen. Also note the separation of the tail feathers, done from the top layer down.

Shown here are the back and primaries of the wood duck hen.

These feathers are accomplished with knives and chisels. The dark colors of the tail and rump allowed for the use of relatively fine texturing, says Schultz.

Primaries were meticulously carved and located on the back of this canvasback drake.

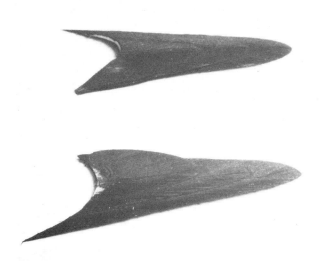

Inserts are not to be done as an afterthought, says Schultz, nor should they consist of bits of veneer "stabbed" into the back of the bird. These are the primary inserts for the black-bellied plover, each set carved from a solid piece of basswood.

A closer view of the canvasback's primaries shows a uniform flow of both those and the tertials.

Working on land once tilled by Danish settlers, Schultz has turned part of this farm into a plantation for pines and hardwoods. Shown here, through a window in his shop, is the original timber frame barn.

In contrast, he speaks of "diorama-type pieces that have water and land and frogs and nymphs emerging from the mud and dragonflies above the water." He admits, "They are intriguing, and sometimes extremely well done, but most go unappreciated except to a tiny fraternity of carvers." Instead, he says, "The trick is to distill your intentions down into the simplest form."

Schultz speaks of a future project which may seem complicated, but really is not. It will consist of two harlequin ducks, one "swimming upstream in turbulent water. The drake will have only a third of its body showing while the hen will be perched on a rock ready to jump in along side." Is this consistent with a simple design? Schultz answers yes, saying that the rocks and water will be carved but not painted. Nor will there be any habitat displays such as pine needles or insects. Instead, the unpainted wood will evoke a strong sense of environment, though, interestingly, he plans on having the carved water partially washing over the harlequin hen's feet.

In defense of wood and not an artificial material such as resin, Schultz says, "I like the direct link to the basic concept of woodcarving and I like what will be a contrast between the unpainted wood and the painted birds."

An Identity Crisis?

Schultz says he is puzzled by the public's interest he has found in bird carving. "I consider it a highly specialized field. Woodcarving in general I consider highly specialized, and to restrict that to birdcarving makes it more so. It's intriguing that such a narrowly defined pursuit can stand on its own right and be recognized for what it is."

Yet, to the Wisconsin people who know him, he has a difficult time convincing them he carves wildfowl for a living. "If I told them I'm an ironworker, they

Schultz can view through the windows of his separate-building shop the rich farmland and forestland of Wisconsin, also the home state of his father, the late William Schultz, a pioneer in the art of bird carving.

A future project for Schultz will be a pheasant hen.

Pheasants inhabit the open fields, brush, and cornfields of Wisconsin near his home. It's there that Schultz can make sketches of them.

A number of attitude sketches of the pheasant hen are done before one is decided upon.

would understand that." He even admits that he is uncertain what to call himself. Is his title woodcarver, bird artist, or wildfowl artist?

The Future

Schultz not only works wood but he also plants it — in the form of hardwoods and pines. He has in fact made his home, a farm established by Danish settlers over a century ago, a plantation for trees. This, he says, will be a legacy for his children.

He continues to hunt wildfowl, though he does take time to sketch it. Another project for the future will be a pheasant hen he has illustrated in a variety of poses.

Its feathers, Schultz says not surprisingly, "have a beautiful, buffy background that works well in wood and paint."

And he will continue to carve, he says, provided he can do birds his way. "I can't speed them up. I just wouldn't know what to leave out if I had to do that."

7

Louis Kean, Jr.

Excerpts from Nature

Louis Kean, Jr., has excelled as both waterfowl and game bird carver. Here he is burning the head of a green-winged teal.

A full-time carver since 1977, Louis Kean, Jr. is that versatile artist who can put wildfowl, with wings spread, into the air, or float full-bodied waterfowl, legs stretched, on water. He is also a master of recreating a bird's habitat, be it cattails, leaves, or even marshy water.

Art Teacher, Hunter, Wildfowl Sculptor

It seems a combination of professional and recreational interests have come together to make Kean one of today's top carvers. An early influence, one that is still pursued, is hunting. Recalling a duck hunting trip in his home state of Virginia when he was only thirteen, Kean says, "I was just fascinated and enthralled seeing all those decoys that were acting like ducks to a certain extent, and being lures to live birds."

Early duck decoys were, however, still representational of a species, but not imitative and decorative. He remembers carving those early birds out of balsa, white cedar, and even cork. It was not until 1973 that he met a fellow carver, Gary Trout, who happened to be competing at the Ward Foundation's World Championships. "Gary gave me a piece of basswood after I showed him some of my decoys. The first competition bird I did was a drake redhead, and that was in 1973. I

Having once made hunting decoys, Kean now does decorative ducks such as this widgeon drake, carved in 1984.

A Moment in Time

Being a hunter, Kean has had an opportunity to observe wildfowl firsthand and in their natural habitats. It should not be surprising that Kean says of his art form, "I try to reproduce the bird as the epitomy of its life-style."

He goes on to say that he attempts to capture "a fleeting moment" in the bird's life. He adds, "I try to capture the feeling of life, whether it's in the pose or habitat, or both." This he calls "an excerpt from nature." It might be anything from "a wing partially raised, a foot lifted, a head partially turned, a bent-over body, a bill opened, or one containing a bug or fish or seed."

A typical excerpt from nature is a bobwhite quail composition. He says that the quail is "upright and alert looking. That gives you a feeling of what the bird is about at this particular moment in its life." He adds, "Birds in nature, when they're undisturbed, may attempt to slow down a bit. They're certainly at peace with themselves because they don't have any real thought processes going on."

Kean's quail composition includes leaves and grasses — in effect, a habitat display. He explains, "With the surrounding habitat, you're trying to complement the carving to make a coming together of bird and natural surroundings. The elements in the quail

also did a pair of ruddy ducks. After entering those at the 1974 World Championship Competition, I was fortunate enough to be awarded, in the novice class, a first place for my ruddy duck drake and a second place for the hen redhead and a third place for the redhead drake." He adds, "I was in awe of what was going on at that show."

But the boy who hunted quail at the age of eleven and ducks two years later grew up, graduated from Randolph-Macon College, earned a fine-arts degree from Old Dominion University, and went on to teach art in public high schools.

Noting that he has drawn and painted from early childhood, Kean says, "My artistic inclination has influenced what I am doing now. Teaching was an outgrowth to be creative and an attempt to pass that creativity on to my students."

Interestingly, he took a detour before he started carving full time: During his teaching years, he custom-made decorative hunting knives. "I thought I could make a living at this and stopped teaching to do it. But I decided," he says more seriously than not, "that I'd rather be eating sawdust than metal filings."

What also helped Kean make that decision was some advice from Michigan carver Larry Hayden (featured in *How to Carve Wildfowl*). Kean quotes Hayden as saying to him, "You can stay in the amateur class and take ribbon after ribbon, but it won't do much good as far as your work is concerned." The advice was well taken, for Kean did turn professional. He now works at wildfowl carving full time and has proven his talent with a number of prestigious Best in Shows and blue ribbons.

This bobwhite quail is typical of his work. He has made some thirty of these game birds. This one is in the collection of A. Neal Rose.

A closeup of the bobwhite quail shows Kean's attention to detail. Kean says that this "relaxed" look represents "an excerpt from nature."

Still to be put into its fall habitat of leaves and grasses is another bobwhite quail. For the browns of the bird, Kean uses raw sienna and burnt sienna. For the whites, he applies a combination of titanium white and raw umber.

piece are dead leaves and winter-type grasses with a bird in winter plumage.

"The quail, in artistic terms, is a heavy object. The leaves and grass, by contrast, are light and airy. So you hope the two together will sort of push and pull to make a complete and pleasing composition."

A Flying Pintail

Another excerpt from nature is Kean's Flying Pintail over Cattails composition. He started it in the fall of 1982, and it took three and one-half months to complete. The piece was commissioned by the Tatler Gallery in Hilton Head, South Carolina.

Kean says this carving, like the quail, "represents one moment in this bird's existence." But that moment is open to interpretation, for, Kean suggests, "It is startled, or perhaps it is going somewhere to find food, or is taking off because other birds in his vicinity are taking off, or perhaps a predator is after him."

When taking on the commission, his reactions were mixed. "I was scared and excited about it," he says. "I knew at that time the accepted and preferred way of doing a bird such as this time was to carve all the tail and wing feathers as inserts and support the bird somehow over the cattails. I hoped I would be equal to the challenge."

Using Frozen Birds

Kean stuffed his own pintail and mounted it in a flying position. But that was a guide for the anatomy,

Here are the feather patterns to be studied on the back of the quail. The bird is carved from basswood, a wood that Kean says holds details well and has good, consistent grain.

Started in the fall of 1982, this full-size flying pintail took three and one-half months to complete. The cattail that supports the bird at a point on its stomach is made of steel. Photo by Edward M. Burrell.

not a bird to generate a pattern from. What Kean does, which is unique among this group of eight carvers, is generate a working pattern from a frozen bird.

Working with birds he has shot, Kean finds he can freeze a bird such as a pintail, let it thaw, pose it, make a pattern, and then refreeze it.

A Cross-Sectional Roll

Another important function of a frozen bird is its feathers. From an extra pintail drake, Kean removed the wing and tail feathers. Laying them out on strips of basswood approximately one-eighth to three-sixteenth inches thick, Kean traced their outlines and cut them out on a band saw.

But, he explains, a feather is not a flat surface.

To help with the flying composition, Kean mounted his own pintail. Photo by Edward M. Burrell.

Here can be seen the mount amid real cattail leaves, which Kean later duplicated using strips of basswood. Photo by Edward M. Burrell.

Kean duplicated nearly 100 feather inserts for the flying pintail. Note the references, including a wing, the feathers, and a mount. The feathers came from a frozen pintail, one of many birds he stores in his freezer for reference. Photo by Edward M. Burrell.

Working with basswood one-eighth to three-sixteenth inches thick, Kean carves in details on these primary feathers. Photo by Edward M. Burrell.

He says that primaries have an S curve that allows them to overlap and underlap each other. To affect the curves, Kean carves away wood on either side of the shaft he made in each feather. Here he uses an offset skew chisel. Sanding is done with a one-half-inch-diameter sanding drum in a Dremel Moto-Tool. Photo by Edward M. Burrell.

Having the actual feathers helps Kean duplicate them. Photo by Edward M. Burrell.

"There is a cross-sectional roll to a feather that some people call an S curve. Its function is to overlap and underlap the preceding and following feather, one to the other, when it's in place."

Kean says there is an aerodynamic function to the S curve. "These feathers are twisted open in their sockets to allow air to pass through them on their upstroke, and they're twisted closed so that the bird gets power on the wings' downward stroke."

What helps to make the S curve is first drawing the shaft, or rib, of the feather. Then a skew chisel can take away wood from either side to raise or lower the contour. Also useful is a one-half-inch-diameter sanding drum and a Dremel Moto-Tool to "turn down the outside edge, and flow the inside edge upward to achieve that overlapping."

Here Kean has laid out the ten primaries, secondaries, and tertials to see how they overlap. This overlapping helps the bird achieve flight. Photo by Edward M. Burrell.

A Hollow Pintail

Kean's methods for inserting the more than 100 feathers into the wings and body of the pintail are not unlike Habbart Dean's in chapter 4. Like Dean, Kean carved axillars and scapulars as part of the body to disguise the wing-to-body joint. He says it was difficult matching a convex to a concave surface, "the convex surface being the top of the wing plus the tertial feathers, the concave surface being the underside of the scapulars."

He also had to deal with the weight of a pintail that had to be suspended on something that looked like a cattail leaf. To facilitate the suspension, Kean had to hollow out the bird.

First, he took two equal blocks of basswood that were large enough to encompass the whole pattern when put together. By careful measuring, he traced the pattern onto the inner and outer faces of the block. Then five drops of glue were spaced around the inner face, well inside the outline of the pattern, and the two blocks were clamped together. The outer pattern was then cut to shape on a band saw. These few drops of glue, he explains, would allow him to separate easily the two halves later on. And by keeping the drops within the outline, there was no risk of tearing away bits of wood at the seam line.

After shaping the laminated blocks with a band saw, files, rasps, and a hatchet, plus making the areas to receive the wings, Kean separated the blocks with a mallet and hollowed each half. (Compare Jett Brunet's shaping techniques in chapter 3.)

If he had hollowed the bird before carving the shape

The feathers are inserted into a slot which was carved with knives and a Dremel Moto-Tool and bits. Photo by Edward M. Burrell.

Here are the top and side profile patterns for the pintail. The basswood bird was hollowed to lighten its weight. Photo by Edward M. Burrell.

All the wing feathers have been inserted with some burned. Note the holding device. Photo by Edward M. Burrell.

So tight is the fit of the wings to the body of the pintail, which can be removed for transporting it, Kean could barely free a carved feather that got wedged in the joint area. Axillars and scapulars are carved as part of the body. These help disguise the wing-to-body joint. Photo by Edward M. Burrell.

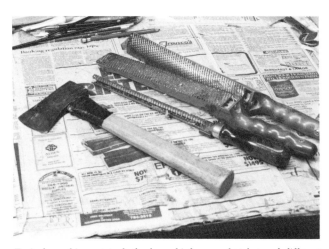

Typical roughing-out tools for large birds are a hatchet and different Surform rasps, available in most hardware stores.

for the wing inserts, Kean explains, he might have removed too much wood from the area he wanted to pin the wings into. "I drilled a hole in the base of each wing and set stainless steel pins into the wood. When I pressed the wings and body together, small depressions were left. I was then able to drill corresponding holes into the body. When the wings were brought up to the body, I had a sturdy, sound joint." Kean adds that the wings can be removed to make it easier to move the piece.

An Inconspicuous Connection

Rising out of a base made from an oval fourteen-by-eighteen-inch piece of walnut are handmade cattails. All but two are made out of pieces of basswood. One is a length of stainless steel that acts as the main support. Another stainless steel strip crosses that to give stability and support, with a notch in one to receive the other.

On the end of the main support cattail leaf, Kean silver soldered a square block of brass in its center. He inserted another square brass block with a square hole into the pintail's stomach to receive the cattail's brass block. These blocks, when joined together, keep the bird from falling over and also from twisting or turning.

"This is an inconspicuous connection," Kean says, "because the width of the cattail is greater than either brass block. Also, there are two convex surfaces coming together, the shape of the pintail's belly and the curving cattail. These curves lead the eye away from the point of contact and this too helps disguise the connection."

Basswood Cattails

When Kean makes cattails for a habitat, whether for the flying pintail or a pair of redwinged blackbirds, he uses strips of basswood.

Starting with basswood boards that measure one and one-quarter to one and one-half inches thick, Kean goes to the band saw to cut out a number of thin strips, only one-sixteenth of an inch thick. He uses a band saw and not a circular saw because the small kerf made by the blade wastes little wood. Mounting a board close to the blade, Kean uses it as a fence along which the basswood board is pushed. This allows for a constant thickness for the cattail leaves.

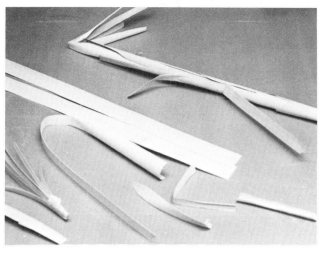

These basswood cattails, bent, broken, and twisted, were made for Kean's redwinged blackbird composition. Photo by Edward M. Burrell.

Kean says that cattail leaves taper.

To make strips for the individual cattail leaves, Kean passes a thick piece of basswood through a band saw.

But the taper is only near the base, so the leaf has parallel edges for most of its length. This leaf is over two feet long.

The thin blade of the tool wastes little wood. Note the clamped block that assures a uniform thickness of the strips, which are about one-sixteenth-inch thick.

A carver's knife is used here to cut out the cattail taper. The tapered end of a real cattail can be as long as twenty inches.

At their bases, cattail leaves have quite a curvature. Also, their ends will get frayed and broken as the results of age and weather.

Once cut to shape, the basswood strips are sanded to remove kerf marks and, at the same time, give them a slightly concave-convex shape. This facilitates the strips wrapping around each other.

Each leaf is soaked in his bathtub until limber, and then the butt end is taped around a half-inch dowel. Then it is bent or twisted and allowed to dry in the sun. Kean says a hair dryer can also be used to dry them.

Cattail leaves fit around each other, making up a stalk of anywhere from fifteen to twenty leaves. Kean uses dowels as temporary armatures around which he wraps the strips of basswood so they form a stalk.

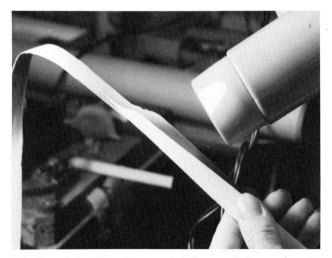

To facilitate drying, Kean does use a hair dryer on the leaves where the sun could not do the job.

The next step is sanding the strips to remove the marks left by the band saw blade and to make them slightly concave on the inside and convex on the outside. This, he says, is the natural shape of the cattail leaves. The tool he uses is a sander grinder with one-inch-wide belts that run from 40 to 600 grit.

Kean points out that cattail leaves are much wider at their bases than at their ends. In effect, they taper. To make their shapes, he draws the outlines on the basswood strips and cuts them to size with a knife.

Telescoping Stalks

Kean says that cattail leaves wrap around each other to form a stalk. "They form a tubular construction. So they are like a solid mass of leaves rolled up almost like a cigar."

His next step in making stalks is soaking all the leaves in a bathtub of water. Once they are saturated, he wraps them around dowels that are one-half inch to three-quarter inches in diameter, keeping the leaves in place with masking tape. He then takes them outside and lets the sun dry them. He will twist or bend the tapered ends and weight them down with heavy objects so they dry in that shape. He uses a hair dryer to be sure all moisture is out of the wood. The leaves are then sealed thoroughly and painted to simulate wintered-over cattails.

Kean says that once the shaping, drying, sealing, and painting are completed, "You can insert them into one another, building them up like stacking up telescoping tubes."

Winter Dormancy and Broken Leaves

"If you go into a marsh," notes Kean, "you will notice real cattails having passed through a winter are in ragged shape. It adds realism and character to tear the end of a leaf or bend it over, or even break it, leave it hanging, and add a little glue to that joint."

To add color, Kean will take a stiff brush and stipple, or spatter, paint on some of the leaves to give the appearance of mold or insect infestations. He will also paint them with acrylics to gray the leaves and add brownish edges. "Ochre tones," he says, "give the feeling of dormancy and wintertime disintegration that allows new growth to take place."

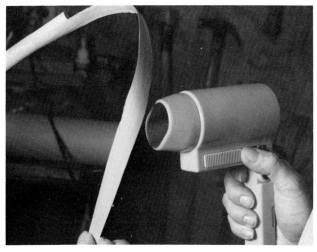

Once absolutely dry, a point when the leaves will retain their new shapes, they will be sealed with a combination of lacquer and lacquer thinner, then painted. Twists and bends like this represent the natural effects of weather on the leaves. If the leaf should crack or split, Kean says that too will represent the effects of wind, rain, and sun.

To get a broken end, Kean will simply snap the basswood leaf in his hands. He may leave it like this without separating the parts.

A broken cattail leaf looks very much like this. The sun and wind make them brittle, Kean says.

Here can be observed broken leaves in the finished redwinged blackbird composition.

The paint for the cattail leaves is ochre-tone acrylics and dark colors spattered on the surface.

Kean makes cattails to appear in murky water and to have the look of having gone through several seasons of inclement weather.

Balsa Wood Heads

Cattails have a central, round stem that ends in a cylindrical seed head. When making stems, Kean will use a one-half-inch-diameter hardwood dowel and taper it to one-eighth inch at its end. For the head, he will use balsa wood. "Balsa does funny things when saturated with water and ground on," Kean says. After carving a piece into a hot-dog shape, he soaks it in a can of water and lets it dry for a while. "I then take a Dremel Tool and bit and chew up the surface. Because the wood is wet, it doesn't create sawdust. The bit actually tears the wood without breaking it away. So you're left with a fuzzy material sticking out that gives the appearance of what a cattail does in the winter-time—that is, it disintegrates into many millions of seeds that are in each head."

Still, he will glue clumps of basswood sawdust to the ground surface to achieve even more fluffiness.

Though Kean has observed that ground balsa is very close in color to the plumes of the seeds, he adds some

Kean makes the cattail heads out of balsa wood, carved to shape, soaked in water, and ground on with a Dremel Moto-Tool and bit. Basswood sawdust is then glued to the surface to help simulate dispersing seeds.

This water is made from plastic casting resin and is approximately one and one-quarter inches deep. Several pourings are necessary to build up the depth. This reduces the risk of the resin warping and cracking from chemical reaction and temperature changes, says Kean.

This redwinged blackbird composition, approximately three feet high, represents early spring, when the birds return from their southern range to mate. Kean says the birds like to land up high. He spent two and one-half months on this piece.

white or unbleached titanium and a burnt sienna to the outer surface not gone to seed.

Plastic Water

Water is another component of the habitats Kean has made for the pintail and blackbird compositions.

Kean says a cattail marsh has dark, murky water. "Where you have so much biochemical reaction going on, you'll find the water dark." He starts with a clear plastic casting resin to which coloring agents can be added. He uses a dark gray agent that results in a nearly black color. For the redwing composition, Kean says there resulted an "interplay of top color [the male

redwing] and the murky water that you might not have had with another species."

Kean advises exercising caution and experimentation when using plastic casting resin. For the flying pintail, the final resin thickness was one and one-quarter inches. To achieve that, he had to make five different pourings. He says that if pourings are over one-half inch thick, chemical reaction problems will cause buckling.

A Chauvinistic Blackbird

Kean says blackbirds will perch high, especially in a cattail marsh, "to be well seen to determine whether

Kean has his male blackbird prominently displaying its red wing-patch. He says this is "a sign of true male chauvinism and territorial proclamation."

there is any threat to their territory." With the male of the species, "male chauvinism is very prominent, so males seek a dominant place where they parade or strut or do their courtship activity."

Kean carved two redwinged blackbirds, a male and a female. "The male's wings are so colorful, I chose to open them up so the bright color would be shown off. That's a natural habit when the bird is making a visual signal for other male redwing blackbirds to stay away. The female is in a relaxed pose to make the piece more peaceful looking."

An Early Spring

Kean says that redwinged blackbirds frequent marshes with cattails. "These are, by their nature, tall plants. So to represent that aspect realistically, I felt the birds had to be a certain height above the base. Also, because the birds are of a good size, I felt the piece needed some height to balance the size of the birds.

"The idea of the composition is to represent early spring," Kean says. "The redwings have just come from their southern range to breed and nest and spend their summer." And the cattails? "They have gone through three seasons. So the elements of sun, rain, sleet, snow, and wind have all worked on these cattails to blow them about, beat them down. Also, the older they get, the more brittle they become. So I showed them bent, broken, and torn to reproduce what naturally occurs."

In fact, Kean has the female sitting on a broken stem, which started as a one-half-inch-diameter dowel tapered to a smaller diameter at the tip. "I used a stem instead of a leaf to faciliate holding her legs and feet, which are made from a brass rod one-eighth inch thick." (Compare Robert Guge's techniques for making feet and legs in chapter 2.)

Stem Joinery

Interestingly, the stems with their redwinged occupants can be removed. Kean says this makes packaging and transferring the piece easier. And, with some flexibility in having separate pieces, there is less likelihood of the composition being damaged at shows or competitions.

He used two different types of joints for the stems that hold each bird. For the female's, he used what he describes as a "clothespin-type notch." He then made a collar out of basswood and glued that around the pointed end of a section of dowel that was put into the center of the cattail stalk. The two pieces could then be dovetailed together, which would keep the bird and stem from twisting.

For the male stem, Kean used what he describes as "a dog leg cut" in the dowel, and he matched the cut on the dowel with one in the cattail stalk. Kean says the upper stem fits down into the wooden collar, and the dog leg cut keeps the stem from twisting.

Kean has the female blackbird perched on a broken stem, lower than the male. Kean says this peaceful look represents her "moment in time."

The legs for the male and female are one-eighth-inch-diameter brass rods. Still to be attached are copper toes, which will be held and built up with plumber's epoxy. Photo by Edward M. Burrell.

One way to remove the stems on which the blackbirds perch to facilitate transporting the piece is this clothespin-type joint. The mating end is deep down inside the stalk. This is the stem for the female.

Centerlines and Laminated Birds

When Kean carves birds such as his redwing pair, he will make each out of two identically thick pieces of wood, laminated along the length of the bird. He did this for the pintail to hollow and make the waterfowl lighter, but the laminating serves another purpose as well.

"The bodies of all my birds, quail, doves, songbirds, except for my floating ducks, are made out of two blocks of wood. When I glue the two pieces of wood together, I always have a centerline reference point. No matter how the carving proceeds, then, I have a centerline running down the middle of the tail, and right up straight through the bird's breast." Why is this line so important? Kean responds, "I take a lot of measurements trying to recreate as accurately as possible the bird's anatomy and symmetry. You have the centerline as a concrete thing. The heads are done the same way, even though they are made separately and attached." Many carvers feel the resulting glue line is a problem. Kean says, "When burning, by the time you get to the center of the bird where the glue line is, the burning lines are pretty much parallel and the glue seam is lost."

Another joint shown here is one that Kean describes as a dog leg joint. This and the previous one rest in collars and keep the stems from twisting. Both are made from three-eighth-inch-diameter dowels. This stem is for the male.

Disguising a Head Seam

Kean admits that burning does not always disguise a head seam where it joins the body. "It's a good idea when putting heads on to put your glue in the center

Centerlines are an important reference to Kean. To achieve a permanent one, Kean glues two pieces of wood together, letting the seam act as a centerline. Photo by Edward M. Burrell.

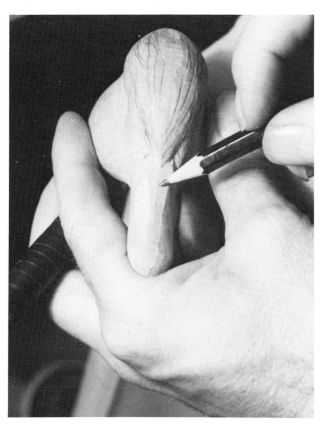

Kean even laminates wood for a head, as he did with this green-winged teal, to achieve a permanent centerline. This, he says, helps with symmetry.

Kean layers his feather groupings with a knife and burns them. He does not stone in texture, though he will shape feather groups with a grinding stone. Photo by Edward M. Burrell.

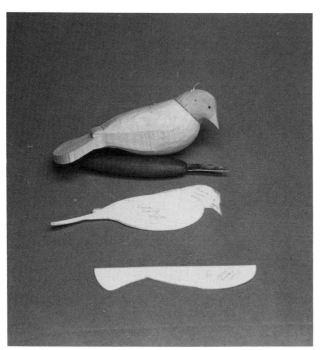

Shown here are the patterns for the female redwinged blackbird. Note that half a top profile is used, which will give an exact centerline. Photo by Edward M. Burrell.

When burned and painted over, the seam line, which runs along the length of the bird, virtually disappears.

of the joint and try not to get any around the outside edges. This way, when the burning lines cross the seam, you don't have a reaction of the glue to the heat."

There is another way to disguise a seam, and that is with the layout of the feathers. When doing a quail, Kean says, "The neck feathers line up so they fit on the seam line in enough places, so that when you carve those feathers, they are raised from the ones below. That breaks up the line where you joined the head to the body."

He adds that at times he has had to go over a seam with a plumber's epoxy and, when hardened, texture that with a grinding stone. "But you may have to carve away some wood from the seam to create a shallow depression that you fill with the epoxy. (Compare John Gewerth's technique in chapter 5.) When textured, it will all flow together."

A Rolling Joint

Kean has yet another unique strategy for making a joint, one he uses on floating waterfowl to join heads to bodies. Instead of making two flat, mating surfaces, he will make a compoundly curving surface. The curve will be from one side of the head to the other, and also from front to back. This technique, Kean feels, also helps to disguise the resulting joint.

He adds, "I do all the shaping and burning on the head before it's attached to the body." As for the rolling joint, "I like to have the shape of the shoulders and breast roll into each other, and it is realistic. When I

He employs a compound curve that is both concave and convex.

With a matching compound curve or contour on the body, a glue joint is nearly impossible to detect.

In preparation for attaching the head of a waterfowl to its body, Kean has a unique way of shaping the mating surfaces.

Here is a head for a shooting stool, a functional and less-than-decorative decoy.

Note how it is nearly impossible to detect a seam line on the head of this widgeon drake.

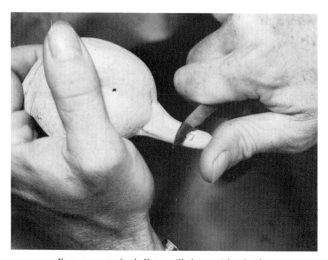

Even on waterfowl, Kean will shape with a knife.

make the patterns for both head and body, I try to use the outline of the shoulders and breast as a guide."

Working Without a Foredom

Kean does not use or even own a Foredom Tool, though, as mentioned earlier, he does use a Dremel Moto-Tool. "A Foredom takes away wood so fast," Kean says. "You can always take wood off, but it's just too hard to put back on." Because the Dremel has a much smaller capacity for removing wood, he uses it for details such as shaping feathers or feather groups.

Much like Jett Brunet (chapter 4), Kean works with a band saw, hatchet and Surform rasps to roughly shape a large bird such as a duck. But much more detailing is done with knives, especially on small birds such as the blackbirds. He uses Cheston Knotts' knives (see appendix for address), which he describes as "the best in the world. I love them. The steel is strong, it holds a good edge, and it's flexible. And the handles are comfortable to hold." Kean adds that Knotts offers over twenty different knives, and, "He will modify an existing pattern, or, if you send him a drawing, he will make a custom knife for you."

Raising Feathers

Kean says he will use a knife to raise feathers, particularly in the back and tertial areas of a bird. Using the point of the knife, he will put it perpendicular to the surface, make an outline of the feather, and relieve

Here Kean works on the body of his redwinged blackbird. Photo by Edward M. Burrell.

Kean prefers the control of a knife over a Foredom when removing wood. Note the separate head which also is laminated from pieces of wood. Photo by Edward M. Burrell.

it from below. Each feather is then rolled down from its center to its edges. He compares this to a staircase effect. "To pronounce the jutting out of feathers, you can take the burner and go underneath and burn wood away. It's another way of undercutting a feather." He adds, though, that the burned area has to be sanded to soften what otherwise would remain a shiny surface.

Ticking and Crisscross Burning

Kean's burning technique is similar to the one used by other carvers in this book. He starts with the tail and works up over the back of the bird, burns the flanks and works into the breast area, so the feathers overlap naturally. What is unique is a burning technique he uses that creates an effect he calls "ticking."

Kean says the back of a bird's head, particularly a duck's head, can be very fluffy with many, comparatively long feathers overlapping each other. "The barbs in their overlay crisscross each other and there is a lot of depth. To achieve the appearance of this depth, I use a crisscross method which entails holding the bird's head in my left hand, the burner in my right, and slightly turning the head back and forth as I work the burner. I'm burning as rapidly as possible with very high heat. The closer to the bill I get, the shorter my strokes, and the less crossing there is."

He will also put the point of the burning pen to the head, still at a very high heat, and literally let it "eat out" sections of the wood. These sections are then

Here can be studied the result of knifework on the breast of the male redwing blackbird.

Kean points out the fluffy head feathers on this mounted waterfowl.

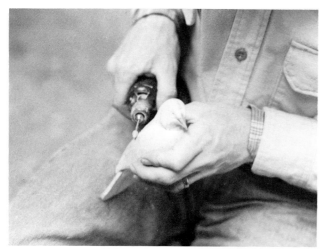

Despite his knifework, Kean will do some fine detailing with a Dremel Moto-Tool and ruby carver, neither of which removes wood too quickly. Photo by Edward M. Burrell.

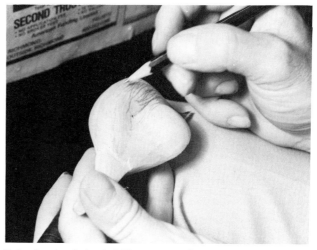

Before burning the head of this green-winged teal, Kean first decides on a feather flow.

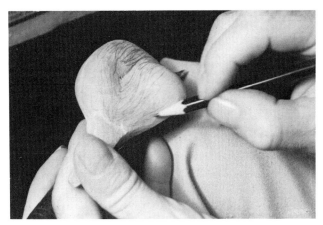

A bird's head feathers, says Kean, overlap from the base of the bill back down the head to the tail.

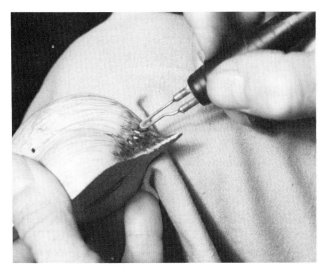

To recreate a bird's fluffy, overlapping head feathers, Kean uses a method he calls crisscross burning. He applies short burn lines as he turns the head back and forth. Then, with high heat, he will burn deeply into areas to give an appearance of depth.

Kean points to the back of his widgeon drake to indicate the effect of deep burning.

Shown here are the results of crisscross burning. Kean describes this texturing as "an attempt at realism."

burned normally to eliminate shiny or flat areas. "This method of texturing," says Kean, "is very valuable in doing birds such as widgeons, black ducks, and most of the puddle duck hens, because of the light and dark feathers on their heads."

This ticking, or raising of feathers to create depth, is really done with the painting in mind. When acrylic washes are applied, patterns of light and dark feathers are created because of the use of contrasting colors and also because of the burned texture. Kean adds that care should be taken not to fill up the burning with paint.

Working Acrylics Without Gesso

When painting, Kean does not prime the wood with gesso. Instead, "I begin with an acrylic color lighter than the one I want to end up with to give some brightness to the feathers." He refers to his widgeon pair, saying, "Their heads have an interplay of dark and light values of color. But the final coats are the lightest of the light values, hitting the high spots, not the deep dark areas."

Achieving a Leathery Bill

When painting bills, Kean strives for a leathery look. This is achieved as much by the preparation of the wood as by the paint. After sanding the carved bill

Kean's widgeon pair was done for the 1984 World Championship Wild-fowl Carving Competition.

When floated, the widgeon hen will have its bill in the water.

with 100- and 220-grit sandpaper, then 360-grit wet/dry paper, and finally steel wool, he seals the bill with Krazy Glue. This toughens the wood, Kean explains, which can then be brought up to a slick, polished surface. This is done two or three times before the head is burned. Kean says that great care should be taken not to get any Krazy Glue on the head area to be burned since toxic fumes will be given off.

"When I start painting, I choose the lightest color and paint the whole bill with that color, then continue building up other colors to affect a leathery look. After painting, I have good luck just polishing the surface with a soft piece of cloth such as soft corduroy." He warns against rubbing too hard, since paint might come off.

Feisty Widgeons

Kean carved his widgeon pair for the 1984 World Championships, widgeons being the designated species. Kean says he enjoys carving this species because they are "colorful and feisty. They love to chase all the other ducks." But, he says, they are a challenge to a carver. "They're hard to paint because of the vermiculation and iridescence and the ticking on the head. Color transitions are hard to achieve, but they're fun birds to do because there are some big colorful tertial feathers you can give flair and activity to."

Kean says he was after a feeding activity for the pair. The drake, he points out, has just swallowed some food or has drunk some water. The female, when floated, will have her bill in the water as if she is about to grab some grass.

Shown here is a good view of the feather layout on the back of the hen.

The widgeon drake has a relaxed look, as if searching for grasses to eat.

The drake's back feather layout can be studied here.

Projecting a Pattern

Though Kean will often use a frozen bird to achieve a pattern, Kean works from slides of live birds on water for ducks such as the widgeons. When the slides are projected onto a screen, he is able to draw patterns from the images of the ducks.

How does Kean know how big to make those images? He answers, "The way you determine the size of the life-size projection is to use a study bill and take a concrete measurement. The bills of dead birds shrink, and this renders them useless. Then you project the slide until it fits the measurement."

Kean says that slides "are an invaluable reference and resource in the carver's repertoire. They capture moments in nature, for you never see things the same way twice."

Hollowing and Sealing a Duck's Interior

As most carvers do, Kean hollows his waterfowl so they will float correctly in competitions.

Kean begins hollowing by taking the side profile wood that had been cut away with the band saw and "tacking it with nails onto the body at the point where the head is going to be glued." This technique leaves no nailholes that have to be filled. The purpose for the waste wood? "This gives you a platform when you turn the bird over on the drill press and start hollowing. And it keeps the axis of the bird perpendicular to the drill bit."

Kean uses a spade bit and then rotary cutters to clear out wood from the interior and smooth the sides. Before he makes a bottom plate, he will seal the interior with straight lacquer. "Hopefully," he says, "this will prevent changes that could occur in the wood such as cracks or water saturating it." He points out that birds left in a competition tank often for hours run the risk of taking in water if the bottom plate or plug is not sealed thoroughly. When gluing the plate, Kean suggests using a five-minute epoxy and then coating the plate with five or six coats of straight lacquer to seal the wood.

Consistent Basswood

It was stated earlier that Kean uses basswood for habitat such as cattails. He also uses basswood for all his birds. Kean says he likes the consistency of the

This fluted conical cutter in a drill press Kean uses after hollowing a duck with a spade bit. This removes excess wood from the interior.

Kean attaches the bottom plate or plug for floating waterfowl with a five-minute epoxy after he has sealed the inside with straight lacquer. This preparation, he says, should keep the bottom from opening up after being in water for an extended period of time, something that has happened to other carvers' work.

Kean says that leaves and grasses go well with a bird like a bobwhite quail.

wood, adding, "There's not a lot of difference between the hard and soft parts of the wood. I've learned how to work it and trust it. And I think it holds details very well."

He does note, though, that basswood has a tendency to raise its grain when textured with a stoning bit. But most of the fuzziness, he says, can be gotten rid of with sandpaper and a wire brush. Burning will get rid of the rest, he adds.

Birds and Grocery Bag Leaves

Basswood cattails are not the only habitat material Kean can recreate. Leaves are another contribution to habitat that seem to go particularly well with game birds.

When he first started making leaves, Kean began with thin pieces of aluminum foil. (Compare Manfred Scheel's metal leaves in chapter 8.) The veins were drawn in the metal with a pick, and he used vinegar to "etch" the aluminum, a means of keeping the paint from coming off.

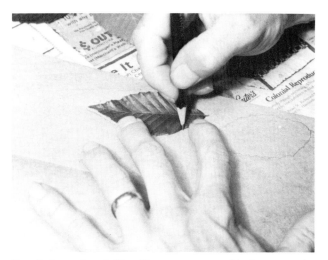

To make leaves for a habitat, Kean traces an actual leaf on grocery bag paper.

But after a while, he turned to grocery bag paper, feeling that its consistency produced a more realistic-looking leaf.

Kean first picks leaves off a tree and traces them onto the heavy brown paper. Then he cuts the patterns out with scissors. The leaves' veins he can inscribe with a burning pen. But he puts a stiff piece of sponge or carpet padding underneath the paper so the burner does not cut through.

"It's best to use a dull burning tip for the leaves because a sharp one will definitely cut through the paper," he says. The heat from the pen can make the leaves curl up, "which is a natural occurrence in the fall and winter months," Kean says, "and you can burn

Once cut out, the leaf's veins can be duplicated with a burning tool at a low heat. But he does this with a piece of carpet padding, which will keep the burning tip from cutting the paper.

Another view of the bobwhite quail base shows a number of leaves and grasses.

Even worm holes can be made with the burning pen. On the left is a real beech leaf, on the right the one Kean made before painting it.

Kean says that in terms of design, the quail is "a heavy object," while the leaves and grasses are "light and airy." He feels the two work together.

holes in the paper as if the leaves were eaten by worms or bugs."

He will paint them after he seals the paper with a Deft spray lacquer that saturates and waterproofs it.

Does he have a preference for a particular leaf? Kean says he prefers to use beech leaves for his bobwhite quail compositions. He notes, "The beech tree is one of the many trees that grows in woods where the bobwhite quail spends a good part of its time. These birds will even feed on small beech nuts."

A Backyard of Mourning Doves

When Kean did his mourning dove composition, he says he had a backyard patio full of doves feeding on corn and other food. And though he had five doves in his freezer to work from, the live birds gave him a chance to study the differences between each one.

"It's true that every bird of a species is going to look different as we look different from each other. On one dove, you may find a back browner than the others. Some can tend toward a raw umber or olive, others toward a raw sienna tone. Or there may be more or less blue on the top of the head. The breast color can vary from a peach to a purplish pink color. Also, the birds will be different in size according to age and diet."

Why is it important to recognize differences? Kean answers, "It's good to have more than one bird to study because you won't be tied down to one representative

Kean says he was lucky to find a branch that mirrored to some degree the shape of this mourning dove. In the collection of Katheryn and Walter Robertson.

Kean worked with slides of live mourning doves and a number of frozen doves to create this bird. He says it represents the best attributes of all that he studied.

Like all his birds, this dove is made from two pieces of wood glued together. The seam, running up the breast, is invisible.

This relaxed dove, carved from basswood, is over eleven inches long. Relieving the wings was done with a skew chisel.

Here can be studied the side of the dove. For the dark gray color Kean used raw umber, raw sienna, titanium white, and Mars black.

Here can be studied the primaries.

On the right is a frozen dove Kean used for study and from which he generated a pattern. After the bird was thawed, he posed it and then refroze it.

bird. You can then pool the attributes of several birds into your carving." And the purpose of that? Kean says, "You want your bird to be as pleasing as possible." Kean says that this dove is a cross section of the birds he studied and worked from.

Doves love to sit a lot, Kean says, so he put his bird on a dead cedar branch. "I liked the different directions of the branch, and the twisting of its grain complements the position and shape of the dove. "Finding this branch was a happy accident, because its twisting design leads back to the bird." The bird itself, he says, is in a relaxed pose, perhaps only partially alert to predators.

Pink Iridescence

A mourning dove has a pink to violet iridescence. To achieve that color, Kean used red, cadmium light, unbleached titanium, raw umber, aqua violet, and Mars black acrylics to make what he calls a grayish pink area. Only then did he add some violet bronzing powder "to give the bird a little bit of shine."

Kean prefers not to overuse bronzing powders to achieve iridescence on a bird like the mourning dove. He will try to paint as closely to the color as he can with acrylics, feeling this keeps him from "overstating the look of iridescence."

8

Manfred Scheel
Wildfowl in Miniature

Manfred Scheel, a master of miniature wildfowl in wood, is shown here working on a diminutive swan.

Cabinetmaker, Marqueterian, Miniature Carver

Of the eight carvers in this book, Manfred Scheel is the only one with an intensive background in wood. He started whittling at the age of six. When he was fourteen, he apprenticed three years to a master cabinetmaker in Germany. Shortly after that, he emigrated with his family to the United States where he continued his trade as a cabinetmaker.

His fascination for birds also goes back to early childhood when he raised owls, grouse, and crows. Even today he houses a variety of species in aviary cages on his land.

It is there, in an area of Pennsylvania probably reminiscent of his former home in Germany's Hartz Mountains, he creates some of the finest miniature wildfowl in the field. They include waterfowl, birds of prey, songbirds, shorebirds, and gamebirds.

Many years were to pass before Scheel started carving full time. For eight years he had his own cabinetmaking shop in Philadelphia, Pennsylvania. During that time, he experimented with marquetry, a technique where different species and colors of wood are inlaid to make designs or pictures. Most of Scheel's pictures were of birds.

His marquetry eventually brought him to wildfowl art and carving shows. The impact of what he saw was dramatic. He says, "Seeing carving in places like the Salisbury Carving and Art Exhibition, I became fascinated with the carving end. I felt it was more intriguing than flat work." He decided ten years ago to carve birds instead of making them from veneers, and he has been carving full-time ever since.

Scheel's property was once a farm with timber-framed buildings. In the lower left corner of the photo is an aviary cage for bobwhite quail.

Why Miniatures?

Nearly all of the birds Scheel carves are miniatures. A number of carvers like Robert Guge (chapter 3) make them, but few do it to the exclusion of full-size work. Why does he do diminutive birds? Scheel says he was always intrigued by them, though he finds them frustrating to do at times. "Most people see one as less than a carving, perhaps rating it second to a life-size piece. But most people have been fascinated by miniatures, even back to the Egyptians. And don't forget that the famous decoy makers did miniatures."

He says he is not opposed to full-size or big birds. "I have done life-size birds, even decorative decoys. But I always go back to miniatures. Maybe it has something to do with not moving a lot of wood around."

Many of Scheel's miniatures are extremely small. A black duck might be only two or three inches tall, a great blue heron only four inches high. But, he says, "If I can make a miniature look as good as a big one, that's just as satisfying to me." And, he admits, "The small one is easier to handle with less wood to remove."

He believes that there is another reason to do miniatures. "People who collect them usually buy a lot. I have customers who own 20, 25 pieces of mine. It's almost impossible to collect that many full-size carvings of birds." He has found, then, that people who buy from him rarely buy just one piece unless it is a gift for another.

He has encountered another frustration, especially with the competitions. He explains, "There are no guidelines for miniatures. A bird might be half-size and called a miniature. So you put a half-size Canada goose next to one of my pieces and mine can't be seen."

Is it easier doing a miniature piece, the time factor notwithstanding? Scheel says the question does not apply to him. "I'm just inclined to do small things. I can relax with them. With a big piece, I'm in tension."

What helped Scheel make a transition from cabinetwork to wildfowl carving was marquetry, the art of inlaying veneer-thin pieces of wood to create patterns or pictures. Shown here is a wood thrush he made from veneers.

This is an inlaid picture of a red-headed woodpecker. Some of the woods are maple, walnut, holly, ash burl, and mahogany.

Typical of Scheel's work is this California quail.

Perky Birds

Most of the carvers featured in this book look for some essence of a bird that can be captured in wood. For Scheel, especially with songbirds, it is a "perky" look. But he also feels the right use of habitat helps create that look. He likes to have his birds in a bright, spring setting or have a cardinal with winter snow. "These are ideal things," he says. "But people don't want to see a rotten log or a base filled up with mud." It is not uncommon, then, to find a flower with one of his miniatures or even an insect like a lady bug.

Learning from Aviaries

What has certainly helped Scheel capture that perky look is that he has not one but five aviaries. (Compare Jett Brunet's use of an aviary in chapter 3.) He defines an aviary as "any enclosure that has a bird in it. A big cage is an aviary. It's where a bird can move freely. Many people think an aviary is something that has to be tremendously big and fancy."

Scheel has a cage in his studio with society finches. This he calls an aviary. But he also has a cage in his yard that measures 10 x 20 x 7 feet high. In it are mandarin and redhead ducks, mallards and teal, and ringneck doves. He says he would like to have a larger one, but he has been told that the smaller the enclosure, the better one can observe the birds without their being overly wild.

He feels that his quail pen, which measures only 3 x 5 feet, is ideal for that. In it are only two bobwhite quail, and the cage, he says, is ideal for that number. "You couldn't observe them in a larger aviary. They would hide from you."

Atop a rock carved from tupelo gum, the quail is only two and one half inches tall.

Scheel describes this winter wren as a "perky" bird, a characteristic his customers enjoy seeing in his work.

He may spend as much time on habitat as he does on a bird. Here he has fashioned leaves from brass and has shaped a lady bug from metal.

Another aviary he has measures 4 x 8 feet. In it are a pair of ring teal, but he also has mallards, redheads, and mandarin ducks.

Scheel in no way underestimates the importance of his aviaries. He says candidly that they helped him go from flat work to three-dimensional art. He is equally frank in his comments on other carvers who do not share his interest in birds. He says, "To do a good bird, you have to be interested in it. I think that's lacking today with a lot of carvers who may have gotten into it because of the popularity carving has achieved today." And what is lacking? He says that the problem is comparable to a horse artist who has never gone to the stable. "It's very hard to do a bird you haven't seen first hand," he says.

But he points out it is not always necessary to have the exact bird on hand that is going to be carved. "I have doves in my aviaries I might never carve, but

This aviary cage measures 10 x 20 x 7 feet high. In it are doves and ducks such as mandarins, redheads, mallards, and teal.

One of the doves in that large cage is this ringneck.

Quail are a favorite subject to Scheel's. In this cage, which measures 3 x 5 x 3 feet high, are a pair of bobwhite quail.

Scheel makes what he describes as pattern sheets on pieces of oaktag. Birds can be removed and replaced. This sheet affords a convenient place to store patterns.

Scheel will occasionally do sketches as he did for this group of yellowlegs he entered in the 1983 World Championship Wildfowl Carving Competition. It took second place. But, he says, drawings do not translate well into three dimensions.

they're so close to other doves, you wouldn't have to have that particular species. Or you might not have a California quail you want to carve, but you have a scaled quail or a bobwhite quail. They will all walk the same, act the same way pretty much."

Aviary Maintenance

Scheel cautions those carvers who want to start their own aviaries. He says the birds need fresh water and food daily. "You have to go out there and provide food and water even in sleet, rain, and snow, and that's tough sometimes. You can't wake up in the morning and wonder if you want to maintain them for that day."

Leaving aviary birds even for a day presents problems. Scheel says, "You have to have someone baby-sitting. Anyone starting this should keep that in mind. And you have to keep it simple and automatic for someone babysitting so that person does not lose interest. The person has to be able to feed and water in minutes, not hours, especially if the weather is bad." He adds that when the weather is bitter, the water has to be changed frequently because it will freeze quickly.

In spite of all these difficulties, Scheel says, "It's a beautiful thing to observe birds whenever you feel like it, especially seeing them in all their best plumage."

Other References

Scheel enjoys visiting a beach to observe shore and wading birds he cannot keep in an aviary. But even observing birds firsthand, or having a mounted bird, a number of which he keeps in his studio, is not enough reference. He says, in fact, "There's no such thing as having too much reference material. I never pass up a photo of a bird in a magazine. I'll cut it out and put it in my files, even if I have fifty photos of that species, because that one extra photo may have exactly that angle or position I'm looking for." So when Scheel carves, he will lay out books and all available photos of a species.

Pattern Sheets

Scheel does not do much in the way of preliminary sketches when starting a carving. In fact, he prefers to "sketch with the wood" rather than on paper. (Com-

This pattern sheet has two condors. But the final composition has three, which he entered in the 1985 World Championships.

Like the shore birds on the previous pattern sheet, the condors can be removed and replaced.

pare Robert Guge's techniques in chapter 2.) "I get too itchy. I want to get to the wood. But that works for me." However, if it is a competition piece, he will spend more time sketching and laying out the setting and positions of the birds.

But for most of his work, Scheel makes what he calls pattern sheets. On a large piece of oaktag, he may have drawings for a dozen different birds. On some there may be background drawings or habitat sketches. But these are not just drawings: They are patterns that can be removed from the pattern sheet and put back for reference.

95 Percent Knifework

"I use the knife 95 percent of the time," Scheel says. He does have a Foredom and all its accessories, but he uses them only occasionally, and only then for sanding areas he cannot do by hand. Scheel explains: "Being a miniature carver, there's not much to remove in the first place from the bandsawed block to the

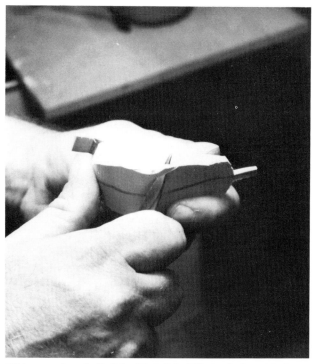

With a very sharp knife, Scheel finds little difficulty dealing with changes in grain direction or even the hardness of the wood.

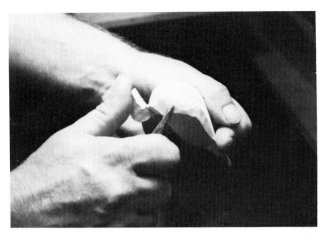

Scheel says he does 95 percent of his carving with a knife. In fact, he feels that if the knife is used properly, it is superior to grinding tools for his kind of work.

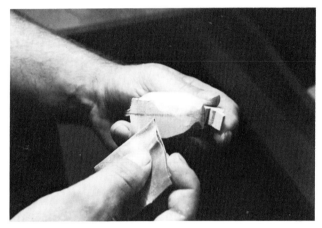

Facets or flat areas left by the knifework can be removed with a fine sandpaper.

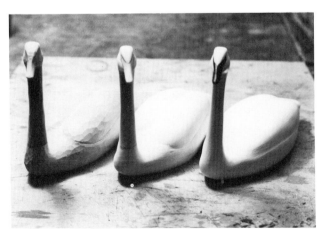

Done with knives and sandpaper, these swans show the transition from an early to a finished state.

finished carving. And I can remove more wood with a single sharp knife stroke than I can with twenty strokes with a grinder."

Scheel wonders how much those who use the Foredom Tool exclusively really know about wood and traditional carving. "With a knife, you have to know the grain, how the wood is to be removed, and have completely, absolutely sharp tools. Maybe that's too much work for a carver today. A grinder has a lot of forgiveness. It takes wood away fast or slow. But one wrong cut with a knife, and that's it."

Still, he says he can do anything with a knife that another carver can do with a Foredom.

Does Scheel have other reasons for using a knife? Aside from having used one since he was six years old, and finding it a comfortable tool, Scheel compares a good, sharp knife-cut to a polished surface. Plus, he can touch up the planes left by the knife with sand-

This sparrow hawk was done with knives. Note the splits on this raptor's breast, also done with a knife.

paper more easily than he can clean up ridges left by grinding stones.

Scheel adds that he does not gesso his birds. What does that have to do with knifework as opposed to grinding? He answers, "When you have ridges left by a grinding tool that were not removed with sanding, they don't go away with gesso. I saw every mistake I made with my Foredom after I painted. With my knife cuts, I can sand and burn and paint right over the raw wood."

Sanding means using 220-grit paper. He says that there are no nicks or scratches made with this sandpaper. "If I worked even with the finest ruby carver, I'd have to start with a 120-grit paper and rough-sand first," he says.

Though Scheel has a dozen different knives at his disposal, he uses only two or three at a time. In fact, he says he could do an entire carving with only two

Scheel claims he can do an entire carving with only two knives, with most of the work being done with the longer blade. Both of these knives were made by Cheston Knotts. (See appendix for address.)

knives. One of them has a short blade he uses in the early stages of carving. The other has a long blade, one that is longer than most of his carvings.

He does admit that the knife is a frustrating tool when the wood tears or doesn't cut the way he wants it to. With a Foredom, however, a carver can "tame a piece of wood any way he wants to." Still, Scheel can make a curlew with a long curving bill out of one piece of wood with little trouble, saying that one has to understand the grain, where to put pressure on the wood, and where not to.

Keeping a Knife Sharp

Scheel states that it is essential that a knife be kept sharp so it can carve against the grain if necessary. So insistent is he on sharpness that he touches up a knife no less than every five minutes when working a piece of wood. To do this, he uses nothing more than a leather strap and a rouge sharpening compound that he puts on the leather. Some of his knives, he says, have been used for seven or eight years without ever having been put to a grinding stone. "It's easy to get the temper [the strength imparted by controlled heating and cooling] out with too much heat. But doing this by hand, you don't even get the tool warm," though he admits that the steel will change shape after years of being stroked on leather.

No Secret to Burning

Scheel says that he textures and burns with a standard burning tool, as finely as he can. Does he use a

Note the layering and definition of the individual feathers. They are made with stop or straight-in cuts. Also, there are no inserts on the bird.

Touching up the blade every five minutes during his carving, Scheel uses a piece of leather impregnated with a rough compound.

He says he burns as finely as he can, letting the burning accentuate the still-to-be-applied paints where he can.

Scheel uses a standard burning tool with a sharpened tip.

Another view of the sparrow hawk, also known as a kestrel, shows the burning details.

Shown here is a miniature wild turkey.

Here Scheel has started burning the turkey's back.

This great blue heron miniature has been completely burned.

special tip? He answers, "I use the same tip used by the guy doing the full-size decorative decoy."

Scheel adds that people ask him if he uses a magnifying glass to do such fine work. He says he does not. And if he did, "What difference would it make? Some people are looking for formulas, or they are skeptical about your work."

Color Sampling on Wood

Scheel says he does not make extensive color charts but does put color samples directly onto wood. However, the woods he uses are maple and birch veneers, left from his years of doing marquetry.

He finds that these veneers approximate the color of the basswood he prefers to use for his carvings. Why does he not use paper as others do? He answers that on paper the colors would be misleading, and they would come out much darker on the basswood.

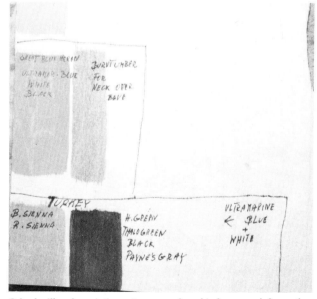

Scheel will make painting notes on maple or birch veneers left over from his marquetry work. These woods resemble basswood, his primary carving material. Also, he uses no primer such as gesso, preferring to paint directly on the wood so that it, the burning, and the paints can interact.

Here he has actually sketched the back of a bird and has made "color notes" on it.

Scheel may even make a sketch of a bird on a veneer piece and paint over that. Or he may make a chart of feather patterns and paint them, making notes of what colors he used. However, he does not mix colors and save them for a future project, saying that he may not be totally satisfied with the mixes.

Wood, Burning, and Acrylics Working Together

Since Scheel does not use an undercoat of gesso, he tries to have the color of the wood and the paint interact to achieve the tones he wants. This is obviously why he samples his colors on unprepared veneers. But he can also take advantage of burning lines to contribute to the color tones. With a bird like a black duck, then, he will burn fairly dark lines, but a duck with white will be burned much lighter.

Of the actual painting, he says that he uses thin layers of paint, sometimes four or five washes. Or he will work with combinations. "I might undercoat with two dark green washes and wash over that with two dark blue washes to get a bluish green sheen instead of trying to mix that color beforehand. To me the color mix would look pasted on. But with only four or five thin washes, you can still see the grain and part of the burning even with a fairly intense color. So everything works together – the wood, the paint, the burning."

Even on a very white bird, he will still apply thin washes of paint, even if it is seven or eight coats, rather than mix up a heavy paint and apply only two coats. "It will look more natural," he says. "There's a softness to the look and it still preserves all the burning details and texturing that a heavy undercoating and wash would cover up."

He adds that though he uses strictly acrylics, he will at times mix in some opaque watercolor or gouache. Particularly with white, opaque watercolor thickens the washes and adds some sheen. But he warns that watercolor by itself is not permanent and will rub off with touching and handling.

Choosing a Wood

Why does Scheel prefer basswood for his birds? He says he has tried all the woods used by carvers today but always returns to basswood. "Jelutong does not carve well," he states. "And the pores I don't like on a small piece. They overpower the carving."

He does say that he likes tupelo. "I would use it more extensively if I were using the Foredom Tool more. It's one of the nicest woods I've seen as far as sanding goes, but it does not carve willingly. So your knife has to be absolutely perfect. Then it will cut well and with clean cuts."

Scheel will use tupelo for habitat. He will even do flowers out of the wood, admitting that the Foredom Tool is ideal for shaping them. "You can get the wood so thin you can almost look through it and see light. And if you're not very clumsy, it will stay. It is very good for flowers because of its not having pores, and it paints so well."

He will also use tupelo for making rocks, saying, "It's light and that makes it perfect for that."

Still another use of the wood is for feather inserts. He says tupelo is very flexible, and when wetted and ironed, it will bend into new shapes. For this, he feels tupelo is superior to basswood.

Though Scheel uses basswood for the wildfowl he carves, he prefers to make rocks out of tupelo.

These diminutive leaves are made from thin sheets of brass.

Here can be seen how small he makes his habitat displays.

A way of holding metallic plants when painting is by inserting them into a cork. These grasses are made from copper, a metal that can easily be shaped.

Still, he says, "Good basswood is good, though some of it gets too hard. You'd think you were carving maple. But the kind I use comes from the lake area of upstate New York. I haven't had a bad piece of it. It's soft with a tight grain and no hard spots."

Metallic Plants

Not all habitat is made from tupelo, however. Many of his plant parts he will make out of brass or copper, though he prefers thin brass. "Brass is springy and does hold its shape well," he notes. Copper is too soft and it does not take much to bend it out of shape.

Why does he not use paper as Louis Kean does (chapter 7)? He answers, "Paper does lend itself to long thin grasses, and makes a more natural looking grass, but I prefer metal. So I make them out of brass even though they take longer to make and are more work."

The wood sorrel, part of Scheel's winter wren composition, is made of brass. Before painting, he primes his plants with a dull white Rustoleum spray, which keeps the metal from "bleeding" through and discoloring the paint.

For a great blue heron composition, brass is used to represent grasses. Brass holds its shape well, Scheel says.

Painting Metal

Scheel says he uses acrylics for painting his metallic plants, though he will undercoat them with a dull Rustoleum white or wrought iron white out of a spray can. These are really primers, he says, for he cannot apply water-based paints like acrylics directly onto metal. He says that both of these primers keep the metal from leaking acids or other chemicals that will discolor the paints.

Making Stones and Gravel

As with the flowers, not all the stones and rocks of his habitat are made out of wood. For some, he will use Durham's Rock Hard Water Putty, a powder that is combined with water. When mixed to a stiff consistency, it becomes like a heavy clay, he says. When that happens, he will break the mass into little pieces. Using two stainless steel bowls, he will put some of the pieces into one bowl, add some of the powder, cover the bowl with the other one, and "shake them like a mixed drink." What forms are small stones or pebbles. What keeps them from sticking together is the addition of some dry Durham powder.

After shaking the mix for a while, he can break the pieces into smaller ones and continue the shaking. When left on a piece of paper overnight, they will dry rock hard and can be placed on a base of still-soft Tuf Carv so that they do not fall off their base.

When acrylic paint is applied, says Scheel, the pebbles act like sponges, soaking up and dispersing the paint. "You don't have to paint every pebble. You can put just drops of paint on them and actually give them a more natural look."

Epoxy Eyes

Unlike the other carvers featured in this book, Scheel rarely uses glass eyes for his miniatures. Most of them would be impossible to obtain, he explains, because they would have to be so small. The eyes of a baby duck would be only one millimeter or less in diameter, he says.

What he does, then, is use a five-minute epoxy. "I take a drop of the epoxy and wait until it is neither watery nor too hard. It has to form a bubble. That is, it must not flatten out but remain beveled. So a fresh mix would flatten out and too hard would not adhere."

However, he prepares the surface of the wood by first painting the eyes inside a circle made with a

The eye for this great blue heron was first painted on the wood. Then a not-too-liquidy drop of a two-part, clear epoxy was put over it.

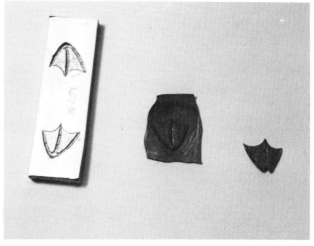

Scheel makes his miniatures' feet out of lead. The mold he uses is a piece of aluminum with the outlines of a left and right foot engraved into it. The piece in the center is lead that was pounded into the mold. The foot on the right was cut out.

Removing the background from the impressed foot is done with a knife.

sharpened tube. He then dips a toothpick into the epoxy and transfers that to the painted eye.

When would he use a glass eye? He says only when the actual eye size gets bigger than one-eighth inch in diameter.

Feet of Lead

Another unique technique Scheel uses is making feet out of lead. He draws onto a hardened piece of aluminum the shapes of the right and left feet of his birds. He then engraves the feet into the metal to the depth and thickness he wants. "This becomes my mold," he says. "Then I take a thin piece of hammered-out lead and pound that into the mold to get an exact impression of the foot I engraved."

He will then cut around each foot to separate excess lead. After that, he rounds the edges with a file.

Burrs of excess lead can be carved away.

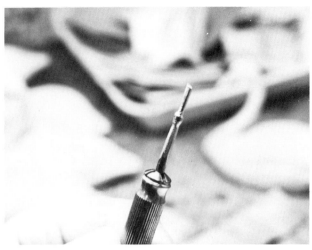

Scheel uses a holding device for the upper part of the foot, which is made out of brass. The narrow part at the end of the foot holds the bird to its base or habitat.

More refining on the foot can be done with small files.

A slot is filed into the foot to accept the lead toes and webbing.

The finished foot is then ready to be inserted into a bird. This foot is for a loon.

On a soldering block, he solders both parts of the foot together.

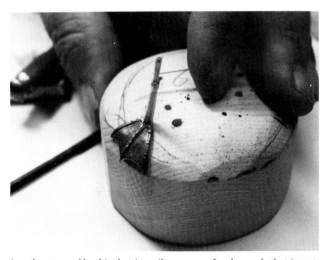

An advantage of lead is that it easily assumes the shape of what it rests on.

What does he use for the leg? This is made from a piece of brass rod, shaped with a file or burrs in a Foredom Tool. The foot is soldered to the leg and the solder is cleaned up and shaped with files.

"The biggest advantage to the lead is that you can shape it to the contour of whatever it is standing on without leaving any gaps. I think this is the biggest thing I've come up with for miniatures. But this wouldn't work the same way for a full-size bird. The lead would have to be poured into a mold."

A Wood Duck with a Turned Head

This wood duck is only two inches tall. It is in a fall setting of dried leaves and grasses. Scheel says, however, that the plumage might be fall, winter, or even spring. Fall leaves and grasses do not clash with the colors of the bird, he explains.

Another feature of this wood duck is that the head was severed, turned, and glued into place.

This wood duck has feet made of lead and brass. Notice how the toes and webbing were bent to conform to the wood it stands on.

The turned head gives more life to a carving, Scheel explains.

Scheel makes his small stones and gravel from Durham's Rock Hard Water Putty. After a quantity is made by adding water to the powdery putty, it is then broken into small pieces and shaken between two bowls, not unlike making a mixed drink.

On this sparrow hawk can be seen a perfect neck joint. If Scheel cannot achieve a perfect fit, he will discard the piece rather than use a filler.

On this egret can be seen the neck joint after the head was cut and glued into its new position.

These swans all show different neck joints.

The primaries for the duck were inserted, and the head was cut off, turned, and glued into place with a five-minute epoxy. "I never use fillers for any joint," he says. "If the joint doesn't fit properly, I'd rather make another piece. I just don't think a filler works well on miniatures." As for the seam line, Scheel says he is not trying to hide it. "That's part of my technique, and that's how they're constructed."

The top of the base was recessed one-eighth inch and filled with Tuf Carv. While that was soft, Scheel pressed pebbles made from Durham's Rock Hard Water Putty into it. The plants, made of brass, were put in later by drilling holes for them.

A Black Duck and Chicks

Scheel sees this piece as having a "cute, motherly look, more likable than if there were a single standing duck."

The black duck was burned dark so that the burning would show through the paint. Also, the base was recessed one-eighth inch to receive the Durham putty stones and gravel.

This black duck has two chicks. Young birds are something Scheel enjoys making.

Carved out of basswood, the chicks were undercoated with gesso and stippled with other paints to create a downy look.

A way to hold the black duck chicks for painting is to put them on a cork.

He adds, "Not many people like to carve ducklings, but I feel comfortable with them." He has also done quail and grouse with baby birds.

These young are, like the mother, carved out of basswood. He explains that they do not have feathers but a down. To create that look, he undercoats the wood with gesso and stipples the surface so that it is rough looking.

A Sparrow Hawk

There are no inserts on this bird, so the primaries were carved from the original block. But he did cut the head and glue it into a different position.

For this composition, Scheel did use paper grasses. "The effect is nice, but I'm not sure about their durability," he says. He also points out that he used glass eyes for this bird rather than epoxy.

This sparrow hawk or kestrel composition stands nine inches high. The habitat comprises brass grasses, tupelo rocks, and Durham's Rock Hard Water Putty for the gravel.

Note the layout of the coverts and primaries on the sparrow hawk.

A Winter Wren

This bird is actual size, though he will do most song birds slightly undersized, even if by only one-half inch. He feels this is a more pleasing proportion.

The wood sorrel that is part of the wren's habitat is constructed from brass with a primer and acrylics applied over it.

A Great Blue Heron with Brass Plumage

This bird, which stands only five inches high, has brass inserts on its head. Scheel felt that any other material would break. But the other feathers are carved from the block.

The head for the sparrow hawk was turned, but the eyes are glass, not epoxy.

This is a good view of the burning details and how the primaries cross.

The winter wren in this composition of wood, gravel, and wood sorrel is full-size.

Shown here is the rump of the wren.

Note Scheel's fine detailing on the breast of the heron.

The great blue heron stands five inches high on brass legs.

Here can be seen the layout of the back feathers and burning details.

Brass inserts were applied to the head to represent the plumage. Scheel felt wood inserts would have been too fragile.

The back of the unpainted heron can be seen here.

This great blue heron has yet to be painted. The blue for it will comprise white, black, Payne's gray, and ultramarine blue.

In contrast to the nearly finished heron is one recently carved with a knife. Note the turn of the head.

This is Scheel's composition of three condors.

Shown here is a good detail of the upper condor.

Endangered Condors

Carved for the 1985 World Championship Carving Competition, these three condors represent not only this country's most endangered species but also its largest flying bird, with a wingspan that can reach nine feet. Scheel says the condor may be extinct in the wild within the next decade since only six birds are left in the wild.

Despite the criticism he has heard about this being an ugly bird, Scheel says that after four weeks of working on them, he grew fond of his condors. Why did he choose them for World Competition? He explains, "Everyone does hawks and owls for birds of prey. To me that's stereotyped. I had the idea to do something different."

Bamboo Neck Feathers

The three birds are each carved from one piece, though the heads were cut and glued. But what is unusual are the neck feathers that form what looks like a collar. These he made from bamboo splinters that were wetted and steam-bent using a burning tool. Each collar has approximately 80 pieces set into a carved groove in the neck, and each was glued in separately.

Why did he choose bamboo? He had experimented with different materials such as basswood splinters, but they broke off too easily. "Finally, I took a look in my shed, saw an old garden rake made out of bamboo and discovered it was so strong. You can splice it down to almost nothing." (Compare Habbart Dean's use of bamboo in chapter 4.) He believes there might be other applications for bamboo. One might be substituting it for the brass used on the great blue heron's head.

Composition and Japanese Design

Why did Scheel choose to make three condors? He believes three birds give a more balanced setting than two. "You can make a nice pyramid shape with three." He says this is his favorite compositional form, with a top bird, a low bird, and one in the middle. In fact, this is the third composition he has done with three birds for the World Competition.

He says there are precedents for this in the art of Japanese flower arrangements, "with things going upward while still bringing the eye back. It's for this

reason I don't have grasses pointing away from a carving, but instead pointing inward." He says that Ernest Muehlmatt (featured in *How to Carve Wildfowl*) taught him much of this. Says Scheel, "He's a master. He can make an arrangement like no one else I know."

Artist Freedom

"I want what I and others are doing to be an art form, not a textbook thing where every feather is accounted for," Scheel says. "I want to have some kind of artistic freedom. So I'm more interested that the bird looks right, is designed right with the right shape and attitude, than is right."

He says he knows carvers who could count every feather and transfer each one to the carving. "There's nothing wrong with that," he says, "but it doesn't really

Here is a detail of its side.

Burning contributes to the color of the birds, though Scheel applies an acrylic mix made up of a warm black with blue and green washes.

mean that much. The person who is going to own that piece isn't going to be aware of that anyway. But if the bird looks wrong, he'll probably know that."

He feels, then, that many carvers lose themselves in details. "And the people who call this a craft instead of an art should keep this in mind. A piece of art has leeway. What we try to do, then, is make the bird look pleasing when nature itself doesn't always look pleasing."

He adds that the artist has the ability to choose the stage at which a bird is pleasing or dramatic, pointing out that even a number of the old decoy makers did this.

The Essence of an Artist

Scheel believes he can distinguish between a craftsman and an artist. "I think someone who doesn't really have the interest in birds and makes a table full of them, he's a craftsman."

He also believes that a craft can be learned far more easily than art. "If you're intelligent and have certain skills and good hands, you can learn. And you can even learn decorative bird carving. But how far can you go?

"Unfortunately, many of those people doing this as a craft are at tables at shows next to those who have brought this to an art form, and many spectators cannot make the distinction."

What, then, is art, and how does he define an artist? Scheel states, "You have to be an artist to do art. You have to have that talent inside of you. You live your art. I eat, sleep, and drink this. No matter where I am, I still catch myself thinking, 'How should I do this pose?' I read books about birds all the time. If I go on

Shown here is another detail of the upper condor. The neck feathers were made from tines of a bamboo rake.

Scheel found that basswood inserts were too easily broken.

Each neck collar comprises some 80 pieces of bamboo.

Scheel has learned much about Japanese design principles, which have the observer's eye moving upward, then back. For this reason, he has these brass grasses bending inward so that the eye does not drift away from the composition.

vacation, I'll probably come back with more ideas than when I left, even though I probably shouldn't have been thinking about the carving.

"So I like to think of myself as an artist, even though I'm a craftsman as well. In fact, when I get an application for something, I write on it 'artist'. I'm proud of that."

Recognizing Fine Art

Scheel believes what he and others do will not be recognized as a fine art until bird carving separates itself from the commercial aspects. These include tool vendors and craftspeople who display their wares in shows and exhibits. "I believe the fine art is already there in the pieces. And I don't believe you can do

very much more with them. You can't make the birds chirp or fly. So now it's got to be recognized. Shows will eventually have to screen their pieces and even put them on pedestals. If you put them next to tools, they don't come off."

He also feels that the public must learn what goes into a composition of bird sculpture. "There's a lot more to doing a piece than making a watercolor. You have to be familiar not only with colors, but also with tools, metals, woods, paper, epoxies, anatomy. You have to have all this in your head just to make one composition. So why shouldn't this be recognized as fine art?"

Bibliography

Audubon, John James. *The Birds of America.* Crown Publisher. 1966.

Ayres, Christopher, and Graham, Frank, Jr. *Gulls: A Social History.* Random House. 1975.

Barber, Joel. *Wild Fowl Decoys.* Dover Publications, Inc. 1954.

Bishop, Richard, and Williams, Russ. *The Ways of Waterfowl.* J.G. Ferguson Company. 1971.

Boyer, Trevor, and Burton, Philip. *Vanished Eagles.* Dodd, Mead & Company. 1981.

Burk, Bruce. *Complete Waterfowl Studies, Volume I—Dabbling and Whistling Ducks.* Schiffer Publishing Ltd. 1984.

———. *Complete Waterfowl Studies, Volume II—Diving Ducks.* Schiffer Publishing Ltd. 1984.

———. *Complete Waterfowl Studies, Volume III—Geese and Swans.* Schiffer Publishing Ltd. 1984.

———. *Game Bird Carving.* Winchester Press. 1972.

———. *Waterfowl Studies.* Winchester Press. 1976.

Burke, Ken, Ed. *How to Attract Birds.* Ortho Books. 1983.

Casey, Peter N. *Birds of Canada.* Discovery Books. 1984.

Chapell, Carl and Sullivan, Clark. Wildlife Woodcarvers. Stackpole Books. 1986.

Clement, Roland C. *The Living World of Audubon.* Grosset & Dunlop. 1974.

Coles, Charles, and Maurice Pledger. *Game Birds.* Dodd, Mead & Company. 1985.

Connett, Eugene V., III. *Duck Decoys.* Durrell Publications, D. Van Nostrand. 1953.

Coykendall, Rolf. *Duck Decoys and How to Rig Them.* Holt, Rinehart and Winston. 1955. Winchester. 1983.

Day, Albert M. *North American Waterfowl.* Stackpole Books. 1949.

Dermid, Jack, and Hester, Eugene. *The World of the Wood Duck.* J.B. Lippincott Company. 1973.

Dougall, Robert, and Ede, Basil. *Basil Ede's Birds.* Van Nostrand, Reinhold. 1981.

Earnest, Adele. *The Art of the Decoy: American Bird Carvings.* Schiffer Publishing Ltd. 1982.

Eckert, Allan W., and Karalus, Karl F. *The Wading Birds of North America.* Doubleday. 1981.

Elman, Robert. *The Atlantic Flyway.* Winchester Press. 1971.

Forbush, Edward H., and May, John R. *A Natural History of American Birds of Eastern and Central North America.* Bramhall House. 1955.

Frank, Charles W., Jr. *Anatomy of a Waterfowl.* Pelican Publishing Company. 1982.

Gilley, Wendell H. *The Art of Bird Carving.* Hillcrest Publishers, Inc. 1972.

Gooders, John. *Collins British Birds.* William Collins Sons & Co Ltd, 1982.

Harrison, Hal H. *Wood Warblers' World.* Simon and Schuster. 1984.

Hochbaum, H. Albert. *The Canvasback on a Prairie Marsh.* Stackpole Books. 1944. University of Nebraska. 1981.

———. *To Ride the Wind.* Richard Bonnycastle Book. 1973.

Hosking, Eric. *Eric Hosking's Waders.* Pelham Books Ltd. 1983.

Hyde, Dayton O., Ed. *Raising Wild Ducks in Captivity.* E.P. Dutton and Company. 1974.

James, Ross. *Glen Loates Birds of North America.* Prentice Hall of Canada. 1979.

Jeklin, Isidor, and Waite, Donald E., *The Art of Photographing North American Birds.* Whitecap Books. 1984.

Johnsgard, Paul A. *Ducks, Geese, and Swans of the World.* University of Nebraska. 1978.

———. *The Plovers, Sandpipers, and Snipes of the World.* University of Nebraska Press. 1981.

———. *Waterfowl.* University of Nebraska Press. 1968.

———. *Waterfowl of North America.* Indiana University Press. 1975.

Kangas, Gene and Linda. *Decoys: A North American Survey.* Hillcrest Publications, Inc. 1983.

Klein, Tom, *Loon Magic.* Paper Birch Press, Inc. 1985.

Kortwright, Frank F. *Ducks, Geese and Swans of North America.* Stackpole Books. 1976.

Landsdowne, J. Fenwick. *Birds of the West Coast.* Houghton Mifflin Company. 1976.

———. *Birds of the West Coast II.* Houghton Mifflin Company. 1980.

Landsdowne, J. Fenwick, and Livingston, John A. *Birds of the Eastern Forest.* Houghton Mifflin Company. 1968.

———. *Birds of the Eastern Forest II.* Houghton Mifflin Company. 1970.

———. *Birds of the Northern Forest.* Houghton Mifflin Company. 1966.

Lawson, Glenn. *The Story of Lem Ward.* Schiffer Publishing Ltd. 1984.

LeMaster, Richard. *Art of the Wooden Bird.* Contemporary Books, Inc. 1982.

———. *The Great Gallery of Ducks.* Contemporary Books, Inc. 1985.

———. *Waterfowl.* Contemporary Books, Inc. 1983.

———. *Wildlife in Wood.* Contemporary Books, Inc. 1978.

Line, Les. *Audubon Society Book of Wild Birds.* Harry N. Abrams. 1976.

Lyttle, Richard B. *Birds of North America.* Gallery Books. 1983.

Mackey, William J., Jr. *American Bird Decoys.* Schiffer Publishing Ltd. 1965.

Matthiessen, Peter. *The Shore Birds of North America.* Viking Press. 1967.

Meanley, Brooke. *Waterfowl of the Chesapeake.* Tidewater Publishing Company. 1982.

Mitchell, Alan. *Lambart's Birds of Shore and Estuary.* Scribners. 1979.

———. *Field Guide to Birds of North America.* National Geographic Society. 1983.

———. *Stalking Birds with Color Camera.* National Geographic Society. 1961.

———. *Water, Prey and Game Birds.* National Geographic Society. 1965.

Mohrhardt, David. *Bird Reference Drawings.* Publication of David Mohrhardt, 314 N. Bluff, Berrien Springs, Michigan 49103. 1985.

———. *Bird Studies.* Publication of David Mohrhardt, 314 N. Bluff, Berrien Springs, Michigan 49103. 1986.

Pearson, T. Gilbert, Editor-in-Chief. *Birds of America.* Garden City Books. 1917.

Peck, Robert McCracken. *A Celebration of Birds.* Walker and Company. 1982.

Peterson, Roger Tory. *A Field Guide to the Birds.* Houghton Mifflin Company. 1980.

Poole, Robert M., Ed. *The Wonder of Birds.* National Geographic Society. 1983.

Pough, Richard H. *Audubon Water Bird Guide.* Doubleday and Company. 1951.

Queeny, Edgar M. *Prairie Wings.* Schiffer Publishing Ltd., 1979. Dover Publications, Inc. 1983.

Schroeder, Roger. *How to Carve Wildfowl.* Stackpole Books. 1984.

———. *Waterfowl Carving with J.D. Sprankle.* Stackpole Books. 1985.

———. *Woodcarving Illustrated.* Stackpole Books. 1983.

———. *Woodcarving Illustrated Book 2.* Stackpole Books. 1985.

Scott, Peter. *Key to the Wildfowl of the World.* Wildfowl Trust. 1957.

———. *Morning Flight.* Watson and Viney Ltd. 1935.

———. *Observations of Wildfowl.* Cornell University Press. 1980.

———. *Wild Chorus.* Robert Maclehose and Company Ltd. 1938.

Simon, Hilda. *The Splendor of Iridescence.* Dodd, Mead and Company. 1971.

Small, Anne. *Masters of Decorative Bird Carving.* Winchester Press. 1981.

Sowls, Lyle K. *Prairie Ducks.* Stackpole Books. 1955. University of Nebraska. 1978.

Stepanek, O. *Birds of Heath and Marshland.* West Book House. 1962.

Terres, John K. *The Audubon Society Encyclopedia of North American Birds.* Alfred A. Knopf. 1980.

Todd, Frank S. *Waterfowl.* Harcourt Brace Jovanovich. 1979.

Tunnicliffe, Charles. *Tunnicliffe's Birds.* Little, Brown.

———. *A Sketchbook of Birds.* Holt, Rinehart and Winston. 1979.

Van Wormer, Joe. *The World of the Swan.* J.B. Lippincott Company. 1972.

Veasey, Tricia. *Waterfowl Illustrated.* Schiffer Publishing Ltd. 1983.

Walsh, Harry M. *The Outlaw Gunner.* Tidewater Publishers. 1971.

Williamson, C.S. *Honker.* D. Van Nostrand Company Inc. 1967.

Wright, Bruce. *High Tide and an East Wind.* Stackpole Books. 1954.

Magazines of interest to wildfowl carvers:

Breakthrough Magazine, P.O. Box 1320, Loganville, Georgia 30249.

Chip Chats, The National Woodcarver's Association, 7424 Miami Ave., Cincinnati, Ohio 45243.

Wildfowl Art, Journal of the Ward Foundation, 655 S. Salisbury Blvd., Salisbury, MD 21801.

Wildfowl Carving and Collecting, Box 1831, Harrisburg, PA 17105.

Sources for Supplies

Al's Decoy Supplies
27 Connaught Ave.
London, Ontario N5Y 3A4
CANADA
519-451-4729

Albert Constantine & Sons, Inc.
2050 Eastchester Rd.
Bronx, NY 10461
212-792-1600

American Sales Co.
Box 741
Reseda, CA 91335
213-881-2808

Big Sky Carvers
8256 Huffine Ln.
Bozeman, MT 59715
406-586-0008

Buck Run Carvings
Box 151, Gully Rd.
Aurora, NY 13026
315-364-8414

Canadian Woodworker Ltd.
1391 St. James St.
Winnipeg, Manitoba R3H 0Z1
CANADA
204-786-3196

The Carver's Barn
P.O. Box 686
Rte. 28
Hearth & Eagle Shopping Plaza
South Yarmouth, MA 02664

Carvers Corner
153 Passaic St.
Garfield, NJ 07026
201-472-7511

Chez La Rogue
Rt. 3, Box 148
Foley, AL 36535
205-943-1237

Craft Cove, Inc.
2315 W. Glen Ave.
Peoria, IL 61614
309-692-8365

CraftWoods
10921 York Rd.
Cockeysville, MD 21030
301-667-9663

Curt's Waterfowl Corner
123 Le Boeuf St.
Montegut, LA 70377
504-594-3012

The Duck Butt Boys
P.O. Box 2051
Metairie, LA 70004
504-443-3797

Electric & Tool Service Co.
19442 Conant Ave.
Detroit, MI 48234
313-366-3830

P.C. English Enterprises
P.O. Box 7937
Lafayette Blvd.
Fredericksburg, VA 22404
703-371-1306

Exotic Woods Inc.
2483 Industrial Street
Burlington, Ontario L7P 1A6
CANADA
416-335-8066

Feather Merchants
279 Boston Post Rd.
Madison, CT 06443
203-245-1231

The Fine Tool Shops, Inc.
P.O. Box 1262
20 Backus Ave.
Danbury, CT 06810
800-243-1037

The Foredom Electric Co.
Rt. 6
Bethel, CT 06801
203-792-8622

Forest Products
P.O. Box 12
Avon, OH 44011
216-937-5630

Garrett Wade
161 Avenue of the Americas
New York, NY 10013
800-212-2942

Gerry's Tool Shed
1111 Flint Road
Unit 6
Downsview, Ontario M3J 3C7
CANADA
416-665-6677

Gesswein
Woodworking Products Division
255 Hancock Ave.
P.O. Box 3998
Bridgeport, CT 06605
800-243-4466
203-366-5400

J. H. Kline Carving Shop
R.D. 2, Forge Hill Rd.
Manchester, PA 17345
717-266-3501

Ken Jones
P.O. Box 563
Salem, NH 03079

Kent's Woodshed
625 W. Main
Broussard, LA 70518
318-837-9470

Lee Valley Tools Ltd.
2680 Queensview Dr.
Ottawa, Ontario K2B 8J9
CANADA
613-596-0350

Lewis Tool and Supply Co.
912 West 8th St.
Loveland, CO 80537
303-663-4405

Little Mountain Carving Supply
Rt. 2, Box 1329
Front Royal, VA 22630
703-662-6160

L. I. Woodcarvers Supply
60 Glouster Rd.
Massapequa, NY 11758
516-799-7999

Master Paint Systems
P.O. Box 1320
Loganville, GA 30249
800-334-8012

Montana Decoy Co.
Route 1
Box 251
Wilsall, MT 59086
406-578-2235

Northwest Carving Supply
P.O. Box 5211
216 West Ridge
Bozeman, MT 59715
406-587-8057

Denny Rogers
309 Daisy Ln.
Normal, Illinois 61761
309-452-8005

Ross Tool Co.
257 Queen Street, West
Toronto, Ontario M5V 1Z4
CANADA
416-598-2498

Sand-Rite Mfg. Co.
1611 N. Sheffield Ave.
Chicago, IL 60614
312-642-7287

Seto Co., Inc.
"Serabian Tool Co."
P.O. Box 148
195 Highway 36
West Keansburg, NJ 07734
201-495-0040

Tool Bin
10575 Clark Rd.
Davisburg, MI 48019
313-625-0390

Veasey Studios
955 Blue Ball Rd.
Elkton, MD 21921
301-392-3850

Joe Veracke and Assoc.
P.O. Box 48962
Chicago, IL 60648
312-824-9696

Warren Tool Co.
Rt. 1 14AS
Rhinebeck, NY 12572
914-876-7817

Welbeck Sawmill Ltd.
R. R. 2
Durham, Ontario N0G 1R0
CANADA
519-369-2144

Wildlife Carvings Supply
317 Holyoke Ave.
Beach Haven, NJ 08008
609-492-1871

Wildlife Woodcarvers
Avian Art, Inc.
4288 Staunton Dr.
Swartz Creek, MI 48473
313-732-6300

Wood Carvers Supply Co.
3056 Excelsior Blvd.
Minneapolis, MN 55416
612-927-7491

Wood Carvers Supply, Inc.
P.O. Box 8928
Norfolk, VA 23503
804-583-8928

Woodcraft Supply
41 Atlantic Ave.
Box 4000
Woburn, MA 01888
800-225-1153

Wood-Regan Instrument Co.
Vermiculation Pen
107 Forest St.
Montclair, NJ 07042

Books
Books Plus
133 St. Joseph's Blvd.
P.O. Box 731
Lodi, NJ 07644
201-777-3033

Highwood Bookshop
P.O. Box 1246
Traverse City, MI 49684
616-271-3898

Burning Tools
Chesterfield Craft Shop
P.O. Box 208
Chesterfield, NJ 08620

Colwood Electronics
715 Westwood Ave.
Long Branch, NJ 07740
201-222-2568

Hot Tools
7 Hawkes St.
P.O. Box 615
Marblehead, MA 01945
617-639-1000

Leisure Time Products
2 Hillview Dr.
Barrington, IL 60010

Carving Knives
Cheston Knotts
106 S. Ford Ave.
Wilmington, DE 19805
302-652-5046

Lominack Knives
P.O. Box 1189
Abingdon, VA 24210
703-628-6591

Makepeace
1482 Maple Ave.
Paoli, PA 19301
215-644-6318

Cast Feet
Richard Delise
920 Springwood Dr.
West Chester, PA 19380
215-436-4377

David Taylor
78 Grove St.
South Braintree, MA 02184

Cast Study Bills
Bob Bolle
26421 Compson
Roseville, MI 48066
313-773-3153

Bob Miller
General Delivery
Evergreen, LA 71333
318-346-4270

Oscar Johnston Wildlife Gallery
Rt. 2, Box 1224
Smith River, CA 95567
707-487-4401

John W. Sebalusky
P.O. Box 1062
Bensalem, PA 19020

Glass Eyes
Carvers Eye
P.O. Box 16692
Portland, OR 97216

Eyes
9630 Dundalk
Spring, TX 77379
713-376-2897

Hutch Decoy Carving Ltd.
7715 Warsaw Ave.
Glen Burnie, MD 21061
301-437-2501

Schoepfer Eyes
138 West 31st St.
New York, NY 10001
212-736-6934

Robert J. Smith
14900 W. 31st Ave.
Golden, CO 80401
303-278-1828

Tohickon Glass Eyes
P.O. Box 15
Erwinna, PA 18920
800-441-5983

Grinding Tool Burrs and Accessories
Pfingst & Company, Inc.
P.O. Box 377
South Plainfield, NJ 07080

Gamzon Bros. Inc.
21 W. 46th St.
New York, NY 10036
212-719-2550
800-223-6464

Molded Birds
Greenwing Enterprises
Rt. 2, Box 731-B
Chester, MD 21619
301-643-3717

Paints and Brushes
Jim and Beebe Hopper
731 Beech Ave.
Chula Vista, CA 92010
619-420-8766

Christian J. Hummul Co.
404 Brooklets Ave.
Easton, MD 21601
301-636-2232

Windsor & Newton Inc.
555 Winsor Dr.
Secaucus, NJ 07094
201-864-9100

Ruby Carvers
Elkay Products Co.
1506 Sylvan Glade
Austin, TX 78745
512-441-1155

Taxidermists
American Wildlife Studio
Box 71, Tuckahoe Rd.
Dorothy, NJ 08317
609-476-2941

Cooper Taxidermy
County Road 50W.
Valparaiso, Indiana
462-0643

Frank Newmyer
5783 Garthby
Union Lake, MI 48085
313-363-1243

Mike's Taxidermy Studio
5019 Lolly Lane
Perry Hall, MD 21128
301-256-0860

Richard Smoker
19 W. Pear St.
Crisfield, MD 21817
301-968-3044

Video Cassettes
"Bird Carving: Art in Detail"
Windsor Promotions, Inc.
127 Bruckner Blvd.
New York, NY 10454

"World Championship Video Series featuring Pat Godin"
Georgetowne, Inc.
P.O. Box 625
Bethel Park, PA 15102

Wildfowl Photos
Cardinal Carvers Supply
P.O. Box 571
Houma, LA 70361

John E. Heintz, Jr.
6609 S. River Rd.
Marine City, MI 48039
313-765-5059

Larry Stevens
3005 Pine Spring Rd.
Falls Church, VA 22042
703-560-5771

Wooden Bases
Birds of a Feather
Box 386
41 Edstrom Rd.
Marlborough, CT 06447
203-295-9469

A Sampling of Competitions and Exhibitions

NOTE: This list was compiled from *Wildfowl Carving and Collecting Magazine*. Addresses given indicate where to write for further information.

California Open and Wildfowl Arts Festival
4351 Whittle Ave.
Oakland, CA 94602
Held in early February, this show is a major competition for carvers. There are some 400 carvers and exhibitors and 8,000 visitors.

Canadian National Decoy Carvers Competition
Sportsmans Association
61 Edgehill Rd.
Islington, Ontario
M9A 4N1
Canada
This show is held in mid March with some 300 entries of wildfowl carvings.

New England Woodcarvers Festival and Competition
Valley Shore Waterfowlers
43 Ridgeview Circle
Guilford, CT 06437
Held in late October or early November, this show debuted in 1985.

U.S. National Decoy Show
5 Flint Rd.
Amity Harbor, NY 11701
Held in middle to late March, it is the oldest show of its kind in this country.

Clayton Duck Decoy and Wildlife Art Show
P.O. Box 292
Clayton, NY 13624
Held in July, this show offers auctions, demonstrations, painting, and carving contests.

Loyalhanna Wildlife Art Festival
Loyalhanna Watershed Assoc.
P.O. Box 561
Ligonier, PA 15658
Held in September, the show offers demonstrations, wildlife films, and an auction.

Pennsylvania Wildlife Art Festival
R. D. #1
P.O. Box 128A
Glen Rock, PA 17327
This show is held in York in mid November with a wide variety of decorative carvings featured.

Annapolis Wildfowl Carving and Art Exhibition
1144 Riverboat Court
Annapolis, MD 21401
Carving and art exhibits are featured in this late January show.

World Championship Wildfowl Carving Competition
The Ward Foundation
655 S. Salisbury Blvd.
Salisbury, MD 21801

Held in Ocean City, Maryland, in late April, this show features some 800 carvers and attracts around 16,000 visitors. This three-day show is a must for anyone interested in bird carving.

The Ward Foundation Wildfowl Carving and Art Exhibition
The Ward Foundation
P.O. Box 703
Salisbury, MD 21801
This early October show, held in Salisbury, is not a competition but an exhibition of carvings and flat work art. Some 150 artists attend with some 9,000 visitors.

Louisiana Wildfowl Festival
3112 Octavia St.
New Orleans, LA 70125
Held in New Orleans, this September show features some 300 carvers and exhibitors with some 10,000 visitors.

Leigh Yawkey Woodson Art Museum "Birds in Art" Exhibition
Leigh Yawkey Woodson Art Museum

Franklin and Twelfth Sts.
Wausau, WI 54401
This show may come the closest to treating bird sculpture as an art form. It is held mid-September to early November.

Easton Waterfowl Festival
P.O. Box 929
Easton, MD 21654
This is an early-November, townwide wildfowl art exhibition, which features 450 carvers and exhibitors and attracts some 25,000 visitors. A number of the carvers in this book and *How to Carve Wildfowl* exhibit their work there.

International Decoy Contest
Decoy Contest
P.O. Box 406
Davenport, IA 52805
This is an early August show which attracts over 100 carvers and some 5,000 visitors.

North American Wildfowl Carving Championship
12620 Southfield Rd.
Detroit, MI 48223
The Holiday Inn, Livonia, is the site for this key show in late September which attracts nearly 300 carvers.

Cajun Hunters Festival
Rt. 2
P.O. Box 337
Cut Off, LA 70345
Held in the Bayou Centroplex in Galliano, this show features over 100 carvers and exhibitors with some 5,000 visitors.